The Perfect Relationship Anxiety Workbook for Married Couples

How Anxiety Destroys Relationships, Stop Feeling Insecure in Love and Worried in a Relationship. Learn to Recognize Anxious Behaviors that Trigger Insecurity.

Kate Homily

A WORD BY THE AUTHOR

I hope you enjoy this book as much as I loved writing it. If you do, it would be wonderful if you could take a short minute and leave a review on Amaz on.com and Goodreads.com as soon as you can, as your kind feedback is much appreciated and so very important. Thank you.

Congratulation on downloading this e-book, currently best-selling in Anxiety Disorder & Phobias Category, and thank You for doing so.

Please Enjoy It!

MY FREE GIFT TO YOU:

As my way of saying thanks for buying '**This Workbook**' I'd like to give you a **FREE COPY** of my book 'Keeping Love and Healthy Relationships Alive'

>>> Click Here to Get the Free Book Instantly<<<

The above book is a gift, given to you as a sincere thanks for buying my e-book. I hope it helps you increase of your life. Download this **FREE BOOK** by clicking the link here
So click the link above to get access now and thanks once again for your support.

Enjoy!

Disclaimer

No part of this e-book may be reproduced or transmitted in any forms of whatsoever, electronic, or mechanical photocopying, recording, or by any informational storage or retrieval system without express writer, dated and signed permission from the author.

I'll send you my future projects, in preview, with nothing in return, if you just want a realistic review on them, which I'm sure will be useful to me. Thanks in advance! Leave me your best email, my staff will send you a copy as soon as possible: digitallifemystery@gmail.com

For a Better Experience, Download Audio Book Version of This Book for FREE

If you love listening to audio books on-the-go, I have great news for you. You can download the audio book version of this book for FREE just by signing up for a FREE 30-day audible trail! See below for more details!

AUDIBLE TRAIL BENEFITS

As an audible customer, you will receive the below benefits with your 30-day free trail:

- **FREE** audible book copy of this book
- After the trail, you will get 1 credit each month to use on any audiobook
- Your credits automatically roll over to the next month if you don't use them
- Choose from Audible's 200,000 + titles
- Listen anywhere with the Audible app across multiple devices
- Make easy, no-hassle exchanges of any audiobook you don't love
- Keep your audiobooks forever, even if you cancel your membership
- And much more

Click the links below to get started!

For Audible US

© Copyright 2020 - All rights reserved.

The content contained within this book may not be reproduced, duplicated or transmitted without direct written permission from the author or the publisher.

Under no circumstances will any blame or legal responsibility be held against the publisher, or author, for any damages, reparation, or monetary loss due to the information contained within this book, either directly or indirectly.

Legal Notice:

This book is copyright protected. It is only for personal use. You cannot amend, distribute, sell, use, quote or paraphrase any part, or the content within this book, without the consent of the author or publisher.

Disclaimer Notice:

Please note the information contained within this document is for educational and entertainment purposes only. All effort has been executed to present accurate, up to date, reliable, complete information. No warranties of any kind are declared or implied. Readers acknowledge that the author is not engaged in the rendering of legal, financial, medical or professional advice. The content within this book has been derived from various sources. Please consult a licensed professional before attempting any techniques outlined in this book.

By reading this document, the reader agrees that under no circumstances is the author responsible for any losses, direct or indirect, that are incurred as a result of the use of the information contained within this document, including, but not limited to, errors, omissions, or inaccuracies.

Table of Contents

TABLE OF CONTENTS

CHAPTER 1: HOW TO USE THIS BOOK

CHAPTER 2: WHAT IS RELATIONSHIP ANXIETY?

    COMMON QUESTIONS REGARDING RELATIONSHIP ANXIETY
    DEALING WITH YOUR RELATIONSHIP ANXIETY

CHAPTER 3: ARE DOUBTS NORMAL IN A RELATIONSHIP?

    LONG-TERM IMPACTS
    WHAT TO REMEMBER

CHAPTER 4: WHAT CAUSES ANXIETY AND INSECURITY IN A RELATIONSHIP?

    THE ROOT OF THE PROBLEM
        Previous Relationships
        Low Self-Esteem
        Attachment Style
        Loss of Trust
        Misunderstanding
        Tendency to Question

CHAPTER 5: WHAT ARE THE MAIN REASONS FOR CONFLICTS BETWEEN COUPLES?

    Religion
    Dominance
    Child Bearing

Poor Communication
Materialistic Difficulties
Perception
Values
Work-Related Stress
Unwritten Rules
Behavior

CHAPTER 6: HOW TO UNDERSTAND YOUR PARTNER AND MASTER THE CONFLICTS IN YOUR RELATIONSHIP

UNDERSTANDING EACH OTHER
RESOLVING ISSUES TOGETHER

CHAPTER 7: RECOGNIZING IRRATIONAL BEHAVIORS THAT TRIGGER ANXIETY AND INSECURITY

EXAMPLES
When Your Partner Doesn't Immediately Reply to Your Text
When Your Partner Can't Spend Time with You
When Your Partner Receives a Call or Text
When Your Partner Appears to Be Distant
When Your Partner Takes Jokes Too Far
When Your Partner Won't Propose to You

CHAPTER 8: HOW DO YOU STOP BEING ANXIOUS AND INSECURE IN A RELATIONSHIP?

STRATEGIES AND EXERCISES

CHAPTER 9: HOW TO USE YOUR RELATIONSHIP ANXIETY TO GROW

ESTABLISH A DEEPER CONNECTION
SPEND QUALITY TIME TOGETHER
GO THE EXTRA MILE
LEARN ABOUT THE WARNING SYSTEM

CHAPTER 10: IMPROVING SELF-AWARENESS AND SELF-PASSION WITH ANXIETY IN A RELATIONSHIP

ACCEPT THAT ANXIETY IS COMMON

- PRACTICE MINDFULNESS
- SEEK OUTLETS FOR YOUR THOUGHTS
- FALL IN LOVE WITH YOURSELF
- UNDERSTAND EXTERNAL INFLUENCES
- WORK ON SELF-CARE
- REWIRE YOUR BRAIN

CONCLUSION

REFERENCES

CHAPTER 1: WHAT HAPPENS TO LOVE AFTER WE ARE IN A RELATIONSHIP?

- KEEPING THE FLAME LIT
- HOW TO HANDLE CONFLICT

CHAPTER 2: HOW TO BUILD LOVE AND AVOID BETRAYAL IN A RELATIONSHIP

- LOVE LANGUAGES
- POWER STRUGGLES
- OPENNESS

CHAPTER 3: THE LOVE HE/SHE DESIRES MOST

- ACTING ON LOVE LANGUAGES
- THE IMPORTANCE OF RESPECT

CHAPTER 4: THE SECRET TO LOVING YOUR SPOUSE EFFECTIVELY

- DISCOVER KEY ISSUES
- HOW TO AVOID NEGATIVITY
- CONFLICT-RESOLUTION SKILLS

CHAPTER 5: THE SECRET TO UNCONDITIONAL LOVE THAT COUPLES NEED, YET FEW FIND

- NAVIGATING YOUR DIFFERENCES
- LET GO OF THE PAST
- DEVELOP FUN AND LAUGHTER

CHAPTER 6: WHAT TRUST REALLY MEANS IN YOUR RELATIONSHIP

- Why Trust Is Important
- Cheating
- Restoring Trust

CHAPTER 7: TRUST — ESSENTIAL AND FUNDAMENTAL TO ANY RELATIONSHIP

- Staying True to You
- How to Be Gentle and Patient

CHAPTER 8: THE SECRET TO ACTIONS THAT WILL GROW TRUST IN YOUR RELATIONSHIP

- Make an Action Plan
- Come to an Agreement

CHAPTER 9: HOW TO REGAIN TRUST IN A RELATIONSHIP THAT IS FALLING APART

- Recognize Emotional Disconnect
- Drop the Excuses
- Identify Chain Reactions

CHAPTER 10: THE LONG-TERM BENEFITS OF REBUILDING LOST TRUST IN YOUR RELATIONSHIP

- Re-Establishing Your Connection
- What You Will Learn
- Long-Term vs. Short-Term

CONCLUSION

REFERENCES

CHAPTER 1: ATTACHMENT STYLES: WHERE DO YOU FALL ON THE SPECTRUM?

- Attachment: A Brief History
- The Four Attachment Styles
- Attachment Styles and Relationships

CHAPTER 2: AN OVERVIEW OF ATTACHMENT THROUGH DIFFERENT LIFE STAGES

ATTACHMENT IN INFANCY AND CHILDHOOD
Attachment Styles: Factors That Influence Your Kids
ATTACHMENT IN ADOLESCENCE AND YOUNG ADULTHOOD
MID-LIFE ATTACHMENT
ATTACHMENT IN LATER LIFE

CHAPTER 3: GETTING STARTED WITH SOME SELF-AWARENESS: EMOTIONALLY FOCUSED FAMILY THERAPY TECHNIQUES

WHAT IS EMOTIONALLY FOCUSED FAMILY THERAPY (EFFT)?
STAGES AND STEPS OF EFFT
WAYS TO CLASSIFY AND IDENTIFY ATTACHMENT STYLES
Core Interventions and EFFT Exercises
FINDING AN EFFT THERAPIST

CHAPTER 4: COGNITIVE BEHAVIORAL THERAPY AND SELF-IMPROVEMENT

WHAT IS COGNITIVE BEHAVIORAL THERAPY (CBT)?
HOW CBT IS USED TO TREAT ANXIETY AND DEPRESSION DISORDERS
CBT: THE PROCESS
COMMON TYPES OF COGNITIVE DISTORTIONS BASED ON YOUR ATTACHMENT STYLE
SELF-IMPROVEMENT PRACTICES AND EXERCISES

CHAPTER 5: FINDING HAPPINESS IN YOUR SINGLE LIFE

YOUR ATTACHMENT STYLE AND YOUR CONFIDENCE
WHAT YOU WANT FROM A RELATIONSHIP, YOU WANT FROM YOURSELF
CHALLENGES TO OVERCOME
SINGLEHOOD MODELS
HOW TO BECOME SINGLE, SECURE, AND HAPPY

CHAPTER 6: STRATEGIES TO BUILD STRONGER, MORE MEANINGFUL RELATIONSHIPS

KEY CONCEPTS IN PROMOTING A SECURE ATTACHMENT
HEALING FROM TRAUMA THROUGH EMOTIONALLY CORRECTIVE RELATIONSHIPS

ATTACHMENT STYLE INTERACTIONS AND THEIR RELATIONSHIP CHALLENGES
EXERCISES TO STRENGTHEN YOUR RELATIONSHIP

CHAPTER 7: LONG-TERM RELATIONSHIP HAPPINESS: WHAT'S THE SECRET?

YOUR EMOTIONAL INTELLIGENCE
STRENGTHEN YOUR COMMUNICATION SKILLS
HEALING YOUR TRAUMA AND MOVING TOWARDS SECURE ATTACHMENT
COMPROMISE
PRIVACY AND PERSONAL TIME
BE OPEN AND HONEST ABOUT DIFFICULT QUESTIONS
SPONTANEITY AND DOING FUN THINGS TOGETHER
THE IMPORTANCE OF TOUCH AND PHYSICAL INTIMACY
DON'T TRY TO CHANGE EACH OTHER, RESPECT YOUR DIFFERENCES
CULTIVATE PATIENCE AND RESPECT
KNOW WHEN IT'S TIME TO GET OUT

CONCLUSION

THINKING, FEELING, AND DOING
FINDING, FIXING, AND HEALING

REFERENCES

IMAGE REFERENCES

Introduction

"Just when the caterpillar thought the world was ending, she became a butterfly." -Barbara Haines Howett

It is the root of many issues. Anxiety can be difficult to manage on a daily basis. As you try to navigate your feelings, you have likely become entirely overwhelmed, even when things are seemingly okay. This is the way that anxiety can be so powerful, convincing you that you aren't capable of living your life. All of the feelings that anxiety brings forward are heightened when you are in a relationship. Not only are you dealing with your own personal struggles, but you also have to make sure that they do not impact your marriage. In worrying about how you are treating your partner, this can create even more anxiety for you to deal with. The good news is that anxiety can be easily resolved once it is identified.

No matter where your anxiety stems from, you need to realize that you deserve to live in peace. Having a stable and happy marriage is one of the many positive things that you are likely aiming for in your life. This might be easier said than done. If you have been struggling with anxiety for a while, getting into a better mindset is going to be a worthwhile challenge for you. Relationship anxiety can appear during any stage of a relationship; no matter how great things have been going. What you need to avoid is placing the blame on yourself or on your partner. Because this happens naturally, the only thing you should be focusing on is how to fix it.

Many different thoughts have likely passed through your head as you have been dealing with your relationship anxiety. You might be wondering if you are good enough for your partner or if they truly care about you. Deep down, you also might know the answers to these questions, yet your anxiety won't let you believe them. This can become a battle between what you know is right and how your anxiety is trying to mislead you. Your whole focus will eventually turn to you soothing the anxiety instead of devoting your time to your marriage. As you can imagine, this is something that can really wear you down after a while.

Studies have shown that nearly 40 million people suffer from anxiety on a daily basis; 20% of this group feeling anxiety toward their partners. This is a very big statistic, so if you find that you are a part of it, know that you are not alone.

With the help of this guide, you will learn how to confront your anxiety head-on. Instead of feeling that it is controlling you and your marriage, you will understand how to cope with it to preserve your relationship. Knowing that you deserve to live a life that is free of worry, the techniques that you will learn will help you feel that you can handle your anxiety.

My name is Kate Homily, and I am a relationship therapist. With over 18 years of experience, I have seen many cases of relationship anxiety. At one point in my life, I even experienced it for myself. It was a battle for me to overcome, but I made it out on the other side. Through my wisdom, I hope to teach others how they can do the same thing.

Today, I am a happily married mother of three with two rambunctious puppies. It took a lot of hard work to get here, but I now know exactly what it takes to create harmony in my life and marriage. I no longer spend my days worrying about the what-ifs or that my life could fall apart. Instead, I have the time to enjoy all of my blessings and remain thankful for everything that I've accomplished.

Chapter 1: How to Use this Book

This book will help you by teaching you more about relationship anxiety. Once you are able to better understand it, you will be able to come up with solutions that truly work for your life. This kind of anxiety can be very hard to deal with because it impacts the closest relationship that you have in your life — your relationship with your spouse. You should be able to share your most personal moments with your spouse while being the truest version of yourself. This level of openness is what makes for a fantastic marriage. Even if you are not yet married to your significant other, this book touches on topics that will likely apply to you if you are in a serious relationship.

The topics that are covered in this book are going to apply to women who are struggling with their anxiety levels to the point where it begins to impact their existing relationship. Though the book is geared toward the woman's point of view, it can still be very beneficial for the man to read as well. Relationship anxiety does not discriminate, so you must make sure that you are taking a look at the bigger picture as you evaluate your relationship. Try not to make any judgments as you examine your relationship for these flaws. Know that once you find them, you are going to fix them to make your relationship great and healthy.

You should feel hopeful and ready for the changes that are to come. While any change can be scary, know that a change in your relationship is going to have one goal — to strengthen and improve your bond. As a couple, it can become very easy to mix your lives and your personality traits, forgetting that you are actually both individuals. While marriage is a union, you must remember that you are two separate parts of this union. You have your own feelings, worries, goals, and interests. Do not allow yourself to become so invested in your marriage that you begin to lose sight of who you are as a person. This can be a way that you will trigger your relationship anxiety.

By mastering all of the concepts that you will learn, you should be able to successfully resolve all of your doubts. Any worries that have developed over time will be put to rest. The things that cause you to feel unsure in your relationship will be broken down into ways that allow you to process them for what they truly are. No one else can put you at ease in your relationship except for yourself. Many people make the mistake of relying on their spouse to do this for them, but that is only part of how you will obtain security in your relationship. Your partner should make you feel stable, but you must also feel stable in your own right.

Brushing off these anxiety issues that you are dealing with is never the answer. When you suppress these feelings, they are only going to return in full force at a later date. It isn't fun to live your life this way, never knowing when your anxiety is going to make another appearance. For this reason, utilizing real methods that work to put these feelings to rest will help you overcome them. You aren't going to be pushing them aside for later. The work that you do will actually eliminate the anxiety and provide you with helpful methods for keeping it away. When you know how to soothe yourself, you will be much better at staying calm no matter what happens. Before you even begin working on these issues, you must tell yourself that you want to work on them.

Being open with your partner is a must. If you cannot talk to your partner about the anxiety that you are feeling, then they are going to be confused when you start treating them differently. This can be a big downfall of any marriage because it leaves your partner feeling like they did something wrong. Plenty of times, the anxiety is not even directly related to something that your partner did recently or has done in the past. It stems from an insecurity that you feel inside of yourself. You must understand that you need to get your own negative thoughts under control before you allow them to become a regular part of your relationship dynamic.

The best way to start this conversation is just by being honest. This book aims to help you stay true to yourself. With the techniques that you will learn, you will have a renewed sense of confidence. If you ever have any doubts about how to deal with your anxiety, you can turn to this book for different tips that you can try. The same methods that work for other people won't necessarily work for you and your relationship, but healing from your anxiety does tend to involve a little bit of trial and error. As long as you are willing and committed to the cause, then you should have the confidence to know that you can break through all of your doubts and live your life with the healthiest relationship possible.

Marriage does take a lot of work, but it is all for a worthy cause. Those who are not willing to acknowledge their marital problems end up living with unhappy marriages that will eventually fall apart. If you want to have the strongest marriage possible, you need to be willing to put in this work. Remind yourself why you are working so hard and what your desired end result is going to be. From this point forward, you do not need to be fearful of your anxiety. You can be comfortable and happy knowing that your anxiety will remain under control, leaving only room for you and your partner to grow happily together.

By becoming more educated on the topic, you will be able to feel more hopeful. Being able to read about the actual causes of your anxiety will allow you to see that it is not all in your head; your thoughts and feelings are valid. With a sense of understanding, you and your partner are going to be able to address the roots of these issues. You will no longer be arguing about the same things because you will be able to find solutions to these problems. Without all of the stress that you were once holding onto, you will see how your anxiety will start to fade away. It is a wonderful feeling knowing that you have what it takes to keep yourself and your partner happy.

Chapter 2: What Is Relationship Anxiety?

At any point during your relationship, you can be subject to anxiety. While it is more common for this anxiety to form in the beginning stages, it does not discriminate. Sometimes, the anxiety can be triggered by certain events or experiences that the two of you have as a couple. No matter where it comes from, you need to be able to pinpoint it so that you can address it. As you know, anxiety that is left untreated can manifest into bigger problems and put a lot of strain onto your relationship. When you are both stressed out, you are more likely to argue and feel that you are not on the same page. This can be very discouraging, especially in marriage. When you want to feel unity, yet you feel like you don't understand one another, this can cause you to second guess your relationship.

It is difficult to narrow down the exact cause for relationship anxiety. Some believe that there is an event that triggers the anxiety, while others believe that it is a combination of factors that lead up to a breaking point. No matter how it forms, being able to recognize that you are acting on your anxious thoughts is important. You might realize that you are secretly questioning your partner's intentions even when they have not given you a reason to. You might also start feeling that you are not good enough for your partner, although nothing has actually changed that would lead you to believe this is true. Anxiety can be powerful enough to make you think that there are all of these problems in your relationship when there might not be any problems at all.

For some, relationship anxiety sets in because of the experiences that you've had in the past. If you have ever been in a manipulative or abusive relationship, it is natural to be fearful that your present/future relationships will also be the same. That is a lot of psychological damage for one person to endure, so getting out of that mindset is going to be very difficult. If this situation applies to your life, know that it is not your fault. If anyone has ever treated you less than you deserved, that is merely a reflection of their own character. One of the most common mistakes made is the internalization of the bad things that others have done to us. If you accept these things and hold them inside, your subconscious is always going to return to them.

Remind yourself why you and your spouse got together. Think about how things were the first time you met and when you first started dating. This spark is the reason you decided to get married. While relationships naturally become less exciting as time goes on, those people who fell in love are still the same people. That natural chemistry should still exist, even when the honeymoon stage comes to an end. By reminding yourself of all the qualities that you fell in love with when you met your partner, you should also realize that they feel in love with your qualities too. These little things can often bring you back to that feeling of how it was when you first got together.

Common Questions Regarding Relationship Anxiety

Having doubts is normal with anything that you do in life. Being able to recognize that you might be making the wrong decision can be a very humbling experience.

On the other hand, it can show you that you know what is best for you. Having the confidence and the ability to make choices is necessary if you want to really get the most out of your life. The person that you have picked to spend the rest of your life with is a very big decision to make. For this reason, anxiety can start to show up over time as you truly get to know the other person. We all have our flaws, and we are usually only comfortable showing them to our partners after we have been together for some time. At this point in any relationship, it should mean that you both feel comfortable enough to be your true selves. This means that all of your personality traits will be seen, flaws and all.

Your flaws make you human; you can learn from them. We all have things that we need to work on in life, but that doesn't mean that we are unlovable or hard to be with. Your spouse should accept you, even despite these flaws. Their love should remain unconditional. As long as you can work on the things that you have to work on about yourself, then there should be no reason why your spouse wouldn't be willing to accept you for who you are. The following are some typical questions that tend to arise as you begin to develop relationship anxiety. If you have ever thought about these things or even asked your spouse these things, you should be able to identify that you do have anxiety in your relationship.

Are we actually right for one another?

Does my partner love me?

Are we moving too fast?

Are they losing interest in me?

Am I ready for this commitment?

All of these questions are fueled by doubt. While you might have seemingly real reasons to ask these questions, try to think about what is causing the insecurity. When you are in a healthy relationship, you should know exactly how your partner feels about you. Both of you should be on the same page when it comes to the stage of your relationship and how comfortable you are with one another. Any commitments that were made have been made on a mutual level. A marriage can start out this way, yet you might still begin to have certain doubts creep into your mind over time. This is normal, and it is nothing to be ashamed of. If you have ever thought about any of the above questions or anything similar, you are not alone.

These questions tend to come up because you have had a moment of doubt. As you know, doubt can be a common feeling for any big life decision. Taking the time to consider if you are making the right choice shows how important it is to you. What you need to be sure of is that you aren't being fueled by doubt. When you develop relationship anxiety, you have likely been experiencing doubts for a while now. It becomes detrimental to your life and your relationship when you allow yourself to become consumed by it. A relationship that has an underlying tone of doubt is always going to be tense. You might be very defensive over certain things, and your partner might not even know why.

It is important that you get your triggers under control. By learning about the roots of your issues, you should be able to have a better understanding of why you are feeling the way that you do. Think about what caused you to get to this point and try your best to be honest with yourself. When you hold back, you might end up taking your worries out on your partner. This is never a good experience in a relationship because it is only going to create an added source of stress. When you are dealing with relationship anxiety, you will become more focused on these worries than actually being a caring partner. All of your priorities will shift until the anxiety is all that you can think about. Imaginably, this is a very difficult way to live. It will also end up impacting your partner in a negative way.

Dealing with Your Relationship Anxiety

To manage the anxiety that you feel in your relationship, you must take accountability for your actions. When you can recognize that you are acting out of insecurity, take a moment to listen to your inner voice. Do you talk to yourself with respect, or are you being too hard on yourself? The way that you communicate with your subconscious can make a very big impact on the way that you are going to take action. When you are acting out of fear or insecurity, you might make some decisions that you wouldn't normally make if you were thinking clearly. Any time that you begin to feel your anxiety, take a few deep breaths. Breathing is super important when you are dealing with anything stressful. It regulates your body and your mind, allowing you to focus on what is most important.

Once you have changed your mindset, think about the problem again. Does it feel any different now that you've had a moment to separate yourself from it? Worry only tends to build the more that you fuel it. By breathing before reacting, you are giving yourself some space from the problem. Try not to be so critical of yourself. Think about the way that you treat your partner. When they have doubts, you are likely going to be there to provide words of encouragement. Do the same thing for yourself. Know that you deserve the confidence boost just as much as your partner does. Even if you already have a supportive partner, you also need to be able to be there for yourself.

It puts a lot of pressure on your partner when you are constantly unloading problems on them. They are going to be there for you, but you also need to make sure that you are putting in the effort to grow as a person. Recognize that your anxious way of thinking isn't going to be permanent. As long as you are able to keep pushing forward, you should be able to get back into a healthy state of being. This is going to be beneficial both for your relationship and for yourself. Keep in mind that you are always in control of your own happiness. While things might happen to you that try to bring you down, you are ultimately in control of your own feelings.

Make the choice to not let your anxiety win. When you begin to experience relationship anxiety, it can cause you to act differently because of the insecurity that you are feeling. Sometimes, people get clingy and become very needy toward their partners. There are also certain instances when it might make you feel that you need more control in your relationship. If you were to act on either of these things, you can imagine the impact that it would make on your partner. Being a control freak or a clingy partner is not going to make your anxiety go away. You might feel better temporarily, but it is still going to be there below the surface.

When you can see that you are gravitating toward negative self-talk, stop yourself. Do not let these thoughts even enter your brain or else they will only grow stronger. Know that you have the choice to either allow this negative self-talk to occur or to redirect it. When you redirect it, you can take the original thought you had and put a more positive spin on it. For example, if you feel like your partner doesn't love you anymore, think about all of the reasons why your partner has said that they have fallen in love with you. Even if time has passed, or if you have been married for a while, remember these small joys because they are still relevant.

If you tend to think that your partner is stuck with you and that they could find someone better, remind yourself that your partner has free will. Your partner can do anything at any time, but they have chosen to commit to you. Take this commitment as a sign of them wanting to be with you, so there is no need to question it. When you worry about problems that don't truly exist, you are giving your anxiety plenty of room to grow. When you take away these negative thoughts and replace them with positive facts, you are taking the power away from your anxiety. This is exactly what you need to do to remind yourself that you are in control of your happiness. You can decide how you are going to talk to yourself and how you are going to treat your partner.

Try to let go of any negativity that you are currently holding onto. You can do so by practicing some breathing techniques and giving yourself the space to clear your head. Spending time alone is healthy, even when you are married. You are an individual with your own set of needs, so make sure that you aren't ignoring them. Only 10 minutes of breathing or meditation can make a huge difference in the way that you feel. Try to focus on the things that you love about yourself and the things that your partner says they love about you. Push aside any of the worries that keep trying to pop up. Remind yourself that your partner has chosen you for a reason, just as you have chosen them.

When you choose to work on yourself from the inside out, this is going to create the biggest change in your mindset. Being able to feel great about yourself and have that renewed sense of confidence is going to make you a better partner. You have likely heard the saying before, but it remains true — if you can't love yourself, then you won't be able to love someone else. Self-love often gets pushed to the back burner when you enter a serious relationship. Make sure that you remind yourself of how important it is. Take some time regularly to unwind by yourself so that you don't lose sight of who you are as an individual.

Chapter 3: Are Doubts Normal in a Relationship?

We have talked a little bit about doubts and why you feel them, but you might be wondering if they are normal to feel if you are in a committed relationship.

What is most important to remember when it comes to feeling doubtful is that you don't need to panic. If a doubt arises while you are in a relationship, this is just your brain picking up on signals that either make you worried or displeased. It is normal to feel doubtful sometimes, even if you are in a wonderful relationship. You are a human being, so you are going to likely feel this way at some point in time. What matters most is where this doubt is actually stemming from and how you decide to handle it.

Many psychologists agree that even the healthiest couples can feel normal instances of doubt and anxiety at times. Much like anxiety, doubt can also happen at any point during the relationship. A lot of people experience doubts in the beginning, but it is also possible to experience them when you are already married and have been for a long time. Anything that leads you to second-guess yourself is a trigger that should be examined. For example, if you begin to doubt that your partner's feelings for you are as strong as they once were, ask yourself what has led you to this conclusion. Once you get to the bottom of the problem, you should be able to take a closer look at why this thought has surfaced in your mind.

Insecurity often fuels doubt. If you believe that your partner doesn't have strong feelings for you anymore, you are likely going to equate this to them being interested in someone else or you not being enough for them. Unless they have actually said these things to you, then you should not allow your mind to run with these ideas. Only allow yourself to think about the concrete facts. Has your partner cheated? Have they told you that you are not good enough for them? If you cannot answer yes to these questions, then you should not have to spend any more time dwelling on these things. Convince yourself to let go of them.

There are certain cases when anxiety can be helpful in a relationship. If you have ever felt butterflies in the early stages of your relationship, this is actually a form of anxiety. Most people feel it as excitement rather than negativity, though. When you and your partner were first getting to know one another, things likely felt very exciting and new. You were discovering all of each other's qualities and learning how to come together as a couple. Each time that you learned something new about your partner or experienced something that brought you closer together, you likely felt these butterflies and took them as a positive sign.

Because you already know one another very well, any feelings of anxiety that develop after you have already been in the relationship for a while are going to feel more bothersome. This is the perfect time for doubts to creep in, preying on your overthinking mind. Pair this with the negative self-talk, and you have a very high chance of making yourself miserable in your relationship. Being with a partner who is struggling can be very difficult, and sometimes, unfair. Keeping yourself in touch with reality is going to prevent you from allowing your doubts to take over. Any negative voices that you hear in your head can be silenced with some positive self-talk.

The more that you choose to focus on your anxiety, the less you are focusing on your actual relationship. As you know, relationships take a lot of effort. When you don't pay attention to your partner and instead pay attention to these problems that you believe need to take priority, you might actually end up transforming into the kind of partner that you are fearful of. Nobody wants to be with someone who isn't considerate of their feelings or attentive to their needs. It becomes difficult to fill these roles for your partner when all you can do is worry about the what-ifs. If something isn't actually happening in your relationship right at the moment, then you shouldn't panic over it.

When you overanalyze things, you are actually distancing yourself from your partner because you are viewing your relationship as a big speculative situation. Instead of seeing your relationship and your partner for what they truly are, you will be acting on fears and worries that might not even actually exist. This is a very exhausting way to live, and it can be damaging to your mental health. Not to mention, it will drive distance between yourself and your partner. None of these things are worth it, so the choice should be very clear when you realize that you can reframe the way that you think. Instead of bringing your worst fears to life, focus on the good things that you already have. Try to attract more of these good things into your life and your relationship.

Long-Term Impacts

You are now realizing how damaging doubtful behavior and relationship anxiety truly can become. If you have been experiencing either for a long time, or if you allow it to get out of control, you are going to be subject to many different problems that are proven to be difficult to overcome. Starting with emotional distress, this will become your permanent state of mind. If you have ever been in emotional distress before, you will know how damaging it can be when it is not treated for a long time. Being in any kind of distress is not healthy for you, and it will not make you a good partner. You will be so caught up in your negative feelings that you likely will not have the time to think about what you can be doing for your partner.

Emotional distress can also lead to some serious mental health issues, such as depression or even thoughts of suicide. When you are constantly viewing your situation with such a negative outlook, you might lose sight of what you are grateful for in your life. Things can seem confusing and scary with no real purpose. This kind of thinking becomes very dangerous because you can easily lead yourself to believe that there is no happy outcome for you or your relationship. Even when nothing at all has happened, your mind is still powerful enough to convince you that your relationship is a disaster. This is why learning how to control your mindset is crucial.

You might begin to lose your motivation in your relationship. This can manifest in many different ways. An upsetting feeling is when you lose all sexual or romantic motivation, leading your partner to believe that they have done something wrong. In reality, you might just be too caught up in your own doubts or anxiety to be able to be there for your partner in this way. Naturally, this can cause a big divide between two people who are in a committed relationship. You might also lose your motivation in other ways, such as being there for your partner. Without your support, your partner might also be led to believe that they have done something wrong or that they have upset you in some way.

When you don't have the motivation, your relationship is going to feel very stagnant. If you are already out of the honeymoon stage, this can really make or break your relationship. With no direction, you aren't going to be focused on moving forward with your partner. Instead, you are likely only going to get stuck in the same habits and routines. This can become very cumbersome, especially if your partner has goals in mind for the future. When only one person is putting in effort toward goals that concern both of you, this can be a very discouraging situation to face. Make sure that you are letting your partner know exactly where you stand on your future and your goals together.

Don't forget how taxing emotional pain can become. When you are constantly fighting with your own emotions, you are bound to become physically exhausted in the process. Fatigue is a very common sign that you are stressing yourself out on a regular basis. Depression can also lead you to this feeling. You might not even feel like you have enough energy to get out of bed each day when you begin to feel the weight from your fatigue. This can be very upsetting for your partner because they will feel helpless. It will also likely upset you more because you won't have the energy to interact with them or reassure them like you once did.

Exhaustion isn't the only physical symptom for you to look out for. If you begin to experience stomach problems, your stress likely has something to do with them. When you are unhappy, your digestive system tends to become very reactive. Even small meals can upset your stomach, causing you to become averse to certain foods. This can lead to some very unhealthy eating habits if you aren't careful. Once your body starts to go downhill, you can bet that your mind will be following closely. Without a healthy body, not only are you going to be unable to be there for your partner like you once were, but your work and other responsibilities are also going to suffer.

When your stomach isn't feeling well, other people are likely going to take notice. This can become an added source of stress because you likely don't want others to know that you are having any problems at all. One of the worst parts about experiencing relationship doubts or anxiety is the shame in knowing that it is happening. Many people will go to great lengths to hide this from others in an attempt to make it seem like they are in a perfect relationship. Know that perfection doesn't exist. You can be in a great relationship, but you and your partner aren't always going to see eye to eye; that's normal. Be realistic with yourself and others because there is no shame in that. You are only human.

What to Remember

Overall, it wouldn't be realistic to say that you will never feel doubts about your relationship. Make sure that you open your mind to the idea that some doubts can be normal, as long as you do not always take them seriously. Before you decide to react to these doubts that pop into your mind, first see if you can locate the source of them. If you cannot, then it is not worth getting upset over. You might end up realizing what the source is and finding an immediate solution. This would mean that your panic and worry happened for no good reason.

Prove to yourself that you can self-soothe when you are in situations where the doubts want to take over. Remind yourself of the concrete facts about your relationship and what it is that you are worried about. If you can't prove it, then it is not a fact. Any remaining insecurities are to be examined. Think about the issues that you are left with. Ask yourself if these are things that you need to deal with or if they are things that you need to discuss with your partner. From there, the choice should be easy to make. When you simplify the process for yourself, all of your doubts won't seem as overwhelming as they once did.

Know that you have everything that you need to get through these moments of doubt. Also, remind yourself that it is natural to feel this way, as everyone is going to experience some moments of weakness. Whether something happened that triggered your doubts or you simply talked yourself into a corner, know that you can just as easily guide yourself to a more positive mindset. When you have positivity, you have a fighting chance of managing your problems. You will also be more likely to find a healthy way to approach this. "Fixing" self-destructive behavior with more self-destructive behavior isn't a solution at all.

Be aware not only of how you are treating your partner but of how you are treating yourself. Both of these are very important components of being a great partner. If you cannot treat yourself with respect, then that is sending your partner mixed messages about the way that you are going to treat them. Any worries that arise should be addressed and handled accordingly. You don't need to dwell on things to fix them. By having a clear understanding of your issues from the very beginning, you should be able to come to a quick solution. The more that you practice this, the better you will get at it. You will find that both you and your partner will be able to grow together when you aren't being chained down by doubts.

Chapter 4: What Causes Anxiety and Insecurity in a Relationship?

In this chapter, you are going to get a more detailed look at what exactly causes your anxiety and insecurity. While it can stem from many different things, even a combination of several things, you need to understand how it happens for yourself personally. You are going to learn about the basics and have a better understanding of where these feelings start. By having this knowledge and this perspective, you should be able to swiftly avoid these things to avoid becoming anxious again in the future. Taking a look at the given examples, you will likely find that you can identify with a lot of them, if not most of them. Don't think about this as a negative thing. Instead, you can think about all of the progress that you are about to make.

The Root of the Problem

Before you work on fixing the problem, you must be able to identify it. While it is often a bad choice to be critical of yourself, in this case, it becomes necessary. To deal with the issues that you are having in your relationship, you must be able to identify exactly what is causing them. Turn inward to see if you can get to the root of your problem. Ask yourself why you are choosing to behave the way that you are. There are no right or wrong answers for this step. No matter how you are feeling, even if it is extreme, you must have a reason for it. Know that this might not be the healthiest choice, but it will soon become a curbed behavior.

If you try to apply all of the different fixes that you know, this is only going to be a waste of time and energy. Don't become frustrated because you aren't seeing an improvement in yourself or your relationship. Take a more targeted approach. See if you can get down to the very bottom of your problems, identifying them and seeing them for what they really are. It can be scary to face your problems in this way, but this is the way that you are going to be able to fix them. Know that you need to trust in yourself and that you need to trust in the process. Problem-solving is difficult for a reason, but you will be happy with the end result. When you only solve the surface layer of problems, the rest of them are bound to come up later. It makes sense to get down to the root of things.

Previous Relationships

If you have ever been in a relationship in which you were mistreated, you are naturally going to be cautious of this in the future. It is a defensive mechanism that is normal for any abused individual to take on. However, it becomes a problem when you start to place this role on your partner, even when they are not abusive. Your constant fear and judgment will eventually lead your partner to many negative feelings, from insecurity to anger. It doesn't feel great to be accused of being controlling or manipulative when you aren't.

Make sure that any fears you have surrounding this issue are grounded in reality. If you have ever been broken up with unexpected, cheated on, physically or mentally abused, or lied to, then you are more likely to develop this kind of anxiety. When you are wronged so badly, it often has the ability to shake you to your core and change you as a person. What you must learn is that you need to heal from the past instead of comparing your present relationship to something that could end up the same way.

To convince yourself that you are being mistreated again, you will often go out of your way to look for "signs" that your partner is not good for you. Whenever you have to search for these things, they are likely not based in reality. You will know if your partner is doing something wrong from the actions that they present to you. Understandably, if you have been manipulated in the past, this can give you trust issues. Again, you need to keep these fears under control instead of taking them out on your partner. If you doubt your partner so strongly, this could be a sign that the relationship is not healthy for you. If your partner is late to get home from work, and the first thing you think is that they were cheating on you, then you should be able to see this as a sign of your anxiety taking over your way of thinking.

Low Self-Esteem

When you have low self-esteem, this can present itself in many ways. Having low-self-esteem often comes with many insecurities. Whether you are insecure about the way you look or your ability to please your partner, you will find that you will start projecting your issues. For example, if you feel disappointed in yourself, you will also start projecting this feeling and will start to believe that your partner is also disappointed in you. The way to tell if you are projecting or not is if your partner has expressed this to you themselves. If they have not indicated their disappointment, then this feeling is coming from your own anxiety and being projected.

As you can imagine, it becomes very unfair when you start to accuse your partner of feeling certain ways when they insist that they do not. It can become a very exhausting battle to fight, one that often proves that it isn't worth it. You will know when you are projecting feelings onto your partner when they constantly feel that they have to prove to you how much they love you or how they see you. Reassurance is important in a relationship, but if they are constantly spending their time reassuring you, this can become exhausting. No matter what answer you receive from them, it likely won't be enough to fix your low self-esteem.

You need to work on bettering yourself, not only your relationship. Realize that you are an individual person with individual needs. You need to be able to look at yourself in the mirror and be happy with what you see and the person that you are. When you feel anything less than this, there will be a risk of you projecting the negative feelings onto your partner. Make sure that you prioritize self-care. Understand that it is not selfish or excessive; it is necessary for your own mental health.

Attachment Style

An attachment style is something that develops when you are a child. Depending on how you are raised, you can either have a healthy sense of how to bond with someone or you might feel that you constantly need to receive reassurance to know that you are cared for. This is definitely something that can end up being projected as you reach adulthood and get into serious relationships. Even though these decisions were made by your parents, they will impact you for the rest of your life.

If your parents were cold and withheld affection, you might have developed a habit of hiding your emotions and needs. Babies who are left to cry for extended periods of time learn how to self-soothe. This can be a difficult process, as they are taught that no one is going to come for them when they are in need. As translated into adulthood, you might feel this way about your partner or you might even believe that your feelings are not important.

Having an anxious attachment means that you are living in fear that your partner could leave you at any moment. These abandonment issues usually stem from having a parent do the same thing during childhood. Children who come from broken homes can often grow to believe that every person in their life is not permanent. If you feel this way, you are never going to feel secure with your spouse because you will be constantly waiting for them to abandon you.

Alternatively, there is an avoidant attachment style. This occurs when you are the one who keeps your partner at a distance, not revealing too many feelings or providing reassurance. This attachment style can make you appear to be cold or not as invested in the relationship, even when you want to be. No matter what kind of attachment style you have, if it is unhealthy and impacting your relationship, therapy will become very beneficial to you. Being able to sort through your issues and understand why you feel this way will provide you with clarity.

Loss of Trust

You can lose trust in your partner for a variety of reasons. It is the way that you handle this feeling that will ultimately determine if it is a problem or not. Typically, when someone loses their trust in another person, that person will have to prove themselves trustworthy again. If you feel that you are too disappointed by their actions to forgive them, or if you choose to live your life while constantly punishing them for what they did, this is an indication that you are being led by your anxiety.

If you constantly feel a sense of disappointment or negativity, it might be possible that you entered the relationship with this mindset. Not having any faith in your partner can be devastating as the years go on. Both of you will feel that your efforts do not matter. By constantly expecting the end of your relationship, you are going to develop a very apathetic mindset. This can form as a defense mechanism, but it is not the healthiest way to deal with your trust issues.

When you can work together with your partner on these trust issues, your relationship is going to stand a fighting chance. Are there concrete reasons why you no longer trust your partner? If you cannot think about factual reasons why your partner is untrustworthy, you might have to turn your focus inward. What is making *you* feel this way and why? Before you react to the surface issues, it is important to get down to the deeper meaning behind the problem. Allow yourself to explore these feelings and realize that they might be stemming from a warped perception of the relationship that you have created. Even if you want the relationship to last, it is going to be difficult when you cannot set aside your negativity. These anxious thoughts are going to eat away at you constantly, providing a distraction. This won't be fair to either of you.

Misunderstanding

Fighting is a normal part of any healthy relationship. Couples should not get along 24/7, even if they are very similar or have a strong bond. By disagreeing, you are showing that you are still individuals. Being able to stand up for what you believe in is important, even if you are standing up to your spouse. When two adults that love each other get into a disagreement, they should also be able to communicate through the issue. This does not signify that the relationship is doomed, but that can often be what your anxiety leads you to believe.

There are certain types of fighting that can be dangerous. This usually happens when anger becomes physical. If you cannot talk about your feelings without getting overly angry, this is going to lead to something bad. Another bad sign is getting into additional disagreements while you are trying to solve the original one. This could indicate that a misunderstanding is taking place. Getting the right words out can be difficult, but you should be able to do so when you are talking to your partner. If they misunderstand you, correct them. Letting things make you even angrier is not going to solve your problem.

All healthy couples must be able to talk their way through fights, even if misunderstandings occur. Both people should be able to express themselves individually without being talked over. If you realize that your discussions usually do not follow this guideline, then you likely need to work on your conflict resolution skills. Be accountable for your own actions and realize when you are being out of line. You aren't always going to be right, no matter how much you believe that you are. Being able to realize that you are wrong can be a big saving grace when you are working through a misunderstanding with your partner.

Tendency to Question

Do you ever overthink situations? When you are given a decision, does it take you a long time to make up your mind? As a partner, being this way likely means that you are also going to question your significant other a lot to best make your decisions. Asking questions isn't always a negative thing; receiving these answers will provide you with clarity. This becomes detrimental to your relationship when you are unable to trust or believe in your partner. Your questions will begin to sound accusatory, which can lead to defensive responses on their end. Telling the truth and not being believed is an incredibly frustrating problem to face, especially coming from the person who is supposed to love and accept you for who you are.

If you are an over-thinker, you will have the ability to quickly create different scenarios in your head of what *could* be possible. For example, focusing on every detail of your spouse's behavior might lead you to an incorrect conclusion that they are being dishonest with you. When you get into this mindset and begin to convince yourself of things that are not backed by valid facts, this is when your behavior is going to be classified as unhealthy. Realize that placing these labels on your partner is unfair.

To correct this problem, you need to shift your focus. Realize that your partner is an individual with a different way of thinking. What they say to you, and the actions that they choose to display, should be the two forms of communication that you should be holding onto. Try to let go of the what-ifs or the various scenarios that you create in your head. If your partner appears to be genuine with you, then you should not have to go on a quest to find a reason why they might not be. Just because you are prone to looking at negative outcomes does not mean that your partner is automatically going to fulfill them. You need to have trust and faith in them.

Chapter 5: What Are the Main Reasons for Conflicts between Couples?

When you are in a serious relationship with another person, you are going to have different opinions frequently. The way that you handle these opinions will showcase the health of your relationships. Not all conflicts are bad, and not all conflicts stem from anxiety. There are plenty of cases when conflict can be healthy. It can show you both differing opinions on the same topic, causing you to re-think your stance on the issue. Even if you do not change your opinion, you should be willing to listen to one another in a respectful way. Those who do not listen to one another tend to engage in conflicts more frequently. These are the kind that can become a burden to any relationship.

This chapter is going to take a look at some of the most common reasons for experiencing conflict in a serious relationship. If you can relate to any of these reasons, then you can consider this the first step toward identifying your problems. As a couple, you should be able to communicate through any problem that you encounter. You do not need to engage in a fight or an argument just because you have differing opinions on a topic. Try your best to remain open-minded, treating your partner the way you wish to be treated. Allow them to express themselves without interrupting them or interjecting with your own opinion. Once you have both had the chance to speak, you should then be able to analyze each side and come to an agreement.

Conflict resolution isn't always going to be direct or simple, but as a healthy couple, you should be able to move past your differences to come to an agreement. When you both want a positive outcome, you are both going to be working toward finding a solution. Those that just want to hash it out are often left disappointed or with unresolved feelings. Both of these feelings can prove to be negative when you suppress them, only to return to them during a later conflict that you encounter. These issues can build up in a very unhealthy way if they are not dealt with properly.

Religion

A topic that often comes with strong opinions, couples can definitely start conflicts over religious beliefs. Whether one of you is religious and the other is not, or you and your partner practice religions, there is a chance that this issue can get brought up during an argument. A lot of the time, issues with religion can be tied to how you plan on raising your children or how your family plays a role in your life.

Understandably, having disagreements about religion can lead to some very tense situations. No matter what you or your spouse believes in, both of you must have respect for one another's beliefs. Any healthy relationship comes with a sense of understanding for each other. If you are intolerant of your partner, then you are contributing to the problem of having conflicts. You need to be able to look at your partner's views as valid, just as you see your own views. Taking an intolerant stance becomes very unhealthy for a long-term relationship, often causing unfixable damage.

Dominance

There are typically roles that are taken in any relationship. Usually, one partner takes a more dominant approach, while the other takes on a submissive role. It would be unfair to assume that either one of you *has* to take on these roles, though. The healthiest relationships have a shared sense of dominance. When only one person is dominant, this places the other person at risk of being controlled while in the relationship. Dominance can appear in the form of who takes care of the household and who makes the decisions. It makes sense that a couple should share these duties, even when one of them typically takes on the role themselves.

There is nothing wrong with settling into these roles, but having the flexibility to do things differently is a sign of a healthy relationship. You will realize that there are dominance issues when one of you protests a change in roles. If this makes you feel lesser than or insignificant, then you are likely in need of some work toward your self-esteem. Understand that dominance does not have to be set in stone. Use your own strengths to your advantage by stepping up when you know that it would be beneficial.

Child Bearing

Planning a family is a huge decision to be made by a couple. It comes along with a lot of pressure and being on the same page is essential. Each of you might have your own opinions and preferences when it comes to how many children you would like to have and how you plan on raising them. If you cannot come to an agreement on these decisions, conflict is definitely going to arise. You need to make sure that you are able to compromise when you disagree.

The birth of a child can also come along with many stressors that will test your limits as a couple. When you are both feeling fatigued and overworked, this opens the door for arguments to occur. If you are not careful, you will become very critical of one another. There is also the possibility of becoming stressed out by your lack of finances. Raising a child isn't cheap and if you have not planned adequately, you will struggle. It is very important that you talk to your partner in a realistic way about how you plan on bringing a child into the world.

Poor Communication

Being able to talk to your spouse is important, but making sure that you respect and understand one another is critical. So often, couples feel that they have great communication skills, yet they are still driven apart by disagreements. Remember, talking is only one-half of your communication skills. The other half comes from your listening abilities. Be an active listener at all times. If you are distracted or unwilling to listen, you are not going to see the bigger picture.

If you ever get into a disagreement, you can test your communication skills by how quickly you are able to end it. Those who have poor communication will raise their voices, insult one another, and even bring up past issues that should have already been resolved. This is why you should always aim to work on your problems immediately. If you wait, you will begin to suppress them. While you won't always agree on everything, you do need to know that there are boundaries that should not be crossed. Having respect for one another will keep you both in line.

Materialistic Difficulties

Even if you do not consider yourself a materialistic individual, your material possessions can drive you apart from your spouse. After you get married, most of your material items are shared. There can be a sense of competitiveness that arises when you realize that one of you is contributing more than the other. Alternatively, you might be tempted to compare what you have to what other couples have. Know that your lifestyle and relationship is unique; your success is not dependent on these material possessions.

If you find that your arguments are stemming from what you both have as a couple, you will realize that too much focus is being placed on material items. You can try to get back to what you love about being together, minus these possessions. Think about why you fell in love with your spouse in the first place. If you didn't have anything except for each other, you would appreciate one another for the qualities that you each possess instead of the items that you can procure. Conflicts can become very messy when you realize that you are simply fighting over things that are temporary.

Perception

You and your partner might see the exact same situation differently, and that is normal. While you are a couple, you also need to remember that you are two separate individuals. Your opinions are going to differ. What you need to do is make sure that you understand where your spouse stands on the topics that matter to you. Part of love is being able to accept one another for who you are, not attempting to change your partner so that their views align exactly with your own. There is a fine line between compatibility and control.

As a general rule of thumb, you should openly discuss the things that you value most. If you find that you and your partner see things differently, try to understand their perspective instead of trying to change their mind. This is going to open dialog rather than a disagreement. You might even find that you will be able to understand them better. This kind of mutual respect is very healthy for a relationship, and it shows that you can still love one another, even if you see certain things differently.

Values

As mentioned above, the things that are most important to you are the things that you value most. There are no right or wrong answers when it comes to these topics. Just as you have your own reasons for why you value what you do, so does your spouse. When these values are not aligned or understood, this opens the door for conflict. This kind of conflict can create difficulties because you will both potentially become stubborn as you try to fight for your cause.

Much like your perception, you need to be able to hear one another out on why you value the things that you do. Try to come from a place of understanding rather than a place of judgment. If you find that your core values do not match, you need to evaluate your relationship to see if you can come to a middle ground. Intolerance is only going to promote unhealthy behaviors and lead to more fighting. Talk about big topics, such as your lifestyle, responsibilities, and religions.

Work-Related Stress

No matter what you do for a living, there will be times when your job is going to stress you out. Being able to keep your work life and your personal life balanced is very important. Your partner should be someone that you can vent to about work without taking your frustrations out on them. Your behavior can become unhealthy very quickly if you realize that you are in a bad mood and are treating your spouse differently because of something that happened at work. It is unfair to subject your partner to this kind of treatment.

Know that when you leave work, you need to try to keep the problems that you cannot control at work. If you bring these worries and stressors home with you, they are bound to appear in your personal life. Overworking is another thing that tends to drive couples apart. If you are too career-oriented, you are going to be lacking in your marriage. Your partner should be someone who will support you and your goals, yet you need to realize that the stress that you encounter during this time is to no fault of your spouse.

Unwritten Rules

Every couple has a set of "rules" in place whether they realize it or not. For example, you should know that if you behave a certain way, this is going to upset your spouse. When you cross these boundaries, not only are you going to upset your partner, but you are going to create a rift in your trust. Betrayal is one of the worst feelings to face, especially from the person who is never supposed to betray you. It can be difficult to create these boundaries when they aren't frequently discussed.

To ensure that you are being fair to your partner, you need to vocalize the things that you are not okay with. This takes away the guesswork and defines a clear line between what you find acceptable and unacceptable. Encourage your partner to do the same thing with you. You might feel that these are things your spouse should already know automatically, but if their actions suggest they do not, you need to tell them. It is healthy for couples to redefine their boundaries, no matter how long they've been married.

Behavior

The way that you behave sends your spouse a very clear message. Even if you are not doing anything that you feel directly impacts your marriage, your actions will speak louder than words. If you cannot do something in front of your spouse, then you should not be doing it when your spouse isn't present. Much like violating the unwritten rules that you have in place, violating certain behavioral patterns can feel just like a betrayal. This will definitely lead to more conflicts and disagreements.

Know that you shouldn't feel controlled by your spouse or vice versa. As long as you both have mutual respect for one another, you should each understand how to act in a way that honors your marriage. This is a tricky balance to find, even for those who have been together for a while. Keep in mind that feelings can also change over the years. The best thing to do is to speak up if your spouse does something that upsets you. This will make it clear as to what you did not care for. Together, you can work on these things.

Chapter 6: How to Understand Your Partner and Master the Conflicts in Your Relationship

After reading about all of the things that could cause conflict, the thought of working through things with your spouse might feel overwhelming. Know that it does not have to be. By having an accurate understanding of how your partner feels and what they value in life, you will be able to make the best decisions for your marriage together. While you have your own values and morals, you have also agreed to engage in a partnership. This means that you must still work together on the issues that you disagree on. If you only pay attention to the ways that you are compatible, the differences are going to divide you over time. It is just as important to discuss the things that you have differing opinions on as it is to celebrate your similarities.

Couples who are able to keep this duality in their marriage are couples who last. You will each feel a lot happier when you are respected and understood. This chapter is going to help you both in different ways. If you have relationship anxiety, it is going to provide you with concrete ways to ease your worries and to identify the things that are causing you to worry in the first place. For your partner, it will allow them to better understand where you are coming from and how to create more reassurance in the relationship. When paired together, you will be dealing with your conflicts in a much healthier and smarter way.

Understanding Each Other

While you might have relationship anxiety, you need to remember that your partner might not. Because of this, your partner might not be able to relate to the things that you are worried about. This is not because they do not care about you or your feelings but simply because they do not understand how you are feeling. Alternatively, your partner might be able to relate, but they communicate their anxiety in different ways than you do. No matter what the case is, try your best to be understanding of where they are coming from. It might seem incredibly difficult, but the easiest way to rid yourself of your anxiety is to talk about it. Allow your partner to have some insight as to how you are feeling, even if you don't know exactly why.

If you choose to keep your anxiety inside, it is only going to build over time. When you are least expecting it, all of your feelings can be triggered by a minor conflict or disagreement, which will cause even more conflict. You should not feel that you have to deal with your relationship anxiety alone, especially when it pertains to your marriage. Know that you are only half of your marriage; your partner plays just as big of a role as you do. For the sake of being fair to both yourself and your spouse, you need to work hard at describing what you are feeling as soon as you feel it. Get to the root of the problem before it starts to spiral.

When your partner is the one experiencing relationship anxiety, know that this is a very real disorder. It is not something that they are consciously choosing to do, even though it might seem easier to just not think about these things. Your partner is worrying because the relationship matters to them. Try not to put them down or insinuate that their feelings are invalid. Do your best to listen to them and to try to put yourself in their shoes. Be a reassuring and supportive partner to help them work through their anxiety. Even if the worries seem ridiculous, hear them out. When you are able to see things from your partner's perspective, this is going to give you a better understanding of their mindset.

Talking about issues that create anxiety can be very difficult, no matter if you are the one experiencing them or not. You need to know how to talk to one another in a way that isn't aggressive or aggravated. Show each other compassion and treat yourself the way that you would like to be treated. It is likely that the anxious individual is going to be speaking emotionally, while the non-anxious individual will try to speak from a logical standpoint. These are two very different approaches, but you will be able to learn a lot about one another once you can identify who is ruled by emotions and who is ruled by logic. You should aim to live your life by both — inquire about your emotions, yet incorporate logic into your decision-making.

The non-anxious partner might need to take a step back when discussing certain issues. To them, nothing is going to seem like it is as big of a deal. The anxious partner will likely already know that their worries stem from situations that are exaggerated in their own head, but that does not mean that they should be made to feel bad about thinking this way; they can't help it. Do your best to really listen to one another and hear both perspectives before you try to fix the problem. When you talk this way, both of you will feel like you are being heard and respected.

Remember that, most of the time, this anxiety does not stem from anything that is personal. Neither one of you needs to be labeled as a bad guy if one of you is experiencing relationship anxiety. Also, neither one of you needs to take a defensive approach. Being accusatory or acting on fear is likely going to end up with one of you saying or believing something that is irrational. The idea that your spouse could leave you due to your behavior, or vice versa, should never be used as a threat. This is a big sign that the relationship is unhealthy. You should be able to talk openly about your feelings without worrying that you are going to say or do something that will cause your partner to leave.

When you are able to truly understand one another, you will feel that your harmony has been restored. Instead of living with your worries and fears, you will be able to put them to rest and focus on the things that you have going for you. A relationship should be a happy part of your life, not one that causes you grief. If you are truly struggling with your feelings, don't keep them inside. Take a deep breath and have an honest conversation with your spouse. When you do, you are already taking a big step toward relieving yourself of your relationship anxiety.

Also, understand that this is going to be one big process. You won't be able to solve all of your problems after having only one conversation. Get into the habit of checking in with one another. Realistically, you will know that talking about an issue only once might not be enough to fully resolve it. After each talk that you have, give yourself some time to think about the things that you discussed. You might also find that your feelings change or your viewpoints are broadened. This is why having follow-up conversations is also essential. Working on your problems together will allow you to feel that you are both contributing equally to the marriage.

Resolving Issues Together

The next step in your process will be learning how to resolve issues together. If you feel any kind of tension or difference in opinions, have a candid talk with your spouse. You do not need to wait until a problem develops before you talk about something that is bothering you. This will prevent you from worrying about issues that you might be intensifying in your head. Either one of you should be able to start the conversation at any time. When you get into this habit, you will be able to manage the anxiety that you once felt. Know that your conversations should be safe spaces where you are able to fully express yourselves.

As a couple, you can both do your best to research the topic of relationship anxiety so that you can each have a better understanding of it. This will make it less scary and less stressful. When you both feel that you are working together at solving the problem, you will be able to feel a true sense of partnership. This is also going to help you avoid experiencing relationship anxiety in the future. Healthy habits are going to continue to yield healthy results. You can be proud of yourselves for knowing that you are working together on this issue rather than struggling with it independently.

The following are some examples of certain conflicts and how to avoid making mistakes while dealing with them:

1. **Being Brutally Honest:** Being too harsh with one another isn't going to solve your conflicts. In fact, it is almost always going to create additional conflicts for you to deal with. Remember to focus on compassion rather than convincing. If you truly respect one another, you should be able to respect where you are

each coming from. When a person with relationship anxiety is met with brutal honesty, this can cause them to shut down or to become flustered. Try to keep the mood as lighthearted as possible, even when you are talking about important issues. As long as you are both reaching for the same result, you will be able to come together. You can be direct without being offensive or defensive.

2. **Only Sharing Feelings:** You might be wondering if sharing feelings is what you are *supposed* to be doing and it is, in a sense. But don't forget that you need to also share with your partner why you are feeling the way that you do. If you are constantly complaining or expressing your emotions without giving your partner some insight into what is causing you to feel this way, this can create problems in your marriage. They won't know how they are supposed to help you or what they need to do to make things better. Be as specific as possible! Practice your best communication skills.

3. **Getting Defensive:** When your partner expresses an opinion that directly contradicts your own, it can be hard to remain neutral as they start to explain why they feel the way that they do. You have likely had moments where you interrupted your partner or cut them off to explain why your opinion is the right opinion. This is a nearly guaranteed way to start an

argument. Respect your partner and their opinions, even when they are different from your own. This kind of tolerance shows them that you value how they feel and that you care about what they have to say. Once you hear both sides of the issue, you can then discuss it. By doing so, you will both find it easier to come to a middle ground.

4. **Not Asking Questions:** Being an agreeable partner is a redeeming quality, but it can backfire if you are too passive. A lot of mistakes that couples make is that they never question one another. While this might keep the relationship free of conflict at the moment, it is only going to create issues that will come up later on. If your partner says something that you do not understand, for whatever reason, ask them about it. Ask them to explain where they are coming from or why they feel the way that they do. When you have a genuine desire to achieve clarity, you are actually going to be able to resolve your conflict. Asking questions to be condescending is only going to add more fuel to the fire.

5. **Being Too Definitive:** When you use language that includes always/never, you are sending your partner a message that states you do not believe there is a solution to the problem that you are facing. If your partner does something that upsets you, it is best to avoid saying "you

ALWAYS" do this or you "are constantly" doing that. Try to pinpoint exactly when your partner has been doing the things that bother you to make a statement that these things can be fixed.

6. **Not Letting Go of Issues:** When working through a conflict, it can spiral very quickly. If you notice that you are both in a negative headspace and that your issues aren't being resolved, you might have to take a step back and come back to the conversation later. When one or both of you won't let go of the issue, this means that you aren't going to be able to get past it. Letting go of it together and working to find a solution shows that you are on the same page. No one likes to fight, but pride gets in the way sometimes. It can be very difficult to admit that you were wrong.

7. **Being Silent:** Using the silent treatment is not a valid way to fix your issues. By ignoring your partner, you aren't helping the situation. Instead, you are further angering them while allowing the problem to linger, and this is all due to immaturity. When you marry someone, you need to be able to have real conversations with them, no matter how tense they are. This is how you grow and learn. Having a healthy amount of conflict in your relationship is much better than experiencing phases of silence. Learn how to talk to one another and

understand that conflict means that you both still have passion.

Chapter 7: Recognizing Irrational Behaviors that Trigger Anxiety and Insecurity

The longer that you are in a relationship with someone, the more comfortable you become. After learning about every aspect of their personality and all of their habits, both good and bad, it is safe to say that you know your partner best. For this same reason, you will often become blind to the fact that you are being triggered by normal behaviors that cause you to act irrationally. When you are feeling anxious in your marriage, you will begin to take a second look at all of these things that you think you know about your partner. In your head, it becomes very easy to start second-guessing certain behaviors and actions. When something used to appear very normal to you, it might trigger you into a battle with insecurity that causes you to act irrationally toward your partner.

These examples might seem trivial because they are

often blown out of proportion. When you start to experience relationship anxiety, these things can make their way into the foreground of your brain. Once you start to question the behaviors, they will grow in severity thanks to your building insecurity. It can become a very toxic cycle if you are not careful. This is why being able to recognize when you are acting irrationally can do a lot for your marriage. By calming down and realizing what is factual and what is fueled by anxiety, both you and your partner will be a lot happier together. This kind of behavior can very easily tear a relationship apart if you let it. Being proactive; noticing if you are triggered by these things will show you a lot about what must be done to improve your relationship.

Examples

When Your Partner Doesn't Immediately Reply to Your Text

It is likely that the two of you text frequently. Texting has become a huge part of our lives in the last few decades, creating an instantaneous way to stay in touch with those we care about. When you and your partner are not together, texting can easily reconnect you and allow you to check on one another. It can be a very helpful way to communicate, but you must be aware of the pressure that it is placing on your relationship. Texting can actually lead to a lot of relationship anxiety, and this typically depends on how fast your partner replies to you.

When you are already experiencing relationship anxiety, any delay in communication with your partner is likely to send you into a spiral of irrational thoughts. You might jump to conclusions and think that they are cheating on you or that they do not want to talk to you. Stop and think about where your partner is and what they could be doing. There are likely endless possibilities. Instead of jumping to the very worst conclusion, ground yourself with a reminder that your partner could simply be busy. Whether they are out running errands, at work, or even driving, it might not be possible for them to get on their phone to text you at that moment.

Obsessing over something like this is only going to leave you feeling sick. It can even get to such an extreme that you start to fear that your partner has been hurt or has died. This is not a healthy way to live as you are waiting for a reply from the other person. Once they text you back, all of the negative feelings likely flee, only further proving the point that you were feeling these things as a part of your temporary anxiety. Try to calm yourself down as much as possible by using only rational and logical thinking. Do not be controlling or angry when they do not reply right away.

When Your Partner Can't Spend Time with You

As a couple, you likely spend a lot of quality time together. By living together, this also increases the amount of time that you get to be around one another. When you get upset with your partner for not wanting to, or not being able to, spend time together, then you are going to be placing a lot of pressure on your relationship. There are many valid reasons as to why your partner can't spend time with you. They might not have the energy because of a busy day at work, or they might have planned a night out with their friends. Understand that your partner is their own person too, not only your significant other.

When you can't spend time together, this doesn't mean that your love is fleeting. This also doesn't mean that your partner's feelings for you have changed. Being able to live your own lives while also being together is a sign of a healthy relationship. You both deserve to have friends and personal time outside of your relationship. Not always assuming that you are going to do everything together allows you to appreciate the quality time that you do have.

Know that it is perfectly normal for couples to spend time apart, even if it is only for a few hours at a time. Don't allow your mind to jump to conclusions. When your partner says that they are not able to spend time together, take that for what it is. Do not assume that you have done anything wrong or that you need to push them to be with you. Allow your love to blossom naturally. Anything that is forced in your relationship is only going to create conflicts. Remember, you do not control your significant other. They can do things on their own while still remaining loyal and faithful to you.

When Your Partner Receives a Call or Text

This is something that tends to start a lot of fights between couples, and it can become very unhealthy when it goes unaddressed — acting angry or suspicious when your partner gets a call/text is irrational behavior. When you are in a relationship, you should have a sense of trust between the two of you. Even if you can't see your partner's phone screen, you should trust that they are communicating in a way that is appropriate and respectful of your relationship. No matter who they are talking to, you should not be worrying about what your partner is saying or doing if you truly trust them. By getting worked up over this, you are only going to become obsessive each time their phone goes off.

Demanding to know who your partner is talking to at all times is taking away their right to privacy. Your anxiety can lead them to feel that they are being controlled, which is very unhealthy for any relationship. There is nothing wrong with asking your partner who they are talking to or what they are saying, but remember that they also deserve privacy. When you give your partner privacy, you are showing them that your trust in them is strong. Privacy does not equate to not caring. Instead, it shows that your relationship is stronger than your anxiety. While you might be curious, you can't allow it to get the best of you.

Remind yourself of the commitment that you made to one another. This should not have to be renewed each time that your partner responds to a text message. Your partner's feelings are not going to change in a matter of seconds. Keep all of those irrational thoughts at bay and try your best to remain calm. If you do not have a valid reason to suspect that anything is wrong, you need to take your partner's word for it. It can be maddening to tell someone that everything is okay, yet they never believe you. The feeling becomes even worse when you try to take matters into your own hands. At no point in time should you ever secretly look through your partner's phone. This is a huge violation of anyone's privacy.

When Your Partner Appears to Be Distant

In your relationship, there are times when you likely just do not feel like talking. This does not mean that your partner has done anything wrong, but it is a valid feeling that you should acknowledge. In life, anything is possible. With all of the stressors that we experience through any given day, this can be enough to lead us to a temporarily reclusive state of being. Sometimes, being quiet and alone is what we need to recharge. As you remind yourself that it is okay to feel this way, also remind yourself that your partner is going to feel this way too sometimes. Not wanting to talk or engage with your significant other does not always mean that they have done something unfavorable or that something is wrong.

By getting out of the mindset that things are always your fault, you will be able to better understand your partner. Know that you can offer your help or guidance, but they still might require some alone time to sort through their feelings. As long as you are able to offer your support, you are a great partner. You will be an even greater partner by respecting their wishes. Do not push your partner into talking to you or being around you after they have already expressed that they need distance. Take away your negative connotations with the idea of needing distance, as it is a healthy human behavior. Being with one another 24/7 isn't realistic, even if you are married and living together. You are both going to need your own space sometimes. Instead of worrying about what the problem is or what you did wrong, you can really step it up by being there for your partner when they express that they need you.

When Your Partner Takes Jokes Too Far

Couples who are able to maintain a sense of humor together often have a very fun and fulfilling relationship. Being able to joke with the person that you are closest to can be very amusing, especially when you know so much about one another. The thing about joking around is that you still need to have boundaries, even with your significant other. When you are being comical, remember that both of you should be laughing. If one person is highly amused while the other is being hurt, then this is not funny. Speak up if your partner takes any joking around too far. By letting it go on, you are only going to be encouraging this behavior. Plus, your partner truly might not have even realized that it upset you. This is why you need to speak up for yourself.

Alternatively, you also need to understand that your partner might ask the same of you. Do not take this personally, allowing your anxiety to tell you that your partner does not love you anymore because you joke around too much. Listen to what they are saying and understand that you might have hurt their feelings. This is not the end of your relationship, but it should be the end of the behavior that caused them to feel this way. Jokes that get taken too far are often based on truths that have not yet been spoken. If you have something important to say, have a proper conversation about it. Any pending issues need to be worked through, not turned into comedy. Know that there is a time and a place for everything. When you are so close to someone, you can't take everything so personally. This is a hard thing to remember, but it will help you manage your anxiety.

When Your Partner Won't Propose to You

For many women, the thought of a significant other delaying a proposal can often lead to anxiety. Doubts will begin to come to mind, wondering if their partner truly wants to commit and questioning why a proposal has yet to happen. Even when both partners agree that they would like to get married, the thought of when this is going to happen can be nerve-wracking. For a lot of men, the pressures are different. Because men tend to be the ones to propose, they usually delay because they are waiting for the right moment. This time in between can be stressful for some couples, causing tension and conflict.

If you have relationship anxiety, all of these feelings can be heightened. You might drive yourself crazy wondering if your partner still sees you as marriage material and questioning why they haven't made the commitment yet. Instead of letting your anxiety turn into insecurity, bring up a conversation with your partner. Without pressuring your partner into proposing, you can discuss your feelings on the topic and get some reassurance that marriage is something that you both still want.

When there is any type of delay in a marriage proposal, it is usually due to the fact that the man wants to live up to the woman's expectations. He will hear about the woman's dream proposal and might feel as though he cannot make it as perfect as she wants it to be. Alternatively, the longer that the woman is waiting to be proposed to, the more she will let the doubts start to creep in. Instead of considering that her partner is trying to make it as wonderful as possible, she might be led to feelings of anxiety and doubt. This situation can easily spiral downward when it really doesn't have to. As long as you know that you are both on the same page, patience should be exercised.

Chapter 8: How Do You Stop Being Anxious and Insecure in a Relationship?

When you are given techniques that are proven to be successful, you will be able to put your anxiety to rest. In many cases, not knowing what to do with the anxiety that you feel can lead to several different emotions. One minute, you might feel that you and your partner have a wonderful relationship, and the next you might be doubtful of everything that you share. This chapter focuses on real methods that you can use in your own life. They will help you manage your anxiety while keeping you focused on the positive reality of your relationship. Everyone experiences anxiety at some point, but it doesn't have to rule over you. Being able to set it aside and focus on making your relationship grow is ideal.

Without traveling too far outside of your comfort zone, you will learn how to combat these feelings in the easiest ways possible. Instead of fighting with your anxious thoughts or trying to push them aside, you will learn how to deal with them head-on. Through practical problem-solving, you will realize that it is never as bad as your mind wants you to believe it is. Anxiety is one of the most powerful mental forces that you can experience. It can even alter the way that you view your reality. Once you are able to see past this, you will feel empowered and ready to take on any challenge that you face. This kind of awareness makes you a better partner and allows you to have a more fulfilling relationship.

Strategies and Exercises

1. Starting with your physical body, you can actually do a lot for your anxiety by making sure that you are getting enough exercise. When you get up and move, this allows endorphins to run through you. Endorphins make you feel good, and it is very healthy to select activities each day that boost your levels. Being mindful while paired with engaging in this physical activity will also give you a new perspective on the things that you are worried about. Staying caught up in your head can promote a clouded mindset. When you take the time to clear your mind and body, you are going to feel the difference.

   Exercise can be done alone or with your partner. Having alone time is essential to any relationship, but getting active with your partner can also have its benefits. Try both! When the focus is on something entirely different, your relationship anxiety is naturally going to subside. It can be very beneficial for you to change your mindset, even if it is only for an hour while you are exercising.

   When you exercise, this changes your perspective automatically. It is a way to take your mind off of your life, and instead, to focus on the exercise or activity that you are doing. Even if you aren't big on going to the gym, you can find other ways that you can get your exercise in at home or through classes. There are endless options that can actually be a lot of fun.

2. When you get into your moments of anxiety, don't suppress them! Talk to your partner about what you are feeling, even if you think that it's stupid. Your feelings should always be valid in your relationship, so your partner shouldn't make you feel stupid for sharing them. Your partner should be there for you during these moments where you are struggling. While they should not have to act as your therapist, having support from your significant other is not a lot to ask for in a relationship. If they were to have the same kind of anxiety and worries, you would be there for them as well.

Even if your partner cannot help you fix your problems, they can provide you with an outlet and help you tackle them. When you speak out loud about your issues, this takes away their power. By having someone who simply understands you, or tries to see where you are coming from, this can allow you to feel less alone as you try to find solutions to fix your problems. This is what a healthy relationship should look like. Keep in mind that your partner might not be able to help you actually heal from your anxiety, but their support should not go unnoticed. When you can be candid about your insecurities, this is going to help your relationship grow. It will show your partner that you are willing to work on your downfalls.

3. Letting go of control can be extremely difficult, especially when you are struggling. Know that it is essential that you are able to let go of this control though. Your anxiety is going to be telling you that you need to have more control or something bad is going to happen. When you accept that you actually cannot control everything, you will be able to work on ways that you can make the good moments even better and deal with the bad ones. Instead of thinking about your life as a doomsday situation, bring yourself back down to reality. Realize that this isn't a matter of life or death and that you are going to be okay.

When you are so consumed by the thought of having control over your life, this definitely impacts your relationship. Your partner might need you, yet you will only be able to see the things that pertain to your control issues. Whether you are bummed about having to work late or a friend getting upset with you, know that these are not situations that should completely derail you. Know that you will get through them, and you can vent to your partner if you need to. There is a difference between talking about the things that get you down and letting them completely take over your life and your decisions. When you learn how to let go of your control, you are actually going to feel a lot more free in your life.

4. When you are in your anxiety mode, your reactions to certain things are going to be a lot different than your normal reactions. Learn how to recognize when you are acting out of anxiety. This is going to help you correct your behavior and allow yourself to get grounded once again. Listen to your partner if they ever tell you that they think you are acting irrationally. As you know, anxiety can often lead to irrational behavior. You should not take this personally, as this hint can actually tell you that you might be letting your anxiety take over your life. Also, know that your partner is telling you this because they care about you and want you to be healthy.

Everything that you do is going to end up impacting your partner in some way. While they might not be able to feel the relationship anxiety that you feel, they are going to notice a difference in your behavior when you are experiencing it. You might be easily angered or even more clingy, but these behaviors should be fairly easy to spot. When you get the hang of identifying them, you can then set your focus on how to put your anxiety to rest. Try to compare and contrast; once your anxiety passes, ask yourself if you would have acted the same way or if you would act differently now. You might find that your reactions are entirely different when anxiety isn't pressuring you.

5. Anxiety comes along with triggers. These are things that can send you into anxious moods or behaviors. A trigger can be something that reminds you of an event that you once went through or just something that causes you to feel insecure. Everyone has different triggers, and there is nothing wrong with this. You cannot help it because they are triggering to you based on what you have experienced in your life. While you cannot avoid them in your daily life, you can make your partner aware of them to help strengthen your relationship. When you inform them of the things that upset you and why, you are allowing them in and shedding light on the issues.

If you find that you are constantly being triggered by things that your partner does, yet you do not let them know, this becomes unfair. You are going to feel upset all the time, and your partner isn't going to know what they are doing wrong. To help this situation, you need to rely on your communication skills. See how important they are and make sure that you do not take them for granted. When you tell your partner about your triggers, try your best to explain each one. To do so, you need to get to the roots of your issues. With enough practice, this shouldn't be too difficult. Place a priority on honesty and openness; it will make a difference.

6. In terms of reassurance, physical affection can do a lot to ease your anxiety. Even something as simple as holding hands can remind you of how great your relationship is and how much your partner loves you. While you should not solely rely on physical intimacy to know that your partner cares, it can be a welcome reminder during the times when you are plagued with anxiety. Without being overly clingy, you and your partner can regain your closeness by displaying a little bit of affection for one another. Know that they likely want reassurance just as much as you do. Even if you are already well past your honeymoon stage, physical affection can remind you about the things that you love about one another.

It isn't wrong to ask your partner for physical affection. Just because they are not being physically affectionate does not mean that they do not want to be. By asking for a hug or asking to cuddle, your partner might realize that they really wanted and needed the intimacy, yet they were distracted by other things in life. This can happen very easily. The longer you are together, the easier it becomes to take physical affection for granted. When you can rekindle the feeling, you are going to feel very loved and very close to one another. Do your best to show one another small acts of affection on a daily basis to keep the intimacy strong.

7. Having a standard in your mind of what your relationship *should* look like or *should* be like is going to become very damaging to how your relationship actually operates. Try your best not to compare your partner or your relationship to the things that you see around you. Each relationship is unique and made up of entirely different people. Instead of placing a comparison on your relationship, do your best to see the great qualities that you share with your partner. Learn how to appreciate them for who they are and respect the things that they love. When you two are able to be completely genuine and comfortable with one another, this is going to create a great foundation for your relationship.

There is no such thing as perfect. If you are only trying to strive for perfection, this is likely going to drive you straight to a state of anxiety. Know that you do not have to maintain your relationship in a certain way to impress other people. Many people admit to making their relationship appear better than it actually is because they do not want others to know that they face problems. Every single couple faces problems. It is not realistic to always get along and live in harmony with your spouse; you are two different people! What matters is how you work through these issues, as you cannot let them divide you. Know that you don't have to impress or convince anyone of your happiness; just be happy.

8. A very valuable option for getting help with your relationship anxiety is to seek therapy. When you see a therapist, you have the option to get all of your anxious thoughts out of your head. This is what the therapist is there for. When you are able to sort through your issues, this is not only going to make you a better person but a better partner. Know that you can see a therapist on your own, or you can begin couple's therapy with your partner. Both are going to have their own benefits. In individual therapy, you will be speaking on your problems from your perspective. The focus will mainly be on you. Engaging in couple's therapy will allow both yourself and your partner to have your own voices.

A lot of stigma is placed around getting help for your mental health, but know that this judgment should not hinder you from getting help. If you think that therapy might be the answer, or if you are curious to try it, listen to your gut instinct. The opinions of others should not be able to dictate what you can and cannot do in your life. By taking back control over what you are doing, this is going to allow you to feel that you truly can tackle your anxiety. A lot of people find that it is just too hard to deal with their anxiety without this outside help. If you are one of them, know that this isn't shameful!

Chapter 9: How to Use Your Relationship Anxiety to Grow

All of the exercises that were provided in the previous chapter follow a certain theme — putting the anxiety in its place. When you can decide how you are going to live your life and how you are going to interact with your partner, you will be a lot happier with the decisions that you make. Your anxiety does not have to control you, so don't give in! In this chapter, you are going to focus on how to use your relationship anxiety to grow. When you can turn your hardships into a way to become a better person and a better partner, this is a true sign of growth. It can seem difficult to get your anxiety under control, but you should also know by now that it is not impossible. When you can find the strategies that work for you, this will show you a small beacon of hope and how your anxiety does not always have to lead you.

Establish a Deeper Connection

When you first began dating your partner, there was likely a lot to talk about. That early stage of any relationship is typically bustling with conversation and the desire to put in the effort to impress one another. This honeymoon stage is something that all couples know is fleeting, but it doesn't have to disappear entirely. Even when you already know everything about your partner, try not to lose interest in them. People can change and grow, so you actually probably don't know everything about your partner. Show them that you still care to know new things and that you still find them just as interesting as you did when you first began dating.

Your connection with one another is limitless. This is the person that you have chosen to spend the rest of your life with, so make sure that you are still able to show them how much you care and how much they intrigue you. When couples lose this magic, the relationship can very quickly become stale. This will often trigger a great deal of relationship anxiety. Not all relationships must fizzle out just because you have been together for a long time. You still need to put in the effort for one another if you want to be in a thriving relationship. It takes work that you must be willing to constantly improve on. Keep learning about what your partner needs from you and think about new ways to give that to them.

When you have an ever-growing connection with your partner, this is going to promote healthy communication skills and excellent conflict resolution skills. In turn, this also strengthens your trust. Overall, you can see that deepening your connection with your partner is going to provide many benefits for the relationship. By having a clear awareness of what one another needs from the relationship, you will both be able to become the best partners that you can be. Understand the ways in which relationships evolve over time. Nothing is going to stay the same forever, but this does not mean that your love or connection will be lost. By accepting these changes, you will be able to learn the ways that you need to grow and work on yourself to adapt.

This is a very powerful way in which you can take your relationship anxiety and turn it around to better serve you. If you feel that you are becoming disconnected from your partner, it is not too late to rebuild your relationship. Having an honest conversation can do a lot for the two of you. Even if you don't want to get into a heavy issue, you can be candid about something that is more lighthearted. By getting back into the habit of regularly communicating with your partner, they are likely going to follow suit. When you can both bounce these ideas off of one another, back and forth, you are creating something that will allow you to bond. Listen to your needs and don't be afraid to ask your partner for more if you require it.

Spend Quality Time Together

Learn about what is important to your partner, from their hobbies to their passions. When you two can spend quality time doing these things together, it will bring you closer together. You will also have a better understanding of who your partner is. It feels great when someone cares to learn about the things that you enjoy doing, so give this feeling to your partner whenever possible. Instead of worrying about what your partner might be thinking or desiring, you can learn about what they actually want. This will allow you some relief with your relationship anxiety. The anxiety stems from a fear of the unknown, so it makes sense that you would feel better when you know exactly what your partner loves to do.

There is a fine line between bonding with your partner and forcing yourself to do things that you do not enjoy.

You are doing to have differences in what each of you finds enjoyable, but when you can find some commonalities, then you are going to be able to become even closer. Just because you are a couple does not mean that you are required to do everything together. Try new things because you want to, not because you feel that you have to force yourself to do them. This will show your partner that you are genuinely interested in doing things that they enjoy without compromising your own interests and passions. If you are having trouble finding common ground, you can even seek out brand new activities that you have both never tried before. Discovering life this way will allow you to grow even closer to your partner. It will allow your anxiety to subside while you are both having fun in the process.

It is a very motivational feeling when you can still find new and exciting things to do with your significant other, even when you have already been dating for a while. Life doesn't have to become boring just because you are married or in a long-term relationship. Having a sense of adventure is going to keep the magic alive. The worst thing that can happen is you will discover that you do not enjoy doing these activities. When this happens, you can come together to try to discover other things that you both want to do. Couples often forget that the discovery process does not end as the years progress. You do not have to settle into a permanent routine. While having a routine provides you with a sense of security, being open to new adventures will keep you feeling refreshed.

You'll notice that the more you try with your partner, the less you will be faced with worries that you are not good enough or exciting enough for them. Instead of succumbing to the fears that pop into your head, you will be taking action. This is going to make you feel great and show your partner that you are invested in the relationship. Couples who have fun together are less likely to get into arguments over trivial things. You will both be able to realize that there is a lot more out there that you can do together to keep your bond strong and to keep your relationship feeling how it did in the beginning.

Go the Extra Mile

Your anxiety can either drive you to a breaking point or motivate you into making a change. When you are willing to go the extra mile for your partner, you can tune out of the same fears that keep popping up in your mind. For example, you can continuously think of new ways to show your partner love and affection without being clingy, as your anxiety might suggest you need to be. Instead of smothering them, do things that are thoughtful and considerate based on their needs. Cooking a meal for your spouse or cleaning up their bedside table can be a simple yet effective way to show them how much you care.

It is important to be true to yourself while you are doing kind things for your partner. If you get to the point where you are sacrificing your own happiness to make your significant other happy, then this is just as unhealthy as letting the anxiety take over. You need to find the right balance that makes sense in your relationship. When you want to do something nice for your partner, think about the little things that you can achieve quickly. Sometimes, less is more when you want to add extra effort into your relationship.

Make sure that you still go on dates. Having a regular date night can be very beneficial to your relationship. Try new restaurants that you've always wanted to try, spend a night exploring your own city, or see two movies back-to-back. There are countless ways that you can have a date with your partner without falling into the same old routines that you are used to. When you do something different, you are showing your partner that you are putting in some extra effort. Instead of focusing on the extravagant things that you want to do together, know that these little things will add up. You can take your relationship further than ever before by incorporating these small gestures into your regular routines.

If something reminds you of your partner, let them know. It can be really nice to hear that your spouse is thinking about you when you aren't together. This showcases your closeness and your bond. It is also a nice way to check-in with one another to see how your days are going. Your goal should be to keep the romance alive. Instead of worrying that the romance is already gone, as your anxiety wants to lead you to believe, you can prove that your relationship is much stronger than your worries. Tell yourself that what you have with your partner is special and then do your best to cultivate it every single day.

When you can prove to yourself that you are enough, your worries will begin to listen to you. Negative thinking can put you into a very dark mindset very quickly. Before you know it, you will have a very warped perception of your own relationship. Focusing on the good things that you know you share with your partner is going to serve as a reminder of why you should always aim to keep improving your relationship. No one else is going to be able to convince you of this except for yourself.

Learn about the Warning System

If you just can't seem to shake your anxiety, there is something that you can do to put a positive spin on it. By becoming great at recognizing your triggers and irrational behaviors, you will also be able to see your anxiety as a built-in warning system. This means that you should be able to recognize your anxious thoughts as an alarm telling you that you need to reframe your thinking. Whether you are being triggered by something or just obsessing over something, this is an indication that you are too deep in your head. Consider if you are seeing your own relationship and your own partner clearly. Confirm that you understand exactly where your thoughts and feelings are coming from. By taking a moment to reflect on this, it can save you a lot of hardship when your anxiety does flare up.

Breathing is so important. Whenever you get really worked up over something that your anxiety creates, take some time to just breathe before you react. When you can stop to breathe, you can also empty your mind. Think about the things that are factual and true. Anything based on worry, fear, or insecurity can be set aside for the moment. This is going to guide you toward the strategy you should already be familiar with — getting to the root of the issue. With a clear mind, you will be able to make more rational decisions.

Your anxiety triggers your fight-or-flight response. No matter which action you take, it is usually one that is based on fear-driven rationality. Instead of living your life based on where your fears take you, try to shift this focus. You can remember the things that make you happy, the things that you are passionate about. Once you have your sights set back onto these things of importance, you will be able to make a much better decision on what to do next. It takes a lot of self-discipline to not give in to the anxiety as soon as you feel it, but it is going to help you tremendously once you are able to see that you *can* control yourself.

Don't be so hard on yourself when you do realize that you are feeling anxious. Remember, you can't help that you have relationship anxiety. The only thing that you can do is work with your symptoms and focus on the good things that you already have going for you. This will automatically put you in a more positive mindset that will make you a better partner in return. Those who live their lives while making thoughtful decisions are often happier with the outcomes of said decisions. You will feel that your choices are made deliberately instead of feeling that these things are simply happening to you.

Chapter 10: Improving Self-Awareness and Self-Passion with Anxiety in a Relationship

While the focus so far has been on how to be a better partner while dealing with relationship anxiety, know that your own feelings are also very important. If you do not like the person you are becoming because of the anxiety that you are facing, know that you are not alone. A lot of people struggle with their own self-worth when they experience relationship anxiety because it can become very easy to punish yourself over your actions. Instead of focusing on the things that you are bad at or the things that you are doing wrong, this chapter is going to teach you how to be kinder to yourself. When you are constantly putting yourself down, this is only going to become more stressful and promote more anxiety. The way that you use your inner-voice can make a big difference in the way that you make your future decisions.

Before you begin with these exercises, make sure that

you are in the right mindset to work on yourself. Understand that you deserve kindness and respect, just as your partner does. Make a promise that you are no longer going to tear yourself down or disrespect yourself just because you are struggling. Instead, you must focus on compassion. If your partner were going through a hard time, it is much more likely that you would act compassionately rather than angrily. Try to uphold these same standards for the way that you treat yourself. It sends a very conflicting message to your brain when you are being so kind to your partner yet so horrible to yourself.

Being kind to yourself can be a lot harder than it seems. It might take you a long time to get out of your negative headspace, but that is okay. Another skill that you are going to have to use is patience. Be patient with yourself and understand that this is going to be a process. You cannot expect results after only one day of positive thinking. However, when you put in the effort each day, you are going to end up seeing results. You are only going to get here by believing in yourself and believing in the process. If you are tired of being ruled by your anxiety, this is all the reason that you need to make a change for the better. Use this as a motivational tool to help you improve yourself. Remind yourself of how hard it can be to constantly feel that you have to answer to your anxiety before you do things.

It can be hard to commit to focusing on yourself, especially when you haven't been very kind to yourself lately. This chapter is going to teach you how to get back to these basics of self-care. It is not uncommon that people forget how to care for themselves when they enter a serious relationship. The focus tends to shift on the other person so much that it can be very easy to lose your own sense of what you need to be happy. Putting a stop to this imbalance as soon as you notice it will also help keep your relationship intact. When your partner sees how much you are doing for them, yet can also see that you are neglecting yourself, this can put pressure on them and on your relationship. For anything to be harmonious, it must be balanced first.

Accept that Anxiety is Common

The first step to working on yourself comes when you are able to let go of any guilt that you might be holding onto. You are not the only person who has felt relationship anxiety before; that is a fact. No matter how great your relationship or your partner is, you can still experience relationship anxiety. This is not your fault, and it is definitely not something that you need to punish yourself for. Before you get angry or frustrated with yourself for feeling the way that you do, stop to think about what this negativity is going to do for your relationship anxiety. Is it going to make it better? The more likely answer is that it is going to stress you out even more, causing you even more anxiety.

People experience relationship anxiety because they just want to be loved. This is one of the most universal human desires that you can experience. It is normal and healthy to desire love because love allows you to feel whole. While you don't need it to survive, having it in your life is very fulfilling. Before you can expect others to love you, it is important that you can love yourself. Try to recognize the amazing qualities that you have to offer. Write down all of the strengths that you have and read the list when you start to sink into a negative mindset. It might be uncomfortable to give yourself this much praise, but this is how you are going to grow. By acknowledging all of these great things about yourself, it will become easier for you to see what your partner sees in you.

If it helps you, speak to your friends and loved ones who also suffer from relationship anxiety. Knowing that you're not alone can provide you with a calming sense of solidarity. Being open to these conversations will normalize the idea of relationship anxiety, further proving that it is nothing for you to feel shame or guilt over. When you can talk to someone other than your significant other who experiences the same things that you do, it might be easier to think about ways that you can handle it. Seek advice and inspiration from those around you.

Wanting to be happy is not something that you should feel wrong for wanting. As long as you are being good to your partner and being good to yourself, there should be no reason why you must hold yourself back from experiencing happiness. The negative voices in your head might be telling you otherwise, but know that you have so much power within. You have the power to silence these voices and to prove that you are worthy of love and happiness. The power behind positive thinking is amazing once you get the hang of it.

Practice Mindfulness

Being mindful is not the same thing as being self-centered. Many people are under the misconception that mindfulness makes you a selfish person. In fact, it makes you the opposite! When you are mindful, this means that you have a heightened sense of awareness and understanding of what is going on around you. This all begins from within, being mindful of the way you are feeling and why. When you can show yourself some empathy, you will be able to do the same for your partner. As mentioned, it sends your brain a confusing message when you are kind to your partner yet degrading to yourself. Your actions need to match your words.

It can be hard to get into the mindset of mindful thinking, especially when the daily tasks of life are pressuring you into thinking about other things. No matter what you have going on each day, devote at least 10 minutes of time in which you can be by yourself. With this time, you are going to work on your mindfulness. The easiest way to do this is by meditating. You do not have to take a yoga class to receive all of the benefits of meditation. Sitting alone in a dimly lit room for these 10 minutes can be enough to shift your way of thinking. Try your best to empty your head as you meditate, imagining that you are being surrounded by a warm ball of light. At the end of your meditation, leave yourself with a positive affirmation about yourself.

Forgiveness is another way to practice mindfulness. You must be able to forgive yourself, just as you are able to forgive others. When you make a mistake, acknowledge that you could have done better without putting yourself down. Think about the things that you can do next time to improve yourself. If you are constantly punishing yourself when you make mistakes, there will be no lessons learned. Mistakes give you an opportunity to do better and to be better. Realize that you need to be constructive with your criticism. Don't let your anxiety get the best of you by pushing you into a negative string of emotions.

When you begin to live as a mindful individual, the little things that once bothered you so much won't hold the same weight. While you might face inconveniences and hard times, you need to always look at the bigger picture. Remember to be thankful for the things that you already have. Counting your blessings each day is another way to remain mindful. It can be so easy to focus on what is wrong that you will start to forget what is right and what is stable. These pillars of stability will provide you with the strength that you need to move forward. Lean on them when you are in need.

Seek Outlets for Your Thoughts

While you can talk to your partner about the way that you are feeling, know that you should not make them your therapist. This is an unfair position to put anyone in, especially the person that you are romantically involved with. Other people, including your partner, are only going to be able to listen to your problems and provide you with advice if they feel that they can relate to these things. They want the best for you, but you have to want the best for you too. Realize that there are other outlets that you can utilize when your anxious thoughts become overwhelming. Going to therapy is a very valuable experience that you should give yourself the opportunity to try. As mentioned, therapy is a very good way to work on yourself with the help of an individual who only has your best interest in mind.

There are other ways that you can express yourself. Writing can be a very healing method to try. When your journal each day, you are allowing a place to store your thoughts. Think about your journaling as a release. Once the negativity and anxiety are placed onto the page, let it stay there. The more that you practice letting go of things, the less likely they are going to be able to torment you later. Clearing your mind will make room for new thoughts and better mindsets. Those who feel that they cannot open up to self-love usually don't have any room to think positively.

Exercise can be another great outlet for you to use. You know how great endorphins can make you feel and when you exercise, you are giving yourself something else to focus on. By turning your attention toward your physical health, your mental health is also going to improve. Sometimes, it takes a little bit of physical activity to remind you that there are other ways that you can take care of yourself. Without the health of your physical body, you would not be able to do much. This is why eating and sleeping properly also become big components of taking care of yourself.

No matter which outlet you choose, make sure that your negative thoughts are staying away once you release them. If you need to, use an outlet more than once to truly get the anxiety out of your head. It might be necessary, but that doesn't make it any less effective. Anxiety can be very stubborn and clingy, but you do not need to give in. Know that you are strong enough to face any thought that comes to your mind, so don't fret if you need to try several times before you feel that you are truly making a difference. The self-love journey is going to become a lifelong journey for you.

Fall in Love with Yourself

Self-love will take practice. If you are having trouble being kind to yourself, you are not alone. Many people find this difficult because it makes them uncomfortable. You must understand that self-love is not selfish. It is within your right to be proud of yourself and to be kind to yourself. If you cannot get to this point right away, you need to remember to be gentle with yourself. Anxiety responds to stress and any added stress in your life is going to make your anxiety a lot worse. If you can eliminate some of the anxiety that you experience by simply being nicer to yourself, then you will see how self-love can be a great tool to use when you are going through a difficult time.

To do this, you must step outside of your comfort zone. If you have a hard time accepting compliments or saying kind things about yourself, this exercise is going to get you in a different mindset. Sit down with a piece of paper and a pen. Put on a 10-minute timer and don't stop writing kind things about yourself until that timer goes off. Do not think too hard about what you write down. These ideas should come to you naturally. When you list the first things that come to mind, you will be able to see an idea of what you really think about yourself. There is always going to be room for improvement, but it is important that you can identify the things that you are proud of yourself for at the moment.

Spend some time with yourself outside of the house. The great thing about alone time is that you can do exactly what you want when you want. Do something that you have been wanting to do for a long time, something that you truly enjoy. When you can be your true self, you are going to be able to see more reasons why you should love yourself. Even around your spouse, there might be times when you feel that you have to hold back from what you are saying or thinking. This happens when you care about people and don't want to upset them. By spending time with yourself, you are really going to get to know yourself.

Some people become really uncomfortable with the thought of being alone because their anxiety mistakenly informs them that they cannot survive without their partner or their relationship. While your partner can feel like your other half, make sure that you know you are still a whole person without them. You have your own hobbies and interests. Your personality is unique to you. Those who get into the codependent mindset usually have a harder time breaking free of their anxiety and loving themselves.

Understand External Influences

Did you know that there are other factors that can contribute to your relationship anxiety? People and situations that exist outside of your marriage can actually give you anxiety. Whether it is a friend with a strong opinion of how you are living your life or pressure that you are feeling from your family, these outside forces actually have a lot to do with the anxiety that you experience within your relationship. Without being too guarded, you always need to protect yourself from these outside factors. There are plenty of other people in your life whom you love and respect, but know that they have the ability to hurt you as well. While working on protecting yourself, you should also work on standing up for yourself.

When you find that something or someone external is impacting your relationship, put a barrier up between the stressor and the relationship. The only people who truly have a say in the relationship are you and your partner. Other people can become very opinionated, but this does not mean that they should dictate anything about your life or your love life. Work on setting these boundaries, not only because you respect your relationship but because you respect your partner.

When a couple does not have boundaries like this in place, they often struggle with conflicts that arise due to issues that other people start.

Getting a handle on the issues that you and your partner face might lead you to realize that it is the external factors causing your stress. By letting go of the outside noise that you cannot control, you will likely find a lot of relief for your anxiety. Unfortunately, you aren't always going to be able to eliminate these stressors, but you do have the ability to control how you react. When you are secure in yourself and your relationship, it leaves little room for anxiety to develop, especially anxiety that is caused by outside forces. Before you react unfavorably to something, consider if it is worth your time and energy. Is there anything else that you could be doing that would be more fulfilling or productive?

You and your partner can actually bond when you both realize that these outside forces cannot hinder your relationship. Couples who get worked up over these things often end up in fights that stem from things that they cannot change. When you two can work together as a team, you are going to feel a lot more secure in your relationship. Remember, you should both be on the same page and working toward the same goals. When you feel that you and your partner are divided, you can work on ways to regain closeness and remind yourself that you both want the same things. Focus on your love and your happiness.

Work on Self-Care

You've heard the term mentioned several times so far, but you might still be wondering one thing — what qualifies as self-care? Anything that you do that allows you to have fun or relax with the sole purpose of making yourself feel good is self-care. This is going to vary for people because everyone has different interests. You might enjoy spending time alone at home, while others might enjoy going out and doing things outside of the house. No matter where you go or what you do, the self-care methods that you select should help you feel happy and stable.

Aside from the activities that you do with yourself, also focus on eating and sleeping better. What you eat and how much you sleep both impact your self-care routine greatly. If you are exhausted and not nourishing yourself properly, this is going to naturally lead you to a bad mood. Your brain and body cannot function without a healthy eating and sleeping routine. Make it a point to go to bed 30 minutes earlier and to eat more fresh fruits and vegetables each day. Small changes that are made consistently will help make a difference in your overall goal of self-care.

If you still feel that your anxiety is flaring up while you are practicing self-care, consider that you might be loading your body with vices that are making you feel anxious. Do you drink coffee? Alcohol? Do you smoke? Any of these things can be habit-forming, causing your mind and body to feel that they are dependent on them. Try your best to work through your vices, showing your body that you can survive without any of them. This is going to be a process, but you will feel a lot better when you can be free of any demanding habits.

You might begin to feel guilty when you practice self-care because you aren't thinking about your relationship as much as you used to. This is okay! It is normal to take a break from thinking about your love life and your partner to better focus on yourself. This does not make you a bad or neglectful partner. Realize that your own needs are important, too. You are your own person, and it is okay that you need time for yourself.

Through the different activities that you decide to do with yourself, you will realize that you probably have a lot of work to do. Many are surprised to find that they are in healthy relationships, yet the one they need to improve is their relationship with themselves. As you work through this journey of self-care, it can be a good idea to write down how you are feeling. This will allow you to have something to compare your current feelings to when you begin to make progress.

Rewire Your Brain

When you feel yourself jumping to the worst possible conclusion, step in and tell your brain that this is irrational. Unless you have been given clear signs that something is devastatingly wrong, then there is no reason for you to stress yourself out. Begin breathing exercises as soon as you can feel your brain jumping to conclusions. Take several deep breaths to get centered. Now, think about what you were originally worried about. Understand that you are likely reacting this way because the situation is out of your control; you must accept this. To soothe your nerves, think about the things that you *can* control. This should be easy because you will realize that you can control your own actions. So, what are you going to do that will allow you to feel better and to remain calm?

If you need to use reason, you can think about realistic outcomes of the situation that you are worried about. Understand that there is only so much that you can do, so there is no point in getting yourself worked up to the point where you experience anxiety. Distractions can also be welcome when you are trying to avoid anxiety. Self-care can be a very nice way to distract yourself because it is also productive. When you can work on yourself and loving yourself, you will be able to feel better about the little things that once worried you.

Your goal is to rewire your brain. When an anxious thought threatens to take over, you need to replace it with something that is more positive. Whether it is a thought about self-love or something that you are looking forward to, you need to give yourself encouragement that it is okay to stop thinking about your relationship to spare your mental health. The more that you learn how to replace your negative thoughts, the better you will begin to feel. You do not have to give in to anxiety, even when it is very persistent.

If you begin to feel insecure in your relationship because of your anxiety, remember the great exercises that you learned that will allow you to strengthen your relationship. Give your partner compliments and do kind things for them without any prompting. When you do things because you genuinely want to, your partner is going to feel your love. Know that your love is enough and who you are is enough. In a healthy relationship, you should feel that you don't have to change yourself to make your partner happy. You also need to be in tune with your own needs to ensure that they are also being met. It is okay to feel insecure at times; this is natural. What matters most is how you handle your insecurities. When you can see that you are a whole person with valuable qualities, you will be able to find ways to love yourself as much as you love your partner.

Conclusion

As you continue on with your relationship anxiety journey, know that you are going to have your own ups and downs. Sometimes, you might feel that you are in total control of your feelings. Other times, the anxiety is going to threaten to take over control. When you can find a balance, no matter what is going on, you are going to be a lot happier in your relationship. You should find solace in knowing that relationship anxiety is normal, and it is not your fault. Anxiety is a very powerful force that can be incredibly hard to control. Now that you understand what you can do about it, your healing journey can officially begin.

You can use this book at any time that you feel you need additional support. When the anxiety is particularly bad, you can review the different methods to combat it. There are also plenty of helpful hints throughout this book that will remind you how to refocus your energy. When you become too focused and obsessive over one thought or idea, this is going to give your anxiety an invitation to come forward. You will be able to tell right away when you are not balanced. This is going to be your number one indicator that you must make a change to preserve your mental health and the health of your relationship.

Having doubts in any relationship is normal, no matter how long you have been together or how well you know each other. What is important is how you handle your doubts. If you keep them inside and allow them to torment you, this is going to impact the way that you feel about relationship anxiety. By having an honest conversation with your partner, you will have an outlet for your doubts while simultaneously receiving reassurance. Understand that it is not up to your partner to make you feel better though. You need to be able to calm yourself down and keep yourself in check.

Your past can trigger you and this is not your fault. If you have had horrible past relationship experiences, then it makes sense that you would carry these worries into your current relationship. What you need to remember is that not every relationship is going to mirror your past experiences. Even if you have been through plenty of hardship, know that not everyone is going to treat you this way. It can be incredibly difficult to separate the past from the present, but it is going to help you a lot. Therapy can become very beneficial for this purpose.

Even if you are not being triggered by your past, you can become triggered by certain things that your partner does. They might not be doing these things intentionally, but their actions could be causing you to experience anxiety. The most important thing for you to do is to tell them as soon as you realize what is happening. When you are able to work through these things together as a couple, you will both feel that you are on the same page. Understand that it might be you who needs to change, but as long as your partner is aware of what is bothering you about their behavior, they might be able to act in a more mindful manner.

You need to create a goal to not allow your anxiety to push you into a pattern of irrational behavior. This can happen very quickly, sometimes without you even realizing that it is happening. Irrational behavior is what leads to conflict. When you start fighting with your partner, this is going to lead to even more insecurity within the relationship. When you can recognize your own irrational behavior, you will be able to prevent or correct it. Understand that this is your anxious self-reacting and that you do not need to be this person all the time. Try your best to keep yourself grounded and in touch with reality. You can only focus on the things that you know are factual.

While this process sounds difficult, it can be a great way for you to reignite the spark that you have with your partner. When you can both get back in touch with the things that you love about one another, you will see that the chemistry still remains. You do not need to let your anxiety get the best of you and get in the way of your relationship. All relationships are work, and you must be willing to put in the effort. When you become stagnant, your partner is going to feel this. Try your best to help the relationship bloom, and during your weaker moments, you should be able to lean on your partner as they put their effort in. All strong relationships have an equal hand from both partners.

Thank you very much for selecting this workbook to help your relationship! Please remember to leave a great review and share all of the ways that you were able to turn your marriage around. Relationship anxiety is very strong, but remember that you are stronger! As I expressed, I have also been through this same situation. It is incredibly difficult to manage at times, but there is a light at the end of the tunnel. You do not have to remain a victim of your own relationship anxiety.

By breaking free of destructive thought patterns, you will be able to rediscover yourself and who you truly are. By allowing yourself to experience self-love, you will become a better partner by default. When times get tough, don't give up! Think about all of the progress that you have made so far. From the instant that you started reading this book, you became more educated on the topic of relationship anxiety; knowledge is power.

References

Birch, J. (2019, January 28). "I Have Relationship Anxiety—Here's How It Affects My Dating Life." Retrieved February 18, 2020, from https://www.health.com/relationships/relationship-anxiety

Free stock photos - Pexels. (2020). Retrieved February 19, 2020, from https://www.pexels.com/

PsychAlive. (2017, September 25). How to Deal with Relationship Anxiety. Retrieved February 18, 2020, from https://www.psychalive.org/how-to-deal-with-relationship-anxiety/

Star, K. (2019, September 29). Are There Potential Benefits to Having Anxiety? Retrieved February 18, 2020, from https://www.verywellmind.com/benefits-of-anxiety-2584134

How to Save Your Marriage When Trust Is Broken

Discover 10 Simple Steps to Turn Your Broken Trust into a Happy Marriage

Chapter 1: What Happens to Love After We Are in a Relationship?

Love evolves just as people do. When you first started dating your partner, it's likely that the sparks were flying. You probably wanted to be around one another 24/7 and were excited to learn more about each other. This is the way that most relationships begin, and this stage is known as the "honeymoon" stage. It is thought that, after some time, you will begin to see one another's flaws. The end of this stage can be a very big make-it-or-break-it point in your relationship because you will begin to see one another for who you truly are. In a healthy relationship, it won't matter when the honeymoon stage ends because the love you have for each other will still remain. You should both be appreciative of one another, all qualities included.

Deciding that you want to get married is a very big milestone in life. This means that you've found the person you want to be with forever. In your commitment to your spouse, you are acknowledging that you are going to be there for them no matter what. However, it becomes easy to find flaws in one another after some time has gone by. Things that used to be minor annoyances can easily grow into major problems if the couple is unable to communicate and reach a solution. Many couples lose sight of the love that they originally found because they're quick to start bickering or blow things out of proportion and get into arguments. Getting back to the root of your love will help you remember that you can still have that honeymoon feeling, even after several years.

Keeping the Flame Lit

Your love should be treated as something precious and rare. It can be hard to think about it this way when you already know so much about your partner and their traits. Understand that nobody is perfect, yourself included. There are always going to be small things that get on your nerves, but at the end of the day, you should remember why you are with your significant other. You need to remember why you chose one another out of all the other people that you could've been with. This is what keeps your marriage special and is something that only the two of you could ever understand. Make sure that you're doing your part in keeping the sparks flying when you're with one another.

The following are some ways that you can aim to bring the romance back into your relationship:

- **Have Alone Time** - For many couples, getting adequate alone time can be difficult. Between work and kids, the amount of time that you get to spend on your marriage is likely limited. It's important that you make this time, though. Anything that is worth putting in effort for will be something that you can make time for. Schedule it on your calendar if you need to. Go on dates with one another and rekindle the feelings that you had when you first met. Being able to enjoy this quality time will showcase all of the things that you first noticed about your partner, what made you fall in love with them.
- **Focus on Intimacy** - Life gets busy and that is no secret. No matter how busy you are, you need to make time for intimacy. That said, the

number of times you have sex isn't going to indicate how successful your marriage is. It should be something that you do because you have passion for your partner and you want to make them feel good. Scheduled sex can become boring and routine. Take your partner by surprise by showing them some extra initiative. Be more daring and try new things. A little excitement in the bedroom is one of many ways that you can rekindle your spark.

- **Work with Tension** - All couples are going to have tension between them at times. You aren't carbon copies of one another, so you are bound to get into disagreements. Instead of working to immediately diffuse this tension, let it play out. Sometimes, passion can arise from tension. Hear one another out and realize why the tension is being created. Once you have a better understanding of this, you might be able to channel it into something positive. No married couple should live without having at least a few disagreements from time to time. Having different opinions is healthy and should be celebrated.

- **Change Your Routine** - Almost all married couples have a routine that they have fallen into. This can include everything from what time they wake up to what they typically eat for dinner. Any routine can become boring or tiresome after a while. If you want to keep your relationship exciting, it's necessary to change this routine occasionally. You don't have to completely take apart the schedule that you share, but try doing things that are more spontaneous. Take your spouse on a surprise date one night or buy them a random gift to show your appreciation. It's little things like these that can really add some passion to your relationship.

- **Practice Emotional Vulnerability** - You need to be open with your partner and this includes being open about your emotions, as well. Many couples find it challenging to be open in this way, but it's necessary if you want your partner to know exactly how you're feeling. They should be the person you go to when you have good news, bad news, or anything in between. Work on opening up more, showing your partner that you trust them when you're in a vulnerable state of being. This can become a mutually beneficial action that brings the two of you closer together.

How to Handle Conflict

As mentioned, conflict is going to happen between yourself and the person that you love. It is inevitable, a part of any marriage. What matters most is your ability to address it and deal with it. When you are married, you need to understand that your actions can impact your partner without you even realizing it. You've agreed to commit to one another in this lifetime, so you need to be mindful of the things that you do. If you upset your partner, whether it was intentional or unintentional, you need to have the patience and the willpower to fix the problem. The longer two people are together, the more likely they are to become lazy when it comes to communicating and problem-solving. In reality, you must work harder than ever as your relationship matures. This is what keeps you both strong.

Negativity

Being negative toward one another is an example of something that causes conflict. Whether you are in a bad mood because of your partner or because of something else, know that bringing negativity into your relationship is not going to end well. When two people who know each other very well begin to argue, this can lead to hurt feelings and even irreversible damage. Make it a conscious decision to find healthy outlets for your negativity. If something is bothering you, do not sit on this information. Instead, speak up about it. You can express your feelings to your partner without blaming them. Explain what you are going through and how they can help you.

By getting rid of any unnecessary negativity in the relationship, you'll both enjoy being around one another more. It isn't fun to enter a room and feel like you can't even sit next to your spouse because of all the tension. You need to work through your issues if you want to move forward from them. Those who don't have the willpower will often become lazy and accept this tension as their new reality. While it has become a cliché to refer to married couples having lots of arguments, your own marriage doesn't have to be this way. You can find harmony and a balanced dynamic with your partner by keeping track of what you do when you're feeling negative.

Before you get into a disagreement with your partner, stop and think about what the underlying issue is. Are they at fault? Is there anything that you can do for yourself before you take this out on them? You are going to experience a lot of trial and error as you begin to navigate through your feelings, but this is normal. What matters most is that you try. When you can identify your feelings and what to do with them before automatically getting into it with your partner, you'll find that it's very beneficial for your relationship. It will also take a lot of the pressure off of you.

Betrayal

Being betrayed by your spouse can be a devastating thing to deal with. No matter what kind of betrayal it was, their actions have caused you to become so upset that you've lost your trust for them. Much like conflicts, it's also important to address and work through betrayals of trust. When they are ignored, they can jeopardize a marriage very quickly. In any instance when you feel betrayed, you need to express this to your spouse. Instead of automatically forgiving them or trying to find a quick solution, you'll need to work together to identify where this behavior stemmed from and how they are going to win your trust back.

Those who are too quick to sweep things under the rug will often find themselves in the same position again later on. There is no easy fix when handling a betrayal, especially one that concerns cheating. If your partner cheats on you, this puts you in a very painful position, and you must decide if you're going to forgive them or end the relationship. It gets messy when so many feelings are involved and tensions are high. Know what you deserve and what you are willing to put up with. Everyone needs to have their own personal limits. For some, cheating is an absolute deal-breaker. For others, cheating can be forgiven over time. You need to decide what makes sense for you and your relationship.

Make it clear to your spouse when you are not on good terms. This leaves less room for misunderstandings. If you're hurt to the point where you no longer think you want to continue in your marriage, you need to tell them. What they do next is going to be very indicative of how much they value the relationship. You should never have to beg someone to be with you or to be good to you. The right partner is going to do this automatically because they want to be with you. Whether you forgive them or not is entirely up to you.

Rebuilding

When you are in the process of rebuilding your marriage, you need to take as much time for yourself as necessary. Do what it takes to make yourself happy and take things day-by-day. Nothing is going to fix itself automatically; it's going to require hard work from both of you. Make sure that your partner understands where you're coming from and why you're upset by their actions. Tell them how you're feeling and let them know that the trust between the two of you will need to be restored before you can continue with a normal relationship dynamic. Own up to anything that you have done on your end. When you can take accountability for your actions, this makes it less likely that blame will be placed on you.

To work on your marriage effectively, you should not be focused on pointing fingers. Instead, you need to focus on your love and how you got to this point. Say that you're sorry when you're in the wrong. Don't delay and don't fall back on excuses. It's better to be entirely honest with your partner than to lead them on with lies. Understand that pain can be very deep sometimes. While they are hurting, they need to know that you are also hurting. Sometimes, an act of betrayal can cause you to look at yourself differently. You may suffer from low self-esteem as a result of being betrayed by your significant other. This becomes a part of the healing process, as you work on ways to get back to the person that you were before this happened.

Avoid defensive behavior. When you are trying to work out your issues, becoming defensive is only going to contribute to your problems. Understand that you might be in the wrong. It can be very hard to admit to these things, but it is necessary. Just as you need to work on doing this, so does your partner. Coming up with excuses is only going to provide you with distractions and prevent you from fixing your actual problems. Accusatory behavior is also commonly seen when couples are trying to rebuild their marriages. When someone does not want to admit that they are in the wrong, they turn the situation around and attack their partner for something. This is very unhealthy behavior and it needs to be monitored.

Acting helpless when you are trying to mend things with your partner is something that should be avoided. This is yet another way for you to avoid taking accountability for your actions. If you notice this behavior in yourself or in your partner, you need to pay attention to it. In any conflict that occurs that results in an argument, you should know that you're both responsible in some way. There was likely no conversation that consisted of only one of you talking and expressing yourself. Acting helpless will not fix anything, and it will not automatically place the blame on the other person. As a couple, you need to both learn how to admit when you were wrong.

Behavior that tends to suppress conflict instead of resolving it can lead to something known as relationship anxiety. This occurs when you feel literal anxiety when thinking of your relationship or of being in a relationship. Even if you've never felt this way before, it's easy to develop these feelings after dealing with stressful situations that are not being resolved. When you get into this state of mind, it can become very damaging for the overall health of your relationship. You might end up feeling like your relationship isn't good enough or that you aren't good enough. A lot of negative feelings tend to pop up when the conflict doesn't get resolved.

Being realistic, no one can simply resolve conflict and immediately go back to feeling happy and fine. Conflict resolution is a process that couples need to master together. It should not be expected that just because you apologize to your partner about something, they will go back to a happy mood with a positive mindset. Hurtful actions and betrayal can take time to get over. Even if you feel okay, that doesn't mean that your partner will automatically feel the same way. Respect their feelings once you have talked about the issues and found solutions. Know that they might need some additional time to process everything.

The best thing that you can do is exercise your patience once you have talked about your conflict and agreed on what you'd both like to do about it. You are each going to have your own unique ways of dealing with this process, so neither one of you can be rushed. It would be unfair of you to take all the time that you needed in order to move forward, yet not give your partner the same treatment. You need to make sure that you're treating them exactly as you would want to be treated. Ask yourself if you would be okay with your own treatment if the roles were reversed.

When you think about all of the different ways that you have shown bias in the past, you might become enlightened about why certain conflicts continue to come back into your lives. When you notice a repeating pattern, this is likely a sign that you aren't truly resolving the conflict. To reach a point of resolution, you must both be willing to move forward from what happened. If there is any resentment or guilt being held on to, then it seems that you need to work on this issue more.

Above all, you need to figure out how to get back to your vulnerability if you want to truly heal your marriage. It can be difficult to convince yourself to be vulnerable with your partner again, especially if they have done something wrong or if you've been betrayed. Keep reminding yourself that this process is going to take time. Be mindful of your own actions as you pay attention to what they're doing on their end. It takes an equal amount of effort if you want to see a real difference. Use your patience and listen to your gut instinct.

Chapter 2: How to Build Love and Avoid Betrayal in a Relationship

All couples want a happy and harmonious marriage, but how do you know that you and your partner have what it takes? Love is a risk that is taken every single day. When you love someone, you're willing to put your feelings on the line in order to experience the happiness that love brings into your life. Many people get hurt, even by those who care about them deeply. It can be inevitable sometimes. As a married couple, you need to focus on how to build your love so that it becomes stronger every day. When you have this strength together, you will both be less likely to betray one another. Having a sense of openness with one another can prove to be very helpful.

In this chapter, you are going to learn how to understand one another. When you don't have to do any guessing in your relationship, you're going to be able to provide exactly what your partner needs. Everyone hopes that they're a great spouse, but with these tips, you can make sure that you actually are one. An effort to understand your partner is going to go a long way. Not only will it clarify boundaries and enhance your communication skills as a couple, but you will both feel that more effort is being put into the relationship. The longer that you are together, the more that you should aim to learn about one another. If you stop trying, this is usually when things fall apart.

Love Languages

There are 5 different love languages that most people can identify with. In this section, they will be explained. As you read through each description, see which one you can personally relate to the most. Also, see if you can spot the one that sounds most like your partner. By having this knowledge, you'll be able to know how to handle different aspects of your marriage. If you know what your partner considers an act of love, then you can do your best to express it to them in the way that they know best.

Affirmation

This love language revolves around the idea that positive words can be used to build your partner up. They likely enjoy being complimented and told what you admire most about them. When speaking to a person who identifies with this love language, they'll be much more responsive to positive reinforcement than demands. For example, saying that you appreciate when your partner washes the dishes rather than criticizing them for not washing them is going to result in a much better response.

Gift-Giving

This love language is exactly how it sounds — your partner will enjoy and appreciate when you get them gifts to showcase your love. People who identify with this love language usually have a great appreciation for material items. If they know that you are willing to buy them the things that make them happy, they will feel very loved and cared for. In their eyes, this will show them that you were thinking about them.

Acts of Service

When you do things for your partner without being asked, they will end up feeling very loved. Some examples include doing the laundry, taking care of the grocery shopping, or cleaning up around the house. To a person who values this kind of love, these tasks are the ultimate way to show your consideration. They know that by taking action, you can see how much hard work they usually put into these same tasks. This love language is based around the idea that you are willing to take some of the weight off of their shoulders.

Quality Time

Being able to spend alone time with your spouse is very valuable to a lot of people. Having uninterrupted time together can definitely be a love language, as life tends to become busy for most people. When you can show your partner that you appreciate them enough to want to spend individual time together on a regular basis, this is going to make them feel special. This can range from anything like going out on a date to sitting down on the couch and having a one-on-one conversation.

Physical Touch

This one is a self-explanatory love language. People who value physical touch want as much kissing, hugging, and touching as possible in their relationship. When they are being shown physical intimacy, they feel the most loved. While this might not be the only way to express your love, it proves to be the most important way for those who value physical touch over anything else.

Getting a better understanding of your partner's love language is going to help you communicate with them. As you know, great communication goes beyond talking. You need to learn how to read them, to see what they truly need from you. When you can identify and respect their love language, this shows that you've spent time getting to know them on an even deeper level. It's a misconception that being together for a long time means that you know everything there is to know about one another. You're both constantly evolving, which means that there is always going to be more to learn.

When you're happy in your marriage, you're both going to treat each other better. In the same way that positive energy is contagious, so is having consideration. After showing your significant other that you not only know what their love language is, but are also doing your best to communicate with them in that unique way, they will likely feel inspired to do the same. This can prove to be a time of exponential growth in your marriage. It will show you both that there is always room for improvement as you learn and grow together.

With an effort to treat one another better, you will find that rebuilding your relationship *is* possible, no matter what you have endured. Getting to this point will prove to be the most difficult part, but once you get there, you'll be able to make significant improvements in the health of your marriage. Both of you have to want it and both of you have to put in an equal amount of effort. When one person is trying very hard and the other person is not, this is going to highlight the inequality in your relationship. It is not a good feeling to discover this. Always try to be mindful of your partner's level of effort and make sure that you check-in with one another if you feel that you need to redistribute the balance.

Power Struggles

When reading the term "power struggles," it makes sense that you would assume they are all bad. A struggle has a negative connotation behind it. What you'll learn is that there can be good struggles and bad struggles. Having a little bit of a power struggle in your relationship can prove to be a positive thing, one that brings out more passion. It is normal to feel this way with your partner, as you do almost everything together. There are certain times when you might want to do something in your own way, yet you have to make compromises because of your partner — this is how marriage works.

As you know, once the honeymoon stage is over, you're just left with two individuals who must work together to accept all parts of each other. Not only do you have to make sure that your relationship keeps growing, but you also need to make sure that you are both compatible with one another in the lifestyle that you're living. You should each understand what the other wants to achieve in the relationship. Both of you should feel happy at the end of the day and secure in the relationship. There are many couples who ignore red flags, only to realize that they weren't actually on the same page.

The best thing to do when you notice a power struggle in your relationship, good or bad, is to pay attention to it. See where this tension is stemming from. The difference between the good and the bad is if it allows you to grow as a couple. Any positive power struggle is going to result in growth for your relationship. This type of dynamic might encourage you to push some boundaries with one another, but ultimately, it will allow you to test one another without causing conflicts. This type of tension can be very beneficial when it comes to your passion and excitement in the relationship.

Negative power struggles revolve around control. When you get into this kind of a power struggle with your partner, the result is usually going to be an argument or a fight. Most of the time, manipulation is a component of a negative power struggle. One person will manipulate the other as a way to control their behavior. When they're able to gain this kind of control, they'll feel that they have more power in the relationship. For some, this can be a good feeling. It seems less likely that you'll be hurt when you have more control in the relationship. The problem is that this is not a representation of an equal partnership. This kind of control results in unhealthy behaviors.

In a healthy relationship, there is no need for any one person to be in control. Sometimes, the control is determined naturally because certain people have more dominant personality traits while others prefer to be more submissive. If you feel that your spouse is demanding more control than is typically held by each of you, this could be an indication that there is a negative power struggle taking place. You need to make sure that control doesn't become the focus of your relationship because marriage is so much more than that. It should be about the life that you're living together, not the life that one person dictates.

After you deal with being controlled for a long period of time, you're going to reach your breaking point. This can manifest as an outburst or a sudden urge to resist being controlled. If you feel that you've had enough of this type of behavior, you're justified in wanting to break free from it. A healthy relationship should be functional and harmonious. There should not be a need for one person to control the other and dictate their actions. As a couple, you need to be able to love and appreciate one another for who you truly are.

Use caution if you feel that you are in this kind of situation. It is possible that toxic behavior will evolve into abusive behavior if you are not careful. The instant you begin to feel unsafe or that you are being treated unfairly, it's always best to speak up or get out of this situation. If you wait too long, you might feel that you have no other choice but to stay. Many couples find that their love cannot last once the power has been shifted too far. The person being controlled is bound to grow tired of it, losing sight of their love.

Practice healthy expressions of power. Let one another take turns making decisions and make sure that you are showing respect, no matter who is in charge of the situation. When you can treat one another equally, any power struggle that you encounter will likely be able to evolve into positive tension. With this, you can turn it into passion or even romance. Being able to find the balance with each other can be tough, even if you've already been in the relationship for some time. You need to ensure that you're aware of your own role and to tone it down when you need to.

Openness

The key to building your love as a couple comes from your ability to be open with one another. These are some steps that you can take together to ensure that you are being as open as possible:

- **Get Rid of Your Fears** - When speaking to your partner, remember that this is a person that should not judge you. No matter what is on your mind, you should be able to fully express yourself to your partner without fear of being rejected or ridiculed. If this happens, it's a sign that points to an unhealthy relationship. You'll know that you have to fix something if this occurs. A great marriage involves the ability to bounce ideas off of one another. You should both feel comfortable talking to each other about anything. Try your best to get rid of any fears that you might be holding on to and remind yourself that your partner loves you and cares about what you have to say.

- **Value Honesty** - Honesty is always going to be the best way to approach any topic. When you can be entirely honest with your spouse, you're showing them that you're being transparent. Healthy relationships do not involve having to lie to one another, whether it be to hide wrongdoings or to ensure that no disagreements happen. Couples aren't always going to get along, but a casual disagreement can be healthy for the relationship. If you notice that you feel a need to lie to your partner, you need to question the health of your marriage.

- **Make Statements** - If you want to talk to your partner about something that makes you nervous, it's best to just speak from the heart. Say exactly what you're feeling and do not phrase it as a question. This invalidates your own feelings by asking the other person for input. Stand behind your statement and allow yourself to say exactly what you mean. This is going to help you open up to your partner by encouraging you to commit to what you're telling them.

- **Let Your Feelings and Behavior Align** - When you tell your partner that you feel a certain way, your actions should be representative of this. Passive-aggressive behavior stems from behavior that doesn't align with feelings that have been expressed. For example, when you tell your partner that you're fine, you don't need to give them the cold shoulder. Speak up when something is actually bothering you and be aware of your actions. If you need some time to collect your thoughts and calm down before discussing something, let them know.

- **Ask for What You Want** - Your spouse cannot read your mind. No matter how well you're getting along, your thoughts are unique. Hinting for things that you want might just leave you feeling upset when your partner doesn't follow through. Be direct and expressive. If you seek something, ask your partner for it. This is a good rule to follow for anything from material items to intimacy. When you're direct, you won't be left feeling disappointed when your partner doesn't pick up on the hints.
- **Have an Open Dialogue** - Try to be expressive when you communicate with one another. If your spouse is telling you something important, it's likely that they want your feedback. Avoid short, one-word answers. Think about how you feel and express yourself openly. It can become frustrating when one person is expressive and the other is only reacting with basic small talk. Your level of communication needs to be on par if you'd like to open up to one another.

It sounds simplistic, yet it's true — if you can be open to romance and intimacy as a couple, you're going to be happier together. As more arguments happen and fights occur, it can become hard to remember the things that first brought the two of you together. Making a relationship last has a lot to do with reminiscing. Whether you are thinking about fond memories that you've shared or how much you've grown together, these things can allow you to feel closer and will remind you that you need to be seeking out new ways to love one another.

In an ideal marriage, you should be able to share every part of yourself with your partner. While you're entitled to your own privacy, there shouldn't be any topics that are considered off-limits because you're afraid that they'll result in an argument or a betrayal. Stability is a very valuable trait that you should seek when you're with your partner. If they can make you feel safe and secure, then you are likely going to be able to open up to them more and vice versa.

It is possible to restore your love after it has been tarnished. If both of you are willing to focus on positivity and figuring out how to help the relationship grow, then you're going to be met with positive results. When you enter anything with a negative mindset, you aren't going to see the results that you truly want. Your mind and your intentions have to align. Show one another that happiness is a priority that you share in the relationship.

Chapter 3: The Love He/She Desires Most

When you can figure out the kind of love that your partner needs to feel happy, you're halfway to making a difference in the quality of your marriage. Being able to determine the love language is only the first step, though. The next step includes taking action and giving your spouse exactly what they need. Through your thoughtfulness and attention to detail, you'll be able to give them the love that they deserve. This is the part of the relationship that will require a lot of hard work, but it's all worth it in order to know that your spouse is happy to be with you. In a relationship that has balance, you'll be receiving the same treatment.

As you know, you cannot become lazy with the way that you express your love for your partner. The same gifts and dates aren't always going to be as impactful as time goes on. This also suggests that you are taking a lazy approach. To put real effort into your relationship, you need to show your partner that you're constantly evaluating their input. You need to show them that you're always paying attention to them and to their needs. Relationships evolve over time and it's normal to experience changes in the way that you express your love for one another and in the way you'd like to be loved.

Acting on Love Languages

In this section, you're going to learn specific ways that you can show your partner you care. Because each one is unique, you need to have a good idea of the actions that fall into each category. With more experience, you will be able to flawlessly shower your partner with love, resulting in a very positive outcome for your relationship. Everyone enjoys feeling special, especially when it is their partner that is helping them feel this way. Once you've gotten a feeling for the types of actions your partner likes, you can get creative and come up with even more ways to make them feel special.

Ways to Practice Affirmation
- Tell your partner you're proud of them
- Compliment their appearance
- Express how hard-working they are
- Acknowledge all that they do around the house
- Remind them of their great qualities
- Support their goals
- Offer emotional guidance

Words are the most powerful way to show your love to a partner who enjoys affirmation. Know that what you say is very important to them. For this reason, you need to be especially mindful of how you express yourself. Your partner is going to crave compliments and encouragement. Make sure that you give this to them frequently in order to show them that you respect their love language.

When you do something that upsets your partner, an apology is going to mean a lot to them. They are going to want you to express yourself and acknowledge what you did wrong. When the situation is reversed, you can expect your partner to be very open about what you did that upset them. This trait is not meant to make you feel bad, but to encourage open communication with one another.

Just because you feel that your partner should already know how you feel about them doesn't mean that you should stop telling them. At the beginning of your relationship, you likely gave them many compliments. The more comfortable you get in the relationship, the easier it becomes to stop giving compliments. You might still feel the exact same way about your partner, but you shouldn't assume that they know this. Imagine that you're telling them for the first time each time that you compliment them.

When you can make affirmations a big part of your dynamic, it will allow your partner to feel important in the exact way that they crave. With a little bit of attention to detail, you'll find that your relationship will effortlessly blossom in a natural way. Many couples become frustrated when they feel that they have to force compliments or express kindness. In order to avoid this, make sure that you are always speaking from your heart. Tell your partner exactly how you feel about them.

Ways to Practice Gift-Giving

- Make them something by hand
- Buy them an experience
- Get them something unexpected
- Buy them something that they mentioned to you
- Surprise them with their favorite food

There isn't much to explain about gift-giving because it can be pretty straightforward when you have a partner who prefers it as their love language. Those who do feel cared for when they receive gifts from their partners. It's a representation of you thinking about them and deciding to get them something that will make them happy. To some, the idea of using material items to express love can seem questionable, but you should know that there are also other ways that you can give your partner gifts.

For example, making something for your partner by hand can be a nice touch. Instead of simply going to the store and buying them something, you can get creative and come up with an idea of something that you can craft yourself. This kind of gift becomes even more meaningful because it's one-of-a-kind. A letter can also be considered a gift. Sit down and write your spouse a detailed letter about how you feel about them. This is another way that you can change up the norm of going to the store and simply buying them something.

The element of surprise becomes useful in this love language. If your partner isn't expecting a gift from you, this gesture can prove to be exciting and thoughtful. Surprise them with little things frequently. Remember that a gift does not have to be expensive or elaborate in order to be appreciated. You know your partner best, so you'll have an idea of what you can get for them based on their current interests. Make sure to keep in mind ideas such as what they've liked to eat recently, any movies that they've been wanting to see, or any new places that they've been wanting to visit. You can buy material items as well as experiences.

Know that your relationship should never revolve solely around you buying your partner gifts. A common misconception of this love language is that the other person will not be happy in the relationship unless they are constantly being showered with gifts. Part of what makes gift-giving so special is that it comes from the heart. No matter what you decide to give your partner, you put thought into it and that is meaningful. Your small, homemade gift is going to be just as valued as a piece of jewelry.

Ways to Practice Acts of Service

- Take care of the household chores
- Go grocery shopping
- Assemble furniture
- Get an oil change for the car
- Organize and clean the closet

You can show your partner kindness in many ways by doing a helpful act of service for them. Those who speak this love language value your hard work. No matter what kind of service you do for them, they are likely going to take this as a sign that you're observant and committed to the relationship. By putting in this effort to complete a task, you are demonstrating to your partner that you're willing to take on some of the work. This is the way that an ideal relationship should function.

If you don't speak the same love language, you probably underestimate the thought that goes into doing simple tasks such as washing a load of laundry or washing the dishes. To your partner, however, these tasks mean a lot. Knowing that they're getting a little bit of extra help will allow them to feel that they're being valued. It's never a good feeling when you know you're pulling more of the weight. This love language promotes balance in relationships.

Much like the other love languages, your gestures don't have to be extravagant in order for them to count. Something as simple as opening the car door can be considered an act of service to your partner. This is a very small task that you likely don't think much about, but realize that your partner could be very positively impacted by it. Another example is when you consider their needs as you're doing something for yourself. If you stop off at the store for something to drink, getting your partner something to drink as well will show them that you were thinking of them.

You don't have to do much to make your partner happy. There is no need to try and take over every chore and task because this will eventually lead your partner to believe that you don't need their help. Much like the idea that goes behind gift-giving, you don't want to speak this love language too frequently or else it will no longer feel special. Do things for your partner because you truly want to and you are feeling inspired to do so. Also, don't feel limited to expressing your love using a single love language all the time, as many partners like to feel loved in more than one way.

Ways to Practice Quality Time

- Go on more dates
- Spend time together without distractions
- Take drives together
- Brainstorm with one another
- Make important decisions together

It seems that most couples agree — more quality time together would be welcomed. To those who speak this love language, quality time is a must. Life tends to get busy, but this does not mean that your quality time together as a couple should be reduced. When something is truly important to you, this means that you should be able to make time for it. In order to effectively communicate in this love language, you need to be great at prioritizing your time. You might need to adjust your time management skills if being too busy is what's stopping you from spending more time together.

Understand that quality time is not the same as simply being around each other. You are likely around your spouse a lot, but what turns this into quality time is the undivided attention that you give to one another. Being distracted by your surroundings or electronic devices is going to take away the meaning from this time that you have. Make sure that you are present when you have the opportunity to enjoy quality time together. Put your phone on silent and go somewhere that you and your partner can be alone.

No matter if you are talking casually or discussing something of importance, what happens during this time is so special because only the two of you share it. If you were to share these intimate moments with others, this can be considered a betrayal by your spouse. Make sure that you're always focused on what is going on in front of you. Your partner will appreciate it and you'll be able to get a lot more out of the time that you spend together.

Ways to Practice Physical Touch

- Hold hands more often
- Spend time in the morning cuddling
- Initiate intimacy when you feel sparks between you
- Spontaneously kiss them
- Place your hand on their back when you are standing near one another

This love language is very straightforward. If your partner enjoys physical intimacy, you should know the basics of what you can do in order to show them love. The one thing that can stand in the way of expressing this is if you don't enjoy physical intimacy as much as your partner does. If you aren't in the mood to touch them or kiss them, this can send signals to them that you don't care about them as much as you once did. Be careful with how you express your love to them and make sure that you are only initiating physical intimacy when you feel the same way.

The best thing that you can do to speak this love language is to listen to your heart. Get close to your partner, both physically and emotionally. Act in a natural way based on the chemistry that you feel between the two of you. If you have a partner who speaks this love language, then you likely have intense physical chemistry. You might have to find ways to reignite this passion the longer that you're with your partner. As you know, intimacy can slow down for couples who have been together for some time, but it doesn't have to.

Never schedule your intimacy. This can cause it to feel forced or ingenuine. You should make time for these moments with your partner because you want to, not because you feel that you have to in order to speak their love language. Acting spontaneously can be a great way to feel the passion once again. It will remind the two of you what it was that first attracted you to one another. Getting back to these feelings is a very healthy thing for couples to do. It can make any trivial issues that you're going through seem like not as big of a deal when you're reminded of how physically compatible you are together. Listen to their signals. Their body language is going to tell you a lot about what they want you to do next.

The Importance of Respect

When you and your partner share a mutual respect for one another, this is going to provide you with a strong foundation for your marriage. In order to determine if you have respect, you must first define it. Ask yourself what respect means to you. For some, it means having a deep admiration for one another. There is no right or wrong answer because what matters most is that you both share the same opinion on what defines respect. A general overview of respect between partner's states that one person should not have authority over the other. This eliminates control issues and promotes individual thinking while maintaining kindness and compassion for one another.

To get a general idea of where you both stand, take a look at how you treat each other on a daily basis. Do you help each other when you're in need? Do you do things for your partner without being asked? If you do these things, they are both signs that you're showing your respect regularly. Your partner can ask you for respect, but they shouldn't have to. It should be something that you want to do because you care and because you love them. In turn, your partner should show their respect for you in a similar way. If anything feels forced, then respect is something that you will likely have to work on together. When respect is forced, this is usually an indication of something unresolved standing in your way.

As you know, unresolved issues can play a big role in your relationship. This is why it's important not to sweep your fights under the rug. You need to talk about them and then discuss ways to make changes for the better. If you continue to do the same things over and over again, you're going to be met with the same results. No one enjoys frequently fighting with their significant other. This is draining and upsetting. Living in harmony is much more desirable. Point out any unresolved issues that you notice when you're gauging the respect you have for one another. Some serious conversations might have to take place before you can go on any further.

Because no relationship is perfect, there might be several things for you to discuss and work out. Don't feel bad about this. Know that each step you take toward clarity; you are taking another step toward having mutual respect. Do your best to have these discussions in a way that is not accusatory because this might just reignite the fight once again. Know that what has already happened cannot be changed, but your actions going forward can be. When you are both able to let go of the things that are bothering you, there is going to be a lot more room for progress. Holding on to negativity, no matter how trivial it may seem, will always find a way to impact your relationship.

If you want to practice acts of respect, you can apply the following to your marriage:

- **Listen to Each Other** - Sometimes, communication isn't going to be about talking. Make sure that you listen to your spouse when they need to express their feelings. You don't always have to think of what to say or how to relate the conversation back to your own feelings. Being an active listener can be very valuable, making your spouse feel that you care deeply about their well-being. Before you respond, ask yourself if you're speaking to add to the conversation or if you're speaking to make the conversation about you.
- **Work on Compromising** - All couples need to be efficient at compromising. There are going to be many instances where you'll want different things, yet you'll have to find a middle ground to keep you both happy. Being able to let go of your original thought or desire can be tough, especially if you're a naturally stubborn person. It takes a lot of communication and effort to be able to come to a middle ground with your partner, but it's necessary if you want a healthy marriage.
- **Give Each Other Space** - This step might seem counter-productive, but it's actually essential if you want to build your respect. When you're constantly around each other, it becomes easier to feel irritable. You are both

individuals and you both deserve some time to yourself. When you're apart, this will show you what you're missing when the other person is not around. This can work out in your favor by showing you all of the great aspects that your spouse brings to your life.

- **Honor All Boundaries** - All couples should have a healthy set of boundaries in place. No matter how much you love one another and how close you are in your relationship, you need to remember that you are two separate people with different limits. When you have boundaries that are to be followed, this is a great way to build respect. Your boundaries are going to be different and that is exactly what will promote you to be mindful of one another's feelings.

Chapter 4: The Secret to Loving Your Spouse Effectively

When you have a strong bond of love, you are going to be able to grow your marriage into something that is happy, successful, and beneficial. It can be hard to remember to focus on the love that you share when your thoughts are clouded by betrayal, confusion, or disagreements that you've experienced with your spouse. When you hurt one another, it takes time for you both to heal. This is going to happen because it is inevitable in all partnerships. You're trusting one another every single day in a big way. By giving your partner your heart, you're showing them that you're willing to take a risk. You know that they want the best for you, but you're also acknowledging that you know you might get hurt.

Love is uncertain, but that is what makes it beautiful. You cannot predict when your partner is going to do something that will upset you. What you can do, however, is learn how to get back to the love that you share no matter what. When it comes to betrayal, you both need to figure out what your breaking point is. Understand that not all negativity can be fixed. If you hurt one another to a point of no return, there is not going to be any hope of reviving the relationship. You need to determine that you are both on the same page, that you both want to make the marriage work.

When you're able to do this, you will be able to love one another in the way that you both need most. You will know when to be there for one another and when to give space. These things cannot be learned overnight, but if you are always making progress, you are going to become a better spouse in the process. Eliminate the idea that certain issues cannot be fixed. This is only true when one or both of you are unwilling to fix them. Remember that it takes two in any aspect of any relationship. When you can both agree that you value your love enough to save it, then you can start to make some progress.

Discover Key Issues

All relationships have certain issues that seem to repeat themselves. These are known as key issues because they seem to remain unresolved. If you notice that a lot of your fights stem from a single topic, it is safe to say that you have found one of your key issues. Examine what your last 5 fights were about. Have a discussion with your partner on what you each believe you were fighting about, down to the very root of the problem. This can become an eye-opening experience in more than one way. You'll be able to see certain patterns in your marriage and you'll also be able to see if you perceive these fights in the same way.

You'd be surprised to discover how many issues you're both misunderstanding, causing more fights in your relationship. When you have misunderstandings that are never clarified, you might be fighting over something that you unknowingly feel the same way about. Realize when you're both saying the same thing in your own unique ways. Many couples don't take the time to break this down and truly examine what is going on in their relationship. This kind of tedious work is necessary if you'd like to see improvement. If you are unclear about where your partner stands on an issue, clarify this by asking them directly. It's better to hear this from their own mouth rather than making assumptions or jumping to conclusions.

Pay attention to anger levels. If the two of you cannot have a serious conversation without resorting to anger, you'll both need to independently work on ways to find outlets for it. When you don't have a way to express your anger and frustration, you're going to end up taking it out on one another. This can prove to be a very big problem in a relationship. It can make your communication seem very unstable and unpredictable. Do your part by making sure that you take a few deep breaths before you express an opinion that differs from your partner's. Try not to think about one of you as right and the other as wrong. Instead, express yourself and listen to what your partner would like to express. Approaching your conversations in this way will lead to much more productive results.

Complaining can come very naturally in a relationship because you are both very comfortable with one another. Be careful that it doesn't become too much of a focus, though. Hearing your partner complain can be very disheartening, especially when it seems like nothing you do is good enough for them. Be mindful of how much you are complaining, as well. If you cannot come up with a solution to the problem, then nothing is going to be resolved. While complaining can feel like a much-needed relief, you need to realize that this can become taxing behavior. Your partner might feel blamed for these things when you don't mean to make them feel this way. It's better to work through your issues on your own when you can before be bringing them into any arguments or disagreements.

When you feel like blaming your partner during an argument, stop to think before you speak. Ask yourself what blaming them would do. Would it help the situation? Most of the time, it's only going to add fuel to the fire. If you aren't careful, constant blaming can eventually turn into abusive behavior. When your relationship gets to this point, it's bound to become toxic. No one deserves to be constantly blamed for things, especially when they aren't doing anything wrong. By taking accountability for your actions and being able to communicate, you and your spouse should be able to get rid of the need to place the blame on anyone and focus on the solutions.

Keep in mind that force is never the answer. When you use force or aggression to try and solve your problems, this creates more tension. You need to be mindful of this because you should always be focused on making peace with your issues and solving problems as you become aware of them. Marriage does not have to be difficult. While you are going to run into disagreements, you don't have to let them change your relationship. What you can do is learn and grow from them.

Also, know that men and women interpret information differently. Women are usually able to access their emotions more easily, while men like to rely on rationalization. Of course, this isn't always the case because everyone is different. However, it is something to keep in mind when you feel frustrated. Your spouse might see the exact same situation and react very differently because that is what they're driven to do. Take some time to learn where they're coming from and why they've reacted in this way before judging them for it.

How to Avoid Negativity

1. **Leave Jealousy Behind** - Jealousy is a large contributor to negative energy in relationships. When one or both of you are jealous, this can cause outbursts and arguments. You both need to be secure in yourselves and in your love so you can avoid distortions in your judgment. Couples who are fueled by jealousy will fall into a pattern of toxic accusatory behavior that should be avoided. It can be tough to let go of your jealousy, but remind yourself that you are the one your partner has chosen. Both of you have made a commitment to one another, so the other people around you should not be able to break down your relationship.
2. **Don't Try to Change Them** - You are with your spouse because you fell in love with the qualities that they possess. When you become more comfortable with one another, it can be tempting to try to guide each other toward the behavior that you favor. Know that when you get into the habit of doing this, you're going to start believing that you can change your partner. Because it's a partnership and not a

dictatorship, you don't get to have that kind of control over them. You need to make sure that you're in the relationship for the right reasons and that you love them for who they are. If something bothers you, speak up about it. It is then up to your partner to make any changes that they see fit.

3. **Laugh Together** - It sounds cheesy, but laughter really is the best medicine. When you can laugh with your spouse, this shows that you know how to have fun together. It's important that you don't always take your relationship too seriously because this can cause tension. Understand that there is a time and place for that. You need to be able to feel comfortable enough with one another to laugh things off sometimes. Joke around and keep them amused, especially when the mood is lighthearted. When you do this more often, you'll be reminded that not every moment of tension needs to turn into an argument. Most can work themselves out and be laughed about when you look back on them.

4. **Don't Pick Apart Flaws** - Your partner is likely already aware of their flaws and insecurities. There is no reason to pick them apart any further. Imagine if they were to do the same thing to you. As you can imagine, this would probably be very hurtful. Know that neither one of you is perfect, so you don't need

to bring this up during a heated moment. A person's flaws do not make up the entirety of who they are, so it's unfair to use this against them. Learn how to let this go.

5. **Don't Ignore Each Other** - It can be very tempting to resort to the cold shoulder when you aren't getting along, but you should definitely avoid this. Not only is this not a healthy way to resolve your issues, but it can turn into a lasting habit. When you don't address your problems, you'll have a tendency to keep ignoring them until they build up and become worse. It's easier to talk about your problems when they're still fresh on your brain. This will ensure that you're able to get to the root of what is bothering you. It can be easy to forget these things when they're ignored, and this can allow them to compound into larger issues that draw you apart from your partner.

By staying calm, you're going to make sure that any negativity you experience does not escalate into a problem. Working on ways to diffuse your temper is important, especially for your marriage. Learn to recognize when you're becoming angry and take a moment to calm down. When you can calm yourself down before you get angry and reactionary, it will allow you to talk through your problems with your partner instead of yelling at one another. Anger never solves anything fully, so know that resorting to it is only going to mean that you'll have to talk about the issue again. It is better to discuss things right then and there in an effort to get to a solution.

While you can be passionate about many issues, ask yourself if it's worth it to argue with your spouse. You might feel that you have a point to make, but consider if there are other ways to do it. By thinking before you speak, you can avoid saying something hurtful that would otherwise come out when you're in a heated argument. These words might not be how you really feel, but they can leave lasting damage to your relationship if you're not careful. This will likely make the problem escalate into something worse rather than resolving it.

Conflict-Resolution Skills

Do

- **Learn to Agree to Disagree** - When you're having a discussion with your spouse, know that you don't always have to agree on everything. This isn't realistic, nor is it healthy. It's a good thing to be able to have your own opinions. In order to get along better as a couple, what must happen is the ability to respect one another. Even if you don't agree with your spouse, learn how to see their side of things and understand where they're coming from. A little bit of respect goes a long way.

- **Work on Things Now** - Instead of waiting to talk about your issues until they pile up, address them as they come up. A big problem that couples face is when certain issues are only brought up when one person starts to feel overwhelmed. This can sometimes come across as a surprise to the other person because it was not addressed sooner. Avoid this by saying what's on your mind as you're feeling it. Know that it's always better to talk sooner rather than later.
- **Make Time to Talk** - If something is important to your relationship, you will make time for it. When discussing something you're arguing about, make sure that you set aside at least 30 minutes of uninterrupted time to discuss it. If the conversation needs to be longer, make sure that you're both able to take a break to regroup. When you give your conversations structure, they'll feel less overwhelming and difficult. Understand that you should both be given equal time to talk about how you feel.
- **Examine Your Unmet Needs** - It's often the needs that aren't being met that cause problems. Identify if you have any unmet needs and then bring them up to your partner. This doesn't always have to be a bad thing. Relationships evolve and people change, but as long as you keep each other in the loop, you can maintain a

healthy and functional relationship. Know that your needs are valid and important. You deserve to feel happiness, so let your partner know what they can do to make you happy. In turn, your partner should do the same so that you'll know what you can do for them.

- **Brainstorm Solutions Together** - You aren't always going to have the right solution, but sometimes you might. Work together with your spouse to explore several different solutions until you both agree on one. What might seem like the right one to you might not be the right one to them. In order to truly resolve a conflict, you both need to feel at ease. Remember this the next time you feel so certain that you've come up with a solution.
- **Pause for Anger** - If you start to feel like you're losing your temper, take a break. Your argument doesn't have to push you to a breaking point, so don't let it. Use your self-discipline to recognize when your temper is flaring up. Take a moment to walk around outside or to go to a different room so that you can clear your head. Remember to take deep breaths and to identify what is making you so angry. After you regroup, go back to your partner and try to approach the issue like you want to solve it rather than fuel it.

Don't

- Have discussions when you're tired
- Use the words "always" or "never"
- Bring up the opinions of others
- Switch topics to fit your point
- Make judgments about their behavior
- Think your partner can read your mind
- Interrupt your partner while they're speaking
- Bring up past issues to make a point
- Compromise your standards to end the argument

Having an idea of what to do and what not to do will make you an effective problem-solver. This is an essential skill for anyone who is in a long-term relationship. You're going to argue with your spouse, but this doesn't have to mean that your marriage will be damaged in the process. With the help of these tips, you'll both be able to get your points across and come to the conclusion that works best for your relationship.

Through having an open discussion about your problems, you'll both be able to feel seen in the relationship. This can be enough to restore the faith that you once lost, reminding you that you're still with the person that is best for you. All couples are going to experience difficulties throughout their marriages, so it's essential to practice these skills whenever possible. Remember, if you haven't worked on communication skills like these before, it can take some practice to become good at them. Learn how to forgive one another and always try to return to the loving bond that you've worked so hard to create. No one else can fix your problems but the two of you, so it's important that you work together.

Chapter 5: The Secret to Unconditional Love That Couples Need, Yet Few Find

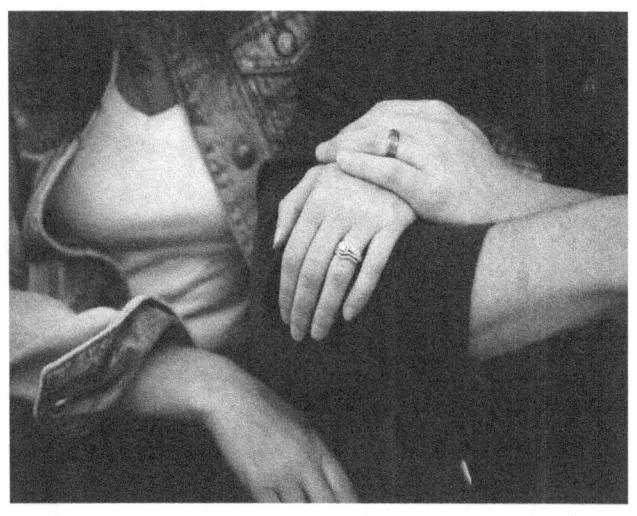

All relationships aren't created equal. You likely know this because of first-hand experience. Think about all of the people that you had to date before you found your spouse. They changed things for you, showed you what true love is supposed to look like. When you decide that you want to marry someone, this is the ultimate display of trust and devotion. It can be hard to get back to this feeling after enduring so many hardships with your spouse. That is the definition of unconditional love, though. It's the ability to still love and care for one another, in spite of any arguments or betrayals that happen over time.

This chapter is devoted to the topic of helping your relationship grow. When you've learned how to love one another unconditionally, you'll be able to enter a stage of growth that will be beneficial for you as an individual and for your relationship. So many people want a love that lasts forever, yet they don't treat their significant other in a way that reflects this. You need to show your partner what you want. Lead by example and there will never be any confusion about where your heart is.

Navigating Your Differences

One-Sided Effort

When one person puts in more effort than the other, this is going to cause problems. You need to work together as a couple to identify if there is an imbalance going on. If you feel that you're putting in more effort than your partner, bringing this issue up can be tricky. You likely don't want to bring this up in a confrontational way because this can lead directly to an argument.

Focus on how this makes you feel. Figure out a way to tell your spouse that you desire more from them. Before you bring this issue to their attention, think about what you would personally like to change about the situation. If you could think about one thing that would make you feel better about it, what would it be? This will prevent you from going into the conversation with an accusatory tone.

If you feel that you aren't pulling your weight, or if your partner has brought this to your attention, do your best to not immediately punish yourself. There is no use in doing this because it will not solve the problem. Instead, you need to think about actionable steps that you can take to improve the situation. Think about how you can be more present for your partner.

There will always be an effective way to solve a problem like this when you're willing to do the work that needs to be done. You must also be willing to listen to what your partner has to say. Nobody is perfect, so it can be a humbling experience to learn exactly what it's going to take to make a difference. Listen to this closely and be open to your partner's feedback.

Emotional Responses

In general, women tend to be more emotional than men. There are exceptions, of course, but this is how it typically is in a relationship. No matter what role you play, understand that your partner might not be as comfortable with expressing their emotions on the same level that you express yours. A problem that can often arise between couples is when one person blames the other for not feeling enough/feeling too much.

Before you become frustrated with your partner because of this, realize that there are many factors that can contribute to their emotional expressiveness. Childhood is one of the first ones. The way that your partner grew up taught them how they should deal with their emotions. Some people are taught healthy forms of expression while others are told that they need to keep their emotions inside. Be mindful of this.

Another factor comes from the way that coping mechanisms are developed. There are unhealthy coping mechanisms that can become a big part of the way that emotions are handled. This can include the suppression of difficult situations and use of aggression to release anger. Your partner might have developed some unhealthy coping mechanisms due to the life experiences that they've lived.

Do your best to meet your partner halfway with emotional expressiveness. If they aren't as open as you are, be gentle with them. It might be hard for them to open up right away. If they are more open than you are, understand that you have every right to say that you aren't there yet if you're struggling to be on the same emotional wavelength. When you can be clear about exactly what you're feeling, this will give your partner all of the insight that they need.

Reservations

A person can become reserved for a wide variety of reasons. This tends to cause problems in a relationship because it can often come across as if your partner doesn't fully trust you when they choose to be reserved. Much like the above example, your partner can have reservations for a wide variety of reasons that have nothing to do with you. From their upbringing to past situations that have impacted them, all of these things come into play.

Don't allow their behavior to lead you to create suspicions. This is a form of jumping to conclusions and it's not likely to work out well for you or your relationship. If your partner seems reserved, the best thing that you can do to gain clarity is to ask them how they're feeling. It sounds simple because it is. The most direct answer that you're going to get is always going to come directly from them, not from your assumptions.

If your partner ever expresses to you that they do not wish to talk about something, respect this. It will show them that you're acknowledging their boundaries. A lot of couples feel that they're entitled to explanations from their significant others, but something that often gets overlooked is the establishment of boundaries. They are important and necessary.

When you can give your partner the space that they need, they will come to you when they're ready. Remember, they don't operate in the exact same way that you do. Give them time to open up and understand that it isn't always personal. They may just need a bit more time before they're ready to talk about their feelings. You don't need to blame yourself for any of this.

Let Go of the Past

We have all been hurt before, but that doesn't mean that the cycle needs to continue. If you let your past slip into your present, this is going to damage your marriage. The things that you've experienced with other people in other situations should no longer hold weight to your current relationship. This can become exhausting and upsetting if you continue to carry the baggage from past relationships. You deserve to live your life free of these burdens and healed from them. By recognizing the things that you're still holding on to, you can learn how to let them go in order to fully move on.

You might believe that you've already dealt with a situation, only to feel it come back to you in full force. The worst thing that you can do in moments like these is to blame your partner for what you're feeling. They were not responsible for this memory, so you need to learn how to separate the two. You must start by identifying why you're still being impacted by this particular situation. Consider how it has shaped you over the last few years.

Despite what you may be thinking, you don't need to ignore the past in order to move on from it. Doing the exact opposite in a productive way is how you'll make progress. Acknowledge what has happened to you and what you've been through. Think about how these situations and people have made you feel and recognize that these feelings are entirely valid. Now, think about how this all ties in with your current life and current relationship.

You are not the things that happen to you, but you are impacted by them. Consider the strengths that you've gained because of what you've gone through in your past. Realize how these experiences have helped shape you into the person that you are today. At the same time, realize that these are not the only things that make up who you are. You were born with a personality and traits that cannot be replaced. You are still you, regardless of what happens to you.

Work on gently letting go of thoughts about your past as they come to you. Remind yourself that they were once a part of your life, but now you're living a different chapter. This step doesn't happen overnight, but a healthy outlook on how to deal with your past can make a significant improvement in your relationship. When you can be focused on the present, you will be a lot more likely to put effort into your marriage and listen to what your partner is saying.

The following are some more tips that you can use to help you let go of your past and stay focused on your present:

- **Write Your Thoughts Down** - It can be helpful to say everything that you need to say on paper. You don't necessarily have to share your thoughts with anyone else, but it can be therapeutic to get them out. Once you've written them down, use this as a way to move forward. Tell yourself that these thoughts no longer need to come to your mind because you've already addressed them. You might have to do this several times before the habit sticks.

- **Keep Your Distance** - If you're trying to let go of memories that involve someone from your past, stay away from them in your present. Big problems can arise when you allow those from your past to linger. If you don't have a healthy relationship with this person, then there is no reason that you need to let them remain in your life. Do your best to distance yourself from them in order to protect yourself. Understand that you do not owe it to them to keep them close.

- **Accept a Lack of an Apology** - You aren't always going to get the "I'm sorry" that you desire. When you're dealing with a past situation that feels unresolved, you must create your own closure. Work with the issues that remain and think about ways that you can build yourself up instead of allowing these memories to drag you down. Know that you don't need to hear an apology in order to move on from someone or something. Find your inner strength.

- **Enjoy Love** - With your partner, you should be experiencing love in many ways. Allow them to make you feel important and cherished. When you are distracted, it can be easy to forget how much your partner does for you and how much they actually care. Learn how to set your sights back on this so that you can fully appreciate how much they love you.

- **Get Help** - If you're finding it difficult to let go of the past on your own, know that therapy is always an option. Talking to a professional can be a big help because this person is going to be someone that you don't already know and who won't have a biased opinion. Sometimes, you just need to talk to someone who is there to listen to you rather than give you advice. It can be very healthy for you to open up to a therapist as a way to begin addressing your past issues.

Develop Fun and Laughter

Being in a marriage that is full of laughter can really open up your abilities to love one another. Over time, arguments and disagreements can come between how you truly feel about one another. It can be very beneficial to get back to the basics of being able to just have fun together. Not only does this keep your relationship lighthearted, but it can also highlight certain things that you first noticed about your spouse as you were falling in love. It's no secret that the beginning of your relationship was probably simpler than it is right now. This is because of the newness that surrounded your love.

It is possible to get back to this carefree version of your love, as long as you're both willing to let go of the petty things. Understand what is actually worth holding on to and what doesn't actually matter. Certain arguments are going to be very temporary, but the anger and resentment can last for a long time. The sooner that you can let go of this negativity, the more fun that you'll begin to experience in your relationship. It can be like a refreshing boost of confidence that will show you exactly what unconditional love feels like.

Your marriage can be fun. Even despite all of the hard work that is involved, it's not impossible to bring back the laughter. Consider these tips for lightening the mood:

- **Keep Dating** - Once you're married, the concept of dating your significant other changes. You already have each other, so less effort needs to be made to win them over, right? Wrong. You should put in extra effort in order to show your partner exactly how you feel about them. One of the most fun parts of a relationship is the chase and just because you're already married doesn't mean that you need to stop this part. Keep flirting with your partner. It will bring back an exciting element to your marriage.
- **Put the Kids to Bed Early** - If you have kids, your life as a couple has shifted to cater to their

needs. Every once in a while, it's okay to put them to bed early in an effort to spend some alone time with your spouse. You both deserve this and it can do a lot for your marriage. It will likely take you both back to an earlier time in your relationship when the feelings were still fresh.

- **Sleep at the Same Time** - When you go to sleep, make sure that you're going to sleep at the same time as your partner. This will signify that you are both living your lives together, rather than being two people who live separate lives that share a bed. This dynamic can bring you a lot closer together as a couple. It will also establish a routine that can make you feel safe and secure. Plus, you will start each day on the same page. Allow your nights to be a time where you can talk freely and laugh as much as you want to. It's likely that you'll also sleep better when you are both resting your heads at the same time.

- **Send Risque Messages** - There is nothing more fun than receiving a risque surprise during your day. Keep your romance alive by spontaneously texting your partner. It's okay to be candid every once in a while, especially if you feel that you need to combat boredom as a couple. Know that these messages will keep your partner thinking about you until you're able to be together in person again. They can bring you closer and even reignite some of your passion.

- **Go on Dates That You Used to Go On** - Getting back to your old habits can bring back those old feelings of fun and excitement that you once had. Revisit restaurants and places that have a special meaning to you both. This will allow you to remember how it felt to fall in love with one another. You can also make new memories while you reminisce about the old ones.
- **Do Something Creative Together** - Creativity can bring out a lot of fun in any relationship. Work on a project together. It doesn't matter how experienced either of you is. A lot of the fun comes from learning together and experimenting with different ways to be creative. Couples who are able to work together in this way are typically able to turn frustrating moments into fun challenges.
- **Try Something New** - While a routine can be nice to have, it's also nice to break free from it every once in a while. Try something new together as a couple. This experience can give you a great chance to bond and see if you both share the same opinion on what you think about the new activity that you're trying. It prevents the relationship from becoming stale and allows you to develop new interests together as a couple.

Chapter 6: What Trust Really Means in Your Relationship

In any relationship, trust needs to be present in order to have a strong foundation. When you have all of the other components of a great relationship, such as romance and fun, this won't mean anything if you and your partner don't trust one another. Trust makes your relationship strong, and it allows you to get through anything together. Consider how strong this bond is. When you're able to fully love your partner, this likely means that you trust them. You can have trust before you have love, but you cannot have love without trust. When you realize how important one is to the other, you will be able to make it a priority in your marriage.

While there are many things that can get in the way of your trust, you should always try to find your way back to having a healthy level. Jealousy is one of the main reasons why couples might struggle with trust. There are many people who might find your partner attractive. This can understandably lead you to feeling insecure, especially if your partner does nothing to reassure you. When you have a healthy and trusting relationship, you shouldn't have to worry about your partner cheating on you. If you've already established that this is a terrible betrayal, your trust in your partner should tell you everything that you need to know. Other people might find them attractive or interesting, but they have chosen you.

If you've already established this with your partner, do your best to let go of your jealousy and insecurity. In a completely loyal relationship, couples can end up getting divorced because of the stress that jealousy brings. When you aren't able to let go of this complex, it can start to put a lot of pressure on your spouse and on your marriage. There's nothing worse than being accused of something that you aren't doing, even when you try to convince the person that you aren't guilty of it. This is why trust is so important. You should be able to take one another's word without having any feelings of doubt.

Why Trust Is Important

Without trust, you're missing the closeness that you should have with your partner. This is the person that you've chosen to spend your life with. You should be able to tell them anything and believe that they will always have your best interest at heart. Trust issues are very capable of tearing marriages apart. They can infiltrate your relationship and make it seem like there is nothing that you can do to fix it. When betrayal has already happened, this makes the trust especially hard to come by. You should always value trust in your relationship and you should do everything in your power to strengthen it.

Sharing trust in a relationship leads to many other great benefits. Trust can open the lines of honest communication. This means that you'll always be able to take what your partner says as the truth. You won't be left wondering if they're leaving out details or changing their words in an effort to mislead you. With a strong, trusting relationship, there is no need to believe that either one of you has a hidden agenda of any kind. It's a very freeing feeling to be able to openly trust your partner in any situation. You'll always know that you have someone on your side.

Life can be unpredictable, so it matters that you can have a partner that you feel comfortable relying on.

Knowing that they're always going to be there to support you can be a great feeling, one that will motivate you to do better and to be better. This kind of mutual support is what creates a strong romantic foundation. As much as your partner is there for you, the same support can be reciprocated. Once you get into this habit, it becomes very easy to find ways to show your support and to encourage your partner in everything that they do. That way, they'll know that they also have someone who is on their side.

One of the biggest benefits of being with someone you trust is the lack of worry you'll face about them cheating on you. Those who constantly feel the need to check-in with their significant other to make sure they aren't being cheated on are likely not in the healthiest relationship. There should be nothing that your partner does that would make you think that they would be unfaithful. The bond of marriage is sacred in that it's only supposed to be shared by the partners who entered into it. When someone else comes between this bond, this creates a very big violation of trust that can be nearly impossible to recover from.

Through trusting one another, you will both get the chance to experience a certain degree of freedom. In the things that you say and do, you will both have clear understandings of what is acceptable and where the boundaries lie. This is why it's so important to let your partner know when they've done something that upsets you. Make it clear when you don't like a certain behavior in order to avoid being hurt again in the future. In turn, work to understand what your partner's boundaries are and respect them. When you can both be honest about your boundaries, there will be no confusion and no trust broken.

Intimacy is another factor in your relationship that is directly impacted by your level of trust. You're going to have difficulty being intimate with your partner if you don't trust them. In order to have sex with someone, you need a special bond and a certain type of attraction. Knowing that you share unlimited trust between the two of you can actually end up becoming a turn-on in your relationship. Use this to your advantage, allowing it to reignite the passion that you both feel for one another. You're also going to be able to become completely vulnerable to each other. This creates another positive element to your sex life by creating an erotic and an enticing mood.

Individually, the trust that you have in your relationship is also going to impact your self-esteem. You're going to feel like a much more confident person when you know that you can trust your partner. Without all of the worries that you would have to face if you didn't share this trust, you'll notice a wonderful sense of freedom and happiness that comes along with it. This confidence can allow you to reach for your goals and to try new things in life. It shows you that you can take opportunities and that you'll have a supportive partner who is going to be rooting for you the entire time. It also helps to know that they'll be there if anything goes wrong in life, comforting you and encouraging you to try again.

Cheating

Arguably the most severe betrayal, it can be incredibly hard to recover from being cheated on. This is an action that destroys trust and makes it difficult to rebuild. If you are experiencing a situation like this in your marriage, you are likely to feel a rollercoaster of emotions. Not only are you left to deal with the pain of being cheated on, but you must also make a very important decision regarding your marriage — are you going to work it out or are you going to leave?

No matter how much you want to rationalize it, you never should. Just because you love your partner does not mean that you need to put up with being treated poorly. You need to ask yourself if this is the relationship that you truly deserve. They need to jump into action, proving to you how they are going to make this up to you by winning back your trust. It can be a very complicated and difficult process. Understand that you call the shots here; you get to make the decision if you want to stay and work things out or if you'd rather move on with your life.

If you decide that you want to heal from this betrayal, know that you aren't the only one. So many couples go through this and end up realizing that their love is strong enough to last. It just takes a lot of hard work to regain the same level of trust you once had. After your partner has been unfaithful, it's likely that you're going to become very suspicious of their actions. Something that once seemed entirely normal, like going to the grocery store, can turn into a big series of what-ifs. You might be wondering if they're really going to the store or if they're going to meet up with someone else. This is a devastating reality to have to deal with.

Remember, if you were not unfaithful, this is not your problem to fix. Your partner needs to find their own ways to prove to you that they want to be with you. They need to establish that this relationship is more important than impulsive and hurtful decisions. Through their actions, they should be making an effort to re-establish the trust between the two of you. If you are doing all of the work, then the relationship still might not last. You don't need to fix something that you didn't break in the first place, but you do need to be aware of the way that you're being treated from now on.

Most couples need to get back to the root of their relationship, remembering how they ended up here in the first place. You need to fall in love with one another all over again, learning about each other's needs and desires. Your partner needs to make a major effort to prioritize you, proving that they want to be with you and only you. Given time, this is possible. You can return to the level of trust that you once had, but this is only going to happen if you both agree to fix the relationship.

A common problem comes when one person agrees to fix things, yet the other person doesn't think the issue can be solved in this way. Now more than ever, it's important that you're both on the same page. You each need to do what feels right individually and for the relationship, as well. This isn't something you can fix alone, nor should you need to. You're going to get your heart broken all over again if you think that you're on the path to fixing your marriage, yet your partner is not displaying the same level of commitment.

When you decide to forgive your partner for such an act, you need to remember that you are making a commitment too. By choosing to forgive them, you need to actively make sure that your actions are matching your words. While you are going to have a lot of built-up resentment, you need to do your best to work through this. Allow yourself to heal from the betrayal while taking care of your own emotional needs first. Couples therapy or individual therapy can be a great option for a situation like this. It can give you the chance to talk to someone with an unbiased opinion and help you work through your problems.

No one is going to know what you need to heal better than you. Once you figure this out, be vocal about it. Your partner should be eager to listen if they're serious about repairing the relationship. Don't feel selfish or guilty for having these requests because you deserve to feel secure in your marriage. Also, remember that your personal issues should stay personal. If you don't want to tell anyone about what has happened, your spouse should be able to respect this and also keep it to themselves. Your relationship issues are for the two of you to deal with, not the rest of the people in your lives.

Restoring Trust

- **Decide on Forgiveness** - When trust has been broken, this is an indication that someone has messed up. In some cases, both of you will be at fault. You need to ultimately decide that you are ready to forgive or to be forgiven. When you can both come to this conclusion, you will be ready to move on and heal your relationship. Staying stuck on the issue without coming to a resolution is very tiring and taxing. You don't deserve to stay in this negative headspace. Move on for the sake of your own well-being.

- **Discuss the Details** - Get all of the details about the betrayal that you need in order to fully understand it. Once you know the whole story, you'll be able to process the information and then move forward. When you're only hearing part of a story, this is going to skew your perception. Make sure you ask your spouse as many questions as necessary until you feel that you're both at this point.

- **Release Your Anger** - It's natural to feel anger, possibly at your partner and possibly even at yourself. Your feelings are valid and you need to have proper outlets for them. Make sure that you aren't holding these feelings inside because they'll begin to eat away at you. This also gives them the chance to appear again during the next confrontation that you have with your partner. Do everything you can for yourself to ensure that you have somewhere to release your negative feelings. Whether you take up a hobby or see a professional therapist, you need to be able to talk about these things openly before you can let them go.

- **Establish Your Desire** - Both of you should be able to express that you want the marriage to work. This is a part of being on the same page as a couple. No matter what you've gone through, the idea that you both want the relationship to work is a promising thought. It shows that you're both willing to do whatever it takes to allow the trust to flow again.
- **Be Open to Self-Improvement** - Sometimes, it takes a little bit of growth as an individual before you're able to grow as a couple. Be willing to do the things that you require until you're entirely happy with the person that you've become. Practice self-care frequently and listen to your own needs. These steps are important because it can be easy to lose sight of who you are as an individual rather than as your partner's spouse. Also, if both of you are willing to improve on yourselves, it makes it much easier to move past challenges in your relationship.
- **Be Aware of Your Feelings** - You are going to experience many different feelings while you're working on healing your marriage. Make sure that you take notice of all of them. They might be able to help you pinpoint exactly what you need in order to move forward. If you get a gut instinct, you should listen to it. These instincts can help you a lot when you're feeling conflicted about your relationship.

- **Shed Your Armor** - There is no need to place walls up with your partner, especially at a time like this. You need to work on staying open and communicating regularly. The conversations might be difficult, but it's a lot better to be honest than to be misled. Understand that this is what it's going to take in order to re-establish that sense of trust that you once shared. You don't need to put up a front; this is still your significant other, the person you once fell in love with.
- **Share Your Thoughts** - Work on making your voice heard at all times. If you have a thought that you feel needs to be expressed, don't hold back. This keeps the power balanced, ensuring that you're able to fully express yourself. If you allow yourself to be overshadowed by the problems that you're facing, there's going to be a lot more work to be done once you finally get over the problem at hand. Know that you are important, too.
- **Get Back to Basics** - Think about how you can restart your relationship. In a way, you're going to imagine that you're back to square one, first getting to know one another. You need to make sure that you're still compatible and that all can be forgiven. You need to have trust and loyalty, reassuring one another that you want this marriage to last.

Chapter 7: Trust — Essential and Fundamental to Any Relationship

Having a basic understanding of trust is great for your relationship, but you should know that trust is something to keep in mind at all times. You can always make an effort to build this trust and make sure that you're always being your best to your partner. This kind of devotion is essential for having a happy marriage. When you can understand that trust is a necessity, you're going to make it a part of your daily routine. Instead of being burdened by the idea of building trust with your partner, you'll begin to adopt and welcome these habits on a regular basis.

This chapter is going to focus on how you can be the happiest couple possible. You'll learn realistic ways to remedy your marriage and to develop healthy habits that will serve both you and your partner. Making a marriage last can definitely be hard work, but that is to be expected. It's one of the strongest bonds you'll ever know and it can evolve over time, just like people can. By remaining true to who you are, you'll be able to keep up with your own needs while also identifying your partner's needs. This ability to remain flexible is going to allow your marriage to feel rewarding and happy.

Remember that you both get to decide what a successful marriage looks like. Some couples value alone time while others value having a big family. You and your spouse don't have to follow any sort of standard. Just strive for the things that you both want and need to be happy. You'll know that you're successful when you feel that you're on the same page. Understand that trial and error is definitely going to be involved, no matter how long you've been together. This is the point of marriage — exploring and growing together while loving one another unconditionally. As cliché as it sounds, practice makes perfect. You need to practice your patience and your understanding in an effort to make your spouse feel heard. You'll also find that both of you need to work on your ability to compromise. With all of these things combined, you'll surely find a way to be happy together.

Staying True to You

It's important that you don't allow yourself to get lost while in a relationship. This tends to happen when you become so comfortable with being with your spouse that you forget to keep your own personal identity. The things that you're interested in and that are important to you matter. What makes you an individual is what made your partner fall in love with you in the first place. See if you can identify things that you enjoy without considering what your spouse thinks. This is a good test to see if you're still being true to yourself. Try to think only about yourself and your interests. This can be a very eye-opening experience for some.

If you have difficulty thinking about this, you might need to take some more time for yourself. There's nothing wrong with requiring a little bit of alone time every now and then. Your partner should understand that you deserve to do the things that you enjoy doing without impacting the love that you have for them. This isn't a personal attack on your partner but a way to make sure that you are still an individual. Most people don't realize that they've lost sight of who they are until it's too late. Getting into a fight with your partner and being forced to think and act on your own can be a way to realize that you don't exactly know who you are anymore.

When you're working on being true to yourself, consider the following tips:

- **Become Self-Serving** - Know that you can still fulfill your partner's needs while also taking care of your own. Do whatever you can for yourself. By knowing that you can take care of yourself and make yourself happy, anything your partner does for you will be extra. True happiness in a relationship starts with individual happiness. Neither one of you should have to rely on each other for your total happiness. When you can remember this, you'll feel more motivated to take action and to take care of yourself.
- **Share Your Thoughts** - As you become more comfortable with your partner over the years, it can become easier to just agree with them rather than expressing your own thoughts. This usually happens because couples tend to think alike as they grow closer. While this can be great in some ways, it's also one of the things that will rob you of your own identity. If you disagree with your partner, or if you have a differing opinion, make sure to let it be known. This will serve as a reminder to both yourself and your partner that you're an individual with a unique way of thinking.

- **Don't Always Aim to Please** - If you have a caregiver personality, it can seem natural to always want to please your partner. You might go out of your way to do things for them, just to make their life easier. This can be a kind gesture at times, but you need to remember to balance this out by taking care of yourself too. Know that you don't always have to aim to please them, especially when the situation involves both of you equally. When you can come together as a couple, you should both be able to put in the same amount of work. It becomes exhausting when you're always the one who is over-exerting yourself.
- **Live Through Your Values** - You should always be aware of the things that you value in life. They can shift over time, but they will always be present in your heart. Make sure that your actions align with these values and be sure to speak up if anything goes against them. By maintaining these values, you are being strong and staying true to yourself. No one else has to share the same values, but as long as they're important to you, then you need to make sure that you're upholding them. Make changes as necessary to ensure that you're living your life in the best way that you know how.
- **Trust Yourself** - This is a very big step to take in order to become the best version of yourself as an individual. While a lot of emphasis has

been placed on having trust in your partner, you must also be able to trust yourself. Much like love, it's hard to trust someone when you don't even trust yourself. Do what you can to build up your self-esteem and prove to yourself why you know what is best for you. This process can be time-consuming, but it's going to be worth it. When you have this strong sense of trust in yourself, you will be able to feel confident about all of the decisions that you make.

- **Seek Growth** - Another downside of becoming very comfortable with your partner is the idea that you've reached a point where you no longer have to grow as an individual. It's understandable that your routines are your comfort zone, but you still need to step outside of them every now and then. Challenge yourself by putting yourself in situations that will encourage you to think outside the box. Do what you think is best for you and for your life at this moment. Ask yourself what you can change in order to promote even more self-growth.

When you value yourself, you're going to be able to value the actions that you take. Any decision that you make in your marriage will be justified and important. It's when you are feeling unsure of yourself that making decisions can seem very difficult. Use your confidence to your advantage and know that you understand your marriage best. While it's between yourself and your partner, only you know what your true feelings are.

In any relationship, there is an unconscious influence that impacts the actions that you take. This influence can come from past experiences in love, childhood upbringing, and more. Learn how to identify these things and know that they aren't always going to apply to your current situation. It can be hard to unravel these ideals because you won't always notice where you've seen them, but know that you can always create your own. Do what you really feel is best, not what your past experiences have shown you.

Placing naive trust in yourself is not the same thing as truly believing in yourself. If you can identify great qualities that you possess, you're going to be a lot more likely to experience a genuine kind of trust. Remind yourself of why you are a good person and what things you've already accomplished that are noteworthy. You might have to give yourself these reminders each day, but that is okay as long as they help you grow as an individual. As expected, the better you can trust yourself, the better the trust in your relationship will be.

How to Be Gentle and Patient

It takes a certain softness in order to be a gentle and patient spouse. When you're able to let your guard down and learn how to recognize when you're wrong, this is going to show your spouse that you care about their feelings. Nobody can always be right because this isn't realistic. There are going to be times when you have excellent points to make, but there will be other times when your ego might get the better of you. By working on ways to combat this selfishness, you're going to be a much better partner and this will lead to a happier marriage.

Seeing the good in your spouse is one of the most effective ways to foster this gentle side of yourself. When you can see where they're coming from and why they're doing what they're doing, you will likely be able to see many redeeming qualities. Know that not everything is a personal attack against you. If your spouse disagrees with an opinion that you have, maybe they believe in something else that matters to them. It's always better to assume the best in your partner rather than automatically jumping to the worst conclusion. This will inevitably lead to fights and disagreements. You don't need this kind of negativity in your life, so you should avoid it at all costs.

Slowing Down

Everyone can benefit from working on their patience. It can be tough to remain calm and patient when there is a lot going on around you. In a relationship, there is always going to be something that requires you to express your opinions or take action. It's a partnership, one that you must work together to maintain. Know that you don't have to quickly jump to making a decision, though. This is one way that you can practice your patience. By thinking carefully about your options when you can, you're going to be more likely to make a choice that you can feel proud of.

This is why it's essential that you think before you speak. Not every conversation will require you to quickly come up with a reply or a retort. By using your active listening skills, identify if the conversation needs a certain reply at all. Remember how valuable a keen listening ear can be. If your response is required, think carefully about how you feel and consider what's at stake. Remember to not only think about what your decision is going to do at the moment but how it will impact you in the future, as well. Considering your responses in this way allows you and your partner to communicate more effectively.

Cut yourself some slack and appreciate all that you do on a regular basis. While your spouse might already express gratitude for this, know that you should acknowledge your accomplishments too. Know that you don't always have to keep pushing for more and overextending yourself. This is going to lead you to feeling burnt out. Understand that your best is good enough and as long as you are giving the relationship your all, you don't have to push yourself past any limits that you have.

Eating Right

The food that you eat is going to make a huge difference in how patient you're able to stay. First of all, if you aren't eating enough, this is going to lead you to an automatic feeling of irritability. You shouldn't let yourself get to this point on a regular basis, and should instead aim to eat a healthy diet. Even if you feel that you aren't in a bad mood, your actions toward your partner might lead you to fight or argue. Be aware that you can come off a little intense when you're battling hunger.

Make sure that you fill up on foods that are actually providing you with nutrients. It can be easy to reach for junk food because it's a quick option, but eating junk food can be just as bad as not eating enough. Eat foods that are going to benefit the health of your brain and your body. These ingredients will fuel you and keep you going throughout your day. Some examples include fish, lean proteins, avocados, leafy greens, and other fruits and vegetables. If you find yourself getting randomly irritable throughout the day, you might need to make some changes in your eating habits.

Breathing

As mentioned, the way that you breathe is very important. It isn't going to be possible to stay patient when you are hyperventilating. Certain conversations might make your heart rate rise and your breathing rapid, but you need to learn how to become aware of this. When you're in this state of being, you're going to be more likely to snap at your partner or to say things that you don't mean out of anger. You need to find valid ways to calm yourself down in tense moments like these. Know that this is going to prevent a lot of difficulties in your relationship.

If you need to take a timeout, let your partner know. Certain conversations can be very taxing. Instead of forcing yourself through them, take a step back when need be. Make sure that you breathe in deeply and imagine yourself exhaling the negativity. It can be helpful to use a mantra such as the following:

"Inhale positivity; exhale negativity."

Recite something that applies to how you're currently feeling. If you need to come back to a conversation at a later time, remember to think carefully about how the first conversation made you feel. Do your best to enter the next one with a calm mindset and a steady heart rate. This is going to help you to remain calm and think rationally. If you feel yourself hyperventilating again, work on your breathing exercises.

In general, yoga can be a great form of exercise to practice because of its calming properties. It allows you to get some physical benefits while also teaching you healthy breathing practices that will clear your mind. Yoga helps you center yourself and is thought to make you a calmer person. When you can handle your temper, you'll feel a lot more confident in your ability to remain gentle and patient.

Doing a little bit of yoga before bed each night can prove to be very beneficial. It will allow you to empty your thoughts so you can start your day off right. Anything that promotes clear thinking is going to be especially valuable to you as you try to manage your anger. Everyone could use some practice with this, so don't feel like you're a bad person because of it. Set a clear focus on how you would like to use more patience and allow it to guide you throughout your day. Sometimes, just focusing your mind on something positive can be enough to change your entire outlook.

If you ever feel that you have gone beyond the point of no return with your anger, take the time to step back from the current situation that is stressing you out.

Breathe in through your nose for 7 full seconds and breathe out through your mouth for the same amount of time. This is going to get your heart rate back down. Know that this moment is going to pass and that you can return to your patience if you try hard enough. Tell yourself that when you go back into the situation, your outlook is going to be different. Remember, these things take practice so try to practice patience with yourself while you learn.

Chapter 8: The Secret to Actions that Will Grow Trust in Your Relationship

Having a great marriage is all about taking actionable steps. It's only the beginning when you can both agree that your relationship needs work. The next part comes when you actually implement it. Like anything that you want to be successful at, you must come up with a plan. By agreeing on steps that you and your spouse can take together, you will both feel that you are making progress toward the end result — a happy marriage that is full of trust.

Think of changes that you can make that will improve your relationship in some way. You don't need to change everything just for the sake of making changes. Be smart about the decisions that you must make together. It's natural for couples to lose trust in one another over time, but your relationship doesn't need to stay this way. Much like love, trust can grow and it can also be lost. This is why it must be cultivated very carefully and paid attention to at all times. The instant that you stop monitoring the trust that you have, the more likely you are to become a spouse who is lazy and unaware of your partner's needs.

Consider that broken trust can come in many different forms. It doesn't necessarily have to stem from a betrayal or a deliberate action. This is why talking to one another openly is so important. A general rule is that if you feel hurt by your partner's actions, say something. What hurts you isn't always going to be apparent to them, so you need to bring it to their attention. Explain how you are feeling and try not to point any accusatory fingers. See what they have to say about your feelings and about how they can potentially correct their behavior. This is how you're going to enter an effective way to grow the trust that you have.

Make an Action Plan

Step 1: Identify why you're having trust issues. This doesn't need to be complicated or drawn out. Simply have an honest talk and discuss the things that stand out to you both. Even if you don't know why this is happening or how you're going to fix it, the very first step comes from being able to identify it. Don't be afraid to mention it if it is greatly impacting the way that you feel. Also, know that your spouse might have issues that are entirely different. Remember to respect one another and listen to both sides of the story. Allow your partner to completely finish talking before you launch into your own opinions.

If you're having trouble thinking about your trust issues, think back to the last time that you felt upset with your partner. What actions did they display that made you feel bad? This can be a very basic way to get into the topic of betrayal and mistrust. During this step, you aren't supposed to analyze anything or fix anything. The main objective is to state what the problem is so that you can both agree on a starting point for your action plan. It's more important than ever that you get on the same page from the very beginning. When you're both clear about what needs to be fixed, your solution is going to work well.

Step 2: Individually, talk about what you feel needs to change in the relationship. Know that this doesn't necessarily have to be the given solution, but hearing this input can help you both by shedding more light on the situation. This part might require some time to think. If you need to each have some space in order to come up with the answers, allow this to happen. Know that you don't need to rush during any part of this plan. Careful thought is going to create better results. As you know, thinking hard before you speak will lead you to your most honest feelings.

Again, let one another fully complete their thoughts before jumping in. When you can communicate without interrupting each other, you will both feel that you had equal time to express your opinions. This is going to avoid any additional conflicts or fighting. Know that talking about sensitive subjects isn't easy, but it must be done in order to truly get to the bottom of things. You might get emotional, but that is okay. It's a sign that you care about fixing the problem. Don't be afraid to wear your heart on your sleeve. This is the step where you'll need to practice vulnerability. Know that your partner isn't listening to judge you. The reason why you're both having this conversation should be clear by now — you want to fix things.

Step 3: Work on healing. This is going to be a diverse step because it can involve a number of different strategies. When dealing with broken trust, this is an indication that you have something to heal from. Whether you need to do this alone or with your partner, now is the time to identify what it's going to take to make you feel better. If you don't know, start from within. Work on yourself in order to become the best version of you that you can possibly be. Incorporate various self-care tasks into your daily routine as a reminder that you matter. As you know, it becomes hard to think about yourself when you're devoted to being a great partner.

If the healing process requires that you both work together, make a commitment to work on this on a regular basis. You can't expect to talk about it one time and for the feelings to disappear. This is going to be a process. Tell your partner if there is anything that they can do to solidify the trust. This isn't going to be a one-sided endeavor. Know that you might also be required to work on certain behaviors or habits that are hindering the relationship. Being stubborn during this step is only going to set you both back. You must be willing to hear this constructive criticism about yourself if you want to see an improvement in your marriage.

Step 4: Brainstorm together. This step is probably going to take the most work out of all of them, but it's helpful because it encourages you to think about the problem together instead of nit-picking it individually. Now is the time to drop any ill feelings about the issue. If you feel that you still need time to heal, then you need to stay on the previous step for as long as it takes to move forward from the issue. Again, there is no set timeline on how long you need to spend on each step. You can take as long as you personally feel that you need. The more thorough that you are, the less likely that the problem is just going to return again in the near future. Many couples make the mistake of thinking that they've solved their problem, yet they've only skimmed the surface.

You need to think deeply about the issue, considering all possible solutions. Don't rule anything out because your solution might be something that you have yet to try. When you make assumptions and remove information from your brainstorming session, you're giving the relationship less of a chance. Understand that the more detailed you are, the more effectively you will be able to find the solution that works best for both of you. Writing down all of your options can be helpful. It will allow you both to keep track of what can be done.

Step 5: Follow through with the solution. It's only one part of moving on to identify what you are going to do. Then, you must put the "action" in your action plan. Take the necessary steps to make the solution your new reality. Make sure that you verbally discuss what these steps are so you can hold each other accountable for upholding them. If you know exactly what needs to be done, there will no longer be confusion surrounding the issue. This part can be a little bit challenging, but it should be clear enough for you to have a guided path. Follow the steps and you won't go wrong.

Give this solution time. Know that your problems aren't going to get better overnight. It can take days, or weeks, to fully implement them. Don't be so quick to give up. If you have gone several months, however, without any changes, then it might be a good idea to go back to the previous step. From here, you can revisit your other solutions to see if one of them is going to work out better. This is also why it's so helpful to have them written down as a reference sheet for you to look back on. Keep doing this until you both feel that you've found a solution that is yielding results. You should be able to identify if it's working if you feel that you are trusting one another more and getting along better.

Come to an Agreement

There are many instances in which you and your spouse will need to reach an agreement. Trust issues are only a part of this practice. There are other ways that the two of you will need to come together in order to achieve a happy and harmonious marriage. An example comes from the way that you run the household. From the very basic actions of doing the dishes to washing the laundry, you'll both need to agree on how you'd like to accomplish these chores. Believe it or not, when you aren't on the same page for the minor things, this can lead to major issues. At the root of the decisions that you make together, understand that a little bit of communication can go a long way.

When you treat one another with love and respect, these small things won't seem like a big deal when you need to discuss them. It's easy to feel the need to take your anger out on someone when other things in your life become stressful, especially the person who you know is supposed to love you unconditionally. You need to avoid this by managing your own feelings. If you're stressed out and it has nothing to do with your significant other, you need to take some time for yourself to figure out how to de-stress. This will keep you from blowing the little things out of proportion. In turn, your partner should treat you with the same level of respect.

Don't go off on one another the instant that you're hit with intense feelings. The idea behind dealing with your feelings on your own means that you'll be able to control your temper. Anger is a big reason why fights start. This anger can quickly evolve into words that you wish you could take back. Before you get to this point, think about what is actually making you angry. If your partner has nothing to do with it, consider going to them for a different reason — venting. If you need to talk about your anger, this is perfectly fine. Your spouse will be willing to listen and it will be a lot healthier to discuss it in this way instead of unintentionally blaming them for the way you feel.

Create opportunities for the two of you to work together instead of focusing on the things that you do differently. Marriage is about compromise, so it can be beneficial to learn directly from the source. See what your spouse can teach you and what you can provide them in return. By coming to an agreement that you will work on things together, this also requires you to focus on the partnership element of your relationship. It will highlight the things that you do well together and it will show you what you need to work on. Both are great and will encourage growth within your marriage.

Nobody likes to focus on the mistakes they've made, but having a sense of understanding when you do make a mistake is important. Not only will it show you what you did wrong, but it will allow you to work on making things better in the future. By turning a blind eye to your mistakes, this is only going to show your partner that you don't want to make any improvements. When you're in a marriage, your actions impact your partner almost as much as they impact yourself. You need to take this into consideration the next time that you feel stubborn or unwilling to change. Growth is a positive thing, both for yourself and for your relationship.

When you come to a certain agreement, it can help to write this down. This will place importance on the issue that you're trying to fix. No matter how big or small it is, both of you should sign this agreement so that you can acknowledge what the problem is and how you're going to fix it. This will serve as both a reminder and motivation for the future. Doing things this way can be unconventional, but it can help provide structure in your marriage. A lot of couples need the reintroduction of structure in order to get better at it and there is nothing wrong with that. Try it out for yourself and see if it makes a difference.

Know that situations change. This is why it's important to review anything that you've agreed upon every so often. If something changes, then it's justifiable that you would have to come together again to think of a new agreement. This is how you're going to practice working together and making successful decisions. As much as your partnership is romantic, it should also be practical. Couples who get along well understand that there are times when they need to be more relaxed and times when they should practice being serious. The more that you work together with your partner, the better you will be at identifying when you need to change the mood.

Overall, being able to agree on things comes down to how much effort you and your partner put into your marriage. If you just sit back and accept what is happening, then you aren't taking much accountability for your actions. You must stay engaged if you want your partner to know that you still care.

How to Engage in Your Marriage

- **Ask Questions** - Instead of assuming how your spouse feels because you already know them very well, ask them how they feel. This is important to stay engaged in the relationship because you should know that their feelings can change. Just as you will evolve as a person, so will they. Make sure that you continue to show an interest in knowing who they are right now, not just who they were when you first met.
- **Spend Time in New Situations** - Experiencing something new together is a great way to even the playing field. Since neither one of you will know exactly what to expect, you can enjoy this bonding experience as a way to work together and to discuss how you're feeling. This can be something simple like going to a new place or going on a double date with another couple. Alternatively, it could be something more complicated like planning a trip together or taking up a new hobby.
- **Put the Phone Down** - When you talk to your spouse, don't be distracted. Being comfortable around one another is a great thing, but not when you're sacrificing your significant other's feelings, this defeats the purpose. Make eye contact and put your phone down. Have a

genuine conversation where you can truly connect without the need for any absentminded distractions.

- **Do Something They Enjoy** - There are going to be plenty of things that your spouse likes to do that you are less familiar with. For a change, engage in an activity or hobby that your spouse enjoys. If possible, let them teach you about it or guide you through it. This is a great way to change the relationship dynamic and the routine without the need to do anything complicated.

Chapter 9: How to Regain Trust in a Relationship That Is Falling Apart

You aren't the only person in a marriage to feel that your relationship is falling apart — many feel that their relationships are broken beyond repair. This chapter asks you to be honest with yourself and to decide on how much your relationship matters to you. If you are willing to fix it and implement the changes, you will be able to give your marriage a fighting chance. All things fall apart at times, but that doesn't mean that you have to live this way. This can bring forward a lot of negative energy, causing you to fall into a downward spiral. No one deserves to live this way and you're going to learn how to break free of these chain reactions.

Starting by getting rid of the idea that you are helpless, you are going to find your inner-strength and recognize what needs to be done in order to fix your marriage. You will be able to effectively communicate these issues to your spouse in an effort to shed some light on what you've been dealing with. In discussing these things, you might be surprised to find that your spouse can identify with you. Making discoveries like this one will bring you closer together. It will serve as a reminder that you are not alone in this and that any relationship is made up of the actions of two people combined.

When you're able to move past making excuses, you're going to see real progress. The passion that you once shared will be reignited and you will both be happier than you've felt in a long time. Getting stuck is natural for all couples. Because no one is exempt, it can often feel as though you are trapped. In order to get out of this mentality, you need to remind yourself of all the freedoms that you still have. From the freedom to make changes in your life to the ability to work on yourself as an individual, there is always more that you can do to help improve the health of your marriage and to regain the trust that you once had.

Recognize Emotional Disconnect

If you feel that your partner is being distant with you, this could indicate that there is some emotional disconnect occurring. You might notice that your partner is pulling away, both figuratively and literally. This can naturally cause you to become very upset, possibly even accusatory at your partner's actions. There is a lot that can lead to emotional disconnect, so it's important that you recognize the signs so that you can talk to your partner about it in the best way possible. This will allow the two of you to have an honest conversation and to help strengthen your trust in one another.

- **Lack of Conversation/Shared Feelings** - One main sign of your partner pulling away might be their lack of interest in talking to you. They're likely doing so to avoid conversations that might have to do with their feelings or problems. If they used to talk to you about these things before, their behavior is going to be very noticeable. When you try to ask them what's wrong, they might change the subject or just lash out at you to avoid getting into a discussion. Naturally, this can be very painful for you to discover because it's going to be apparent that the trust you once shared is no longer present.
- **Distant Behavior** - When you do get the chance to talk to your partner, you might notice

that they seem distant or distracted. You might be telling them all of your feelings and yet they only give you short answers or try to change the subject. This is definitely a sign of emotional disconnect and it might be stemming from their inability to connect with the conversation that you're presenting to them. It can be very frustrating, especially when you feel that you are giving it your all. As you know, it takes two people to be in a healthy relationship. If one person is putting in all of the effort, this will create an imbalance.

- **Blind to Emotions** - If you express your emotions with sadness, rage, or even tears, this might still not be enough to elicit a response from your partner. Whether they're unaware of your emotions or ignoring them, they're likely not going to respond to you or ask you what's wrong. This can often be a coping mechanism for when situations get emotionally intense. By keeping themselves distanced, they won't have to launch into the discussion with you. This behavior will end up making you feel that they don't care at all. In reality, they might just not know how to cope with what is going on and thus be trying to avoid the situation.

- **No Conflict Resolution** - Your partner will begin to show a lack of interest in resolving any conflicts that you get into. When a fight occurs, they will likely find a way out of it or simply express that they don't want to discuss it any further. You might notice that they even seem indifferent when something is impacting you or your relationship. Frustration is probably going to be one-sided because your feelings will be hurt and they will keep going as if nothing is wrong. It can seem difficult to get through to your partner on any level, even if there is a big issue that is hindering your relationship.

- **No Quality Time** - Part of being in a relationship means that you and your partner should have quality time together. This is your chance to regroup and hear what is on each other's minds. If your partner stops showing interest in being alone with you or keeps changing the plans so that other people are involved, this can be an indication that they're feeling emotionally disconnected. The thought of this might make them uncomfortable or nervous, causing them to find ways to change the situation so there is little chance that you'll have to talk about their behavior. They might even go as far as pretending that they have other plans or that they're too busy doing something else.
- **Non-Existent Sex Life** - Having sex is one of the most emotional acts that a couple can engage in together. If your partner isn't connecting with you emotionally, the sex is likely to become sparse or stop altogether. If

intimacy becomes an issue like this, bringing it up to your partner is probably only going to cause a fight or be met with excuses. In some cases, your partner might even blame you or something that you've done for their lack of sexual interest. This is something that can hinder couples very easily. It can cause insecurity and, sometimes, resentment. You will notice that you'll start to feel uncomfortable when the idea of having sex with your partner comes to mind.

Drop the Excuses

In relationships, it becomes very easy to fall into certain habits. When you get into conflicts with your spouse, it can be easier to just say what they want to hear or give them an excuse in order to prevent the situation from escalating. What you must be mindful of is the fact that this will not fix the problem. It's simply going to delay it until it comes up again in the future. Making an excuse for something that is wrong is not a valid way to resolve it. While it might seem like it fixes things, for the time being, it's likely to come back as an even bigger issue later on. Be aware of this habit and recognize if you do this.

If you want your partner to fully trust you, then you need to show them that you aren't just going to come up with an excuse when you hurt them or betray them. Issues should be discussed when they're fresh on your mind. This will allow you to fully tap into the emotions that you're feeling. Together as a unit, the two of you should be able to work things out. When your partner displays this kind of behavior, let them know. Without blaming them for any of the issues that you're having, try to bring it to their attention when they're telling you excuses instead of explaining how they really feel. This can potentially open up a new dialogue. While it might be hard to have conversations like these, they are necessary.

Open yourself to the idea that you might be wrong about something. A lot of people have a fear of being wrong and this is one way that excuses tend to appear. Know that you aren't perfect and your spouse knows that, too. They love you for who you are. It's a very humbling experience to realize that you've gotten something wrong, but you can learn a lot from it. Try your best to be open to these instances. When you do not have an answer for something, be honest with your partner instead of trying to make one up. This is going to further humble you and encourage you to be completely honest instead of hiding behind your mistakes with excuses.

Allow yourself to apologize to your partner if you do find that you've made a mistake. Honest mistakes require honest apologies. It will show them that you care about hurting their feelings or lying to them, two very big factors of any relationship. The more that you are honest with them, the more you'll be able to be honest with yourself. If you do have to apologize for something that you've done, consider this a new starting point. Once you've made amends, you can try again and be better. You don't need to punish yourself or prevent yourself from speaking up again in the future, just learn from the experience and move on.

Try not to compare yourself to other people. You are who you are, and you should be proud of that. Again, your partner is with you because of this, not because you're a copy of someone else. It can be easy to make excuses when you're trying to fit a certain mold. You might have to focus on some self-love in order to get back to what is important. Understand what qualities you have to offer and what you bring to the relationship. Give yourself credit for all that you've accomplished. You shouldn't have to change who you are to make your marriage work, but small efforts of self-improvement will be noticeable.

Make sure that you remain realistic during any discussions that you have with your partner. If you're expecting them to drop their way of thinking to adopt your own, you're going to be met with frustration. Understand that they are going to have their own process of working through issues and that you need to respect it. Not being able to think the exact same way shouldn't be an excuse that is used as to why conflict cannot be handled. You should still be able to come together as a couple to identify what actually can be changed and what will improve the situation.

Don't blame other people for your own actions. This is another common excuse that is made, and it allows you to get out of taking accountability for the things that you've done. Just because another person might have influenced you doesn't mean that they forced you to act the way that you did. All of your actions were chosen because you made the decision to implement them. It's important that you always keep this in mind, even if you mess up badly. Instead of making excuses for what you've done, you need to come up with ways to fix the situation and prevent yourself from making the same choices again in the future.

Identify Chain Reactions

When your decisions activate a chain of results, this is what is known as a chain reaction. Some people might refer to it as a domino effect. You need to be aware of these reactions in your relationship, as they can tell you a lot about why you have trust issues and what is holding you back as a couple. A chain reaction can be either positive or negative. If you can eliminate the negative chain reactions by avoiding what triggers them and strive for more positive ones, you'll notice a significant improvement in your relationship. The only way for you to do this is by being aware of these cycles and what behaviors set them off.

Positive

Some examples of positive chain reactions include:
- Regular laughter together
- The ability to be relaxed/happy
- Feeling close to one another

- Enjoying one another's company
- Understanding that trust and confidence is your foundation
- Feeling respected and heard
- A sense of attraction present
- Love flowing on a daily basis
- A noticeable desire for one another

Negative

Some examples of negative chain reactions include:

- Anger experienced on a regular basis
- A built-up feeling of resentment
- Blaming one another for issues
- Not respecting boundaries
- Feeling personally attacked
- Distance being present
- Talk of breaking up happening frequently
- Feeling jealous/insecure
- One person losing interest in the relationship
- Feeling that the marriage is falling apart

Given the above examples, you should be able to identify if any of these things are present in your current situation. A chain reaction is something that usually cannot be stopped once it is started, this is why it's important to identify it at the source. Take a look at which behaviors lead to bigger issues or greater benefits. This is how you'll be able to tell what to eliminate and what to do more of in your marriage. For this step, it's going to take some attention to detail as well as some patience.

Work on rebuilding your trust by letting your partner know that you want to eliminate negative chain reactions. When you can explain that both of you are going to have work together to accomplish this goal, this will make it less of an attack and more of a process. With both of you paying attention to what triggers these reactions, you should be able to come together and find a way to operate in your marriage without causing anything so extreme. Know that you can stop this series of reactions if you put in the effort to do so. By allowing your partner to know what you'd like the goal to be, they'll have a clear understanding of how much the relationship means to you.

If one of you seems to always be the cause of these chain reactions, this should become apparent once you start observing them. Pay attention to how each of you reacts when something bad is happening to you both. Know that your actions might be fueling the fire. If you're doing something that is causing a reaction and either you notice it or your partner points it out, you'll be able to know when to stop and think of ways to fix it. If you notice that your partner is at-fault, bring the issue up with them. Instead of trying to correct it, allow them to come up with their own way of doing so. This will show them that you aren't trying to control or nit-pick them but simply attempting to improve the quality of the relationship.

When you're both acting on your best characteristics, you're going to feel like the relationship has entered into a new chapter. You will both likely feel refreshed and able to handle whatever comes your way. It's amazing how tiring it can be to constantly have to deal with the same problems repeatedly, especially if these problems tend to lead to stressful arguments. Showing your best characteristics encourages you to live your life with your best foot forward. It will allow you to think about the smartest decisions that will ultimately lead you to the most harmony possible within the marriage.

Make sure that you're always as approachable as possible when your partner tries to come to you with a problem that they would like to fix. If you are truly on the same team, you'll be willing to work with them to improve the relationship. An unwillingness to talk comes across as standoffish. This can create fights as well as chip away at the trust that you have already built up together. In any relationship, there is going to be a time when you must do away with your complaints and simply handle what is going on. You'll be glad you did, and your partner will see that they don't have to work on things alone.

Chapter 10: The Long-Term Benefits of Rebuilding Lost Trust in Your Relationship

The work that you put into your relationship does not only help at the moment but in the future as well. All of the efforts that you put into your marriage right now will carry over into your future interactions. This means that you aren't only solving problems and dealing with current issues together, but you're also learning how to practice longevity. All couples strive for longevity in their marriages. Because you want to be with your partner for the rest of your life, you need to understand that everything that you do right now is going to make a difference in your relationship. Be cautious about what you say and do in times of anger or stress. These things that might seem insignificant right now can become magnified over time, leading to fractures within the bond you share.

As you work through this guide together, you are both making a commitment to the overall health of your marriage. You are stating that you believe in the relationship and that you see it working out in the long-run. Those who have to question their significant others about whether they still want to be together will likely not be going through these exercises together. Know that if your spouse is willing to make changes and improvements, they are likely to believe that the love *is* going to make it and that the relationship *will* last. You need to have faith in one another as you explore this together. Rebuild your trust and enjoy the newfound connection that you discover.

Re-Establishing Your Connection

1. **Make your intentions clear.** This is a way for you to be extremely genuine with your spouse. Even if you do not align on certain ideas, if you both have the same intentions behind your actions, you are going to be met with results that both of you are happy with. Oftentimes, couples will try to make this more complicated than it really is. You don't need to adjust your ideals to the point that they're identical, just get them moving in the same direction.
2. **Understand that love is powerful.** While a relationship is built on a lot more than the love that you share, it's still a very powerful element of any marriage. Use this love wisely and allow it to guide you when you are at a loss for what to do. This connection is one of the most genuine aspects of the relationship that you share. It was there in the beginning and it should continue to remain present until the very end. This is a constant that you can rely on.
3. **Agree to disagree sometimes.** You should know that not all arguments or conflicts need to be held in the same regard. Some are going to be pointless and you both need to recognize these limits. If you can just agree to disagree and then move on, this is a very healthy practice to learn as a couple. In doing so, this is going to save you a lot of time and effort while also allowing you both to potentially look back and laugh about this issue. It is a way that you can

make your connection strong by realizing that you both don't need something like this in your life.

4. **Choose honesty over a white lie.** While telling a small lie to your partner might seem harmless, know that it's always going to get back to them. If you lie with the intention of making them feel better, you're doing a lot more than you need to be doing. It is easier to just express how you really feel and deal with it instantly rather than letting something go on for an extended period of time. Also, being honest with them keeps them in the loop. There is no worse feeling than being the last to find out about something, especially relating to your marriage, so remember to be honest with each other.

5. **Brainstorm together frequently.** Even if you aren't fighting and looking for a solution, it's a great idea to continually brainstorm with your significant other. You can discuss ideas and opinions this way. It provides you with a great outlet for your thoughts while also encouraging you both to make the best decisions that will benefit the overall health of the relationship. Use these brainstorming sessions to learn new things about one another. You can also use them to help each other figure out how to achieve your goals as individuals and as a couple.

6. **Allow yourself to let go of control.** There will be times when you really don't want to let go of being right. This is a form of control that you need to be aware of. It shows your partner that you trust them when you are able to step away from something that you believe in because you see value in their approach, as well. This becomes a great way for you to show that you're able to compromise and stick with decisions that aren't always your own. Every couple should be able to reach this point together if they want a sense of balance in their relationship.
7. **Give a sincere apology when you need to.** Stepping down when you have done something wrong can be incredibly difficult, but it's time to swallow your pride. Give a heartfelt apology to your partner when you need to say that you're sorry. Don't do it because you have to or because you feel that you should. This will only come off as ingenuine. The words should come from your heart and the timing should make sense based on what is currently going on. These things matter if you want to have a thriving marriage that is full of trust.
8. **Know not to push certain buttons.** You know your partner better than anyone else and this means that you definitely know what tests their limits. It can be tempting to push them close to their boundaries without crossing any lines, but

this is known as button-pushing. It's a negative action because it's normally done in a deliberate fashion. Don't allow yourself to take things to this point. You need to exercise your own form of self-control in order to avoid pushing your partner's buttons. This is a sign of respect and of how you value your partner.

9. **Always think positively.** No matter what is going on in your life or in your marriage, you need to set your sights on positivity. If you get too caught up on what is negative, it's going to be difficult for you to move forward. Envision the positive results that you're hoping for and your actions will begin to align with your efforts. There is no use in tormenting yourself by replaying the negative possibilities over and over again in your head.

10. **Enforce your boundaries.** While you might not want to remind your spouse of the things that you aren't okay with, it becomes necessary to do so if your boundaries aren't being respected. In the same way, you shouldn't feel offended if they remind you of their own. Boundaries are important for every couple to have, regardless of how long they've been together. Your boundaries are a set of your own personal beliefs that matter to you. If your spouse truly loves you, they should have no problem respecting these boundaries and being sure to listen to you when any lines have been

crossed. You should also be able to do the same for them without taking the request as a personal attack.

What You Will Learn

- Instead of coming up with ways to pick apart flaws and point out weaknesses, you will learn how to accept these things about your spouse.
- Holding on to resentment/bitterness is only going to end up hurting you after a while. You will learn how to let go of it and to move on from it.
- The focus will shift to the qualities that you can appreciate most about each other instead of the qualities that could use some improvement. Being able to acknowledge these things will allow you to pay your spouse better compliments.
- Talking about hardship or difficulty doesn't always have to result in a fight. As a mature couple, you should be able to get into these discussions and talk about these things honestly.
- The longer that you work toward overcoming your differences, the shorter your fights will last. Once you get into a method that works well for both of you, this process is going to become easier.

- Instead of keeping your distance when things get hard, you will learn to come together and begin working on your issues immediately. There is nothing worse than allowing separation to overtake your relationship, causing emotional distancing.
- On a daily basis, you should be able to do things for one another that show you truly care. These things should be unprompted and done because of the love that you share.
- When healing is necessary, you will both be able to rely on constructive methods of getting to this point instead of continually resorting to behavior that ends up hurting you or the relationship.
- Reframing your approach can be beneficial when you're trying to solve problems. Instead of jumping straight into possible solutions, you will learn how to see things from new perspectives to see if it helps make things easier.
- Issues in the past can stay in the past if you move on from them properly. There shouldn't be anything residual that you're holding on to that is hindering your marriage today.
- When you see negativity, you will start with the attitude that you do not wish to carry it with you. After having this in your mind, you will be a lot more likely to find a solution for it rather than starting fights over it.

- You will learn how to enjoy what feels like a new life with your significant other. It can be a very refreshing feeling to realize that you do not have to be controlled by your trust issues and your problems.
- Couples should also be friends. When you can have a genuine friendship with your spouse, this is going to make your bond even stronger and show you different sides of each other.
- The two of you should be able to come to an agreement of what your "dream relationship" looks like. This kind of vision should come from how you wish your relationship could be in an ideal world. Together, you can strive to make this a reality.

This is only the beginning of what you will learn as you work through this guide. All of these examples can serve as motivation for you to use moving forward. A part of changing your behavior is changing your mindset. When you have the above examples to think about, you should be able to let go of any negativity that you might still be holding on to. Think deeply about why you might still feel the need to hold on to it, then let go of it in the best way that you know how. Understand that you don't need to remain in a state of worry or anxiety if you can personally clear your head enough to focus on the positive things about your marriage. If any issues come up, trust that your spouse will make them known and then you can work on solving them together.

Long-Term vs. Short-Term

When thinking about their problems, couples usually make the mistake of only considering what is going on in the present moment. Think back on the things that frustrated you the most last year. Do these things matter as much to you this year? Do you even remember what they are? Your mood has a lot to do with your reactionary impulses and you cannot necessarily help that. If something bothers you, then you're going to react to it — it's that simple. What you can do, however, is to learn how to think about the bigger picture. Understand that what might be bothering you right now might prove to be insignificant in the future.

When defining "the future," know that this can be anywhere from years later to weeks later. You need to consider if any issue is important enough to hold on to and if it will impact you in the future. If the issue is very temporary, meaning that it is likely to be resolved quickly, this is something that you shouldn't need to hold on to and take with you into the future. It is only going to take up negative space in your brain and hold you back from being the best partner that you can be.

For more serious and ongoing issues, you might need to carry them for a little while. This still does not warrant carrying them in a way that places weight onto your relationship. Know that the only reason problems need to go unresolved is if they need additional time to fix. For example, it might take time to rebuild trust once it has been broken. For anything that has a clear solution, do your best to consider it as handled. This way, you won't feel the need to bring it up again unnecessarily or use it against your partner in the future. You will feel a lot better when your conscience is free of these things that simply take up space.

Consider this example:

You and your spouse have been fighting a lot over the amount of time that is spent going out with friends rather than the amount of time that is spent with each other. It has been causing fights that come to the same conclusion — you want your partner to stop going out. This has then caused a negative chain reaction and your spouse has become emotionally distant, avoiding you and avoiding having this conversation again. They continue to go out with friends and it continues to make you upset. There is no resolution.

Short-term solution: You don't talk to your partner until they stop going out as much. This causes a lot of tension in the relationship and the issue often gets brought up in fights, even when they have nothing to do with this subject. Your partner develops a defensive type of aggression that tends to come out when you nitpick at them for going out. The cycle repeats itself until you both feel exhausted. You both keep doing it because it seems easier than addressing the issue and working on finding a solution that you feel would benefit you both.

Long-term solution: You both sit down and talk about the issue, expressing both sides of the story. Your partner wants to feel that they have their own individual life, but you don't want them gone late into the night. You come to a compromise, showing one another that you both value your marriage. Instead of going out all the time, your partner has their friends come over. This no longer makes you mad because your boundaries are respected. With this solution, you both feel that the issue has been taken care of, therefore, you don't continue to bring it up again in the future.

As you can see, each solution would result in very different outcomes. When you think that you are "handling" a problem, you might realize that you're only coming up with a temporary and short-term solution. Recognize these instances and see how you can change them for the better. Adjust what you're doing so that you can make them long-term, instead.

The latter is going to leave you feeling a lot better about the solution and it will encourage you both to speak up about what you feel should be done.

Passive-aggressive techniques should not be used, as they are solely meant to make the other person feel bad. Remember, you need to always make sure that you are acting out of love. No matter what the situation is, that love for your partner should not simply disappear. Allow it to guide you and provide you with a new way of thinking. Understand that you aren't always going to get exactly what you want, but there are ways to come up with a compromise that will leave you feeling just as satisfied. It's all about being willing to work with one another. Long-term solutions leave you with long-term results. You know how frustrating it can be to repeat the same cycles, so do everything that you can to avoid this from the beginning.

Conclusion

This guide has given you valuable resources that you can now use to identify any problems that you are having, heal from the things that have hurt you in the past, understand why you have the habits that you do in your relationship, and work together as a couple to come up with the best solutions. It serves as a comprehensive look at exactly what it takes to be happy in your marriage. All of these tips and exercises stem from real ways that couples communicate and interact with one another in healthy relationships. Both of you should feel that you're being equally respected while being treated with care. The happiness that you're able to work toward together is not going anywhere, as long as you are both on board with the process.

After exploring all of the new ways that you can improve your marriage, you should be feeling inspired and proactive. Any relationship can be hard work, but the promise of being together forever brings forward a different kind of pressure. Understand that you are both going to change as individuals and this will, in turn, impact your relationship. You do not need to lose trust or betray each other in the process, though. Your ability to remain flexible to changes and your willingness to think outside of the box is going to greatly benefit both of you as you aim to rebuild your trust in the relationship.

Aim to understand your spouse and do your best to listen attentively to their needs. You don't need to rush this process because it sends them the message that you don't care about how they are feeling or what they are thinking. After taking their side into consideration, you should be able to come up with solutions together on how you want to fix your problems. In any harmonious marriage, this part needs to be balanced. This means that you both need to come up with solutions and agree on one together. When you're both putting in the same amount of work, fewer problems are likely to surface as a result.

Stop with the excuses and the avoidance that you have when you encounter problems. The best way to handle any issue in your relationship is going to be addressing it head-on. If you wait until it upsets you to the point of breaking, then you're likely going to lash out at your partner which will cause even more damage. Talking openly and honestly can be difficult, but it is necessary. Your communication is a direct way to identify if your marriage is healthy or not. You should be able to talk to one another about anything at any time without holding back or feeling judged. Make sure that you are doing your part to keep this communication flowing.

By choosing to take deliberate action, you will start to notice significant improvements in the way that you get along and are able to keep your happiness flowing. Not only will your efforts be beneficial when you're working through problems, but they will also set a strong foundation for the future. Your significant other should be a priority to you, so you should let them know by allowing your actions to match your words. Do kind things for them and remember to consider their love language. At the end of the day, you should both feel appreciative of one another and lucky to be in the relationship that you are in.

As promised, you were given all of the tools that you need to move forward in your marriage. Instead of getting caught up in past issues and the same problems, you will be able to make decisions that are going to benefit the health of your relationship. Your marriage is going to feel stronger and happier, allowing you to feel that you can be yourself without any consequences. The best marriages are a true partnership with a sense of freedom that is still present. You should do things together because you want to, not because you feel that you have to. The love that you share should shine through any difficulties that you encounter because it is going to be stronger than ever.

References

Browne, D. (2018, August 31). *How to Let Go: 12 Tips for Letting Go of the Past.* Healthline. https://www.healthline.com/health/how-to-let-go#1

Dean, F. (2013, June 5). *How to have more patience.* Chatelaine. https://www.chatelaine.com/health/sex-and-relationships/how-to-have-more-patience/

Fensterheim, S. (n.d.) *Relationship Advice: Why is Trust so Important?* The Relationship Expert. https://www.thecouplesexpertscottsdale.com/2017/08/relationship-advice-trust-important/

Gans, S. (2019, November 19). *Ways to Rebuild Trust in Your Marriage.* Verywell Mind. https://www.verywellmind.com/rebuild-trust-in-your-marriage-2300999

Gaspard, T. (2016, December 7). *10 Ways to Rekindle the Passion in Your Marriage.* The Gottman Institute. https://www.gottman.com/blog/10-ways-rekindle-passion-marriage/

Herrin, T. (2020, March 16). *How to Recognize Emotional Disconnect in Your Relationship and What to Do to Reconnect*. ReGain. https://www.regain.us/advice/general/how-to-recognize-emotional-disconnect-in-your-relationship-and-what-to-do-to-reconnect/

Ishak, R. (2015, December 10). *Little Ways To Be More Open With Your Partner*. Bustle. https://www.bustle.com/articles/128557-6-ways-to-be-more-open-with-your-partner

Lancer, D. (n.d.). *24 Tips for Conflict Resolution in an Intimate Relationship*. Gracepoint Wellness. https://www.gracepointwellness.org/51-family-relationship-issues/article/56557-24-tips-for-conflict-resolution-in-an-intimate-relationship

Linder, A. (n.d.). *Ideas for How to Add Fun Back Into Your Marriage*. All Pro Dad. https://www.allprodad.com/ideas-for-how-to-add-fun-back-into-your-marriage/

Mirchevski, B. (2019, June 16). *Stop with the Excuses — It's Time to Make a Change*. Medium. https://medium.com/the-logician/stop-with-the-excuses-its-time-to-make-a-change-87990fc6a9d6

Moody. (2018, May 16). *The Five Love Languages Defined*. The 5 Love Languages. https://www.5lovelanguages.com/2018/06/the-five-love-languages-defined/

Morin, A. (2020, April 9) *15 Ways to Rebuild a Broken Relationship*. Lifehack. https://www.lifehack.org/articles/communication/10-tips-make-positive-thinking-easy.html

Smith, K. (2018, July 8). *Does Your Relationship Have Positive or Negative Power Struggles?* PsychCentral. https://psychcentral.com/blog/does-your-relationship-have-positive-or-negative-power-struggles/

StockSnap.io - Beautiful Free Stock Photos (CC0). (n.d.). Retrieved March 2, 2020, from https://stocksnap.io/

Pegler, L. (2019, October 7). *How to Remain True to Yourself in a Relationship — The Ascent*. Medium. https://medium.com/the-ascent/how-to-remain-true-to-yourself-in-a-relationship-c836554ac631

PowerofPositivity. (2019, December 16). *10 Ways to Keep Negativity Out of Your Relationships: Power of Positivity*. Power of Positivity. https://www.powerofpositivity.com/10-ways-to-keep-negativity-out-of-your-relationships/

What is Respect in a Healthy Relationship? (2017, February 3). LoveIsRespect. https://www.loveisrespect.org/content/respect-in-healthy-relationships/

The Adult Attachment Workbook

Powerful Strategies to Promote Understanding, Increase Security, and Build Long-Lasting Relationships

Kate Homily

MY FREE GIFT TO YOU:

As my way of saying thanks for buying 'The Perfect Relationship Workbook' I'd like to give you a FREE COPY of my book 'Keeping Love and Healthy Relationships Alive'

>>> Click Here to Get the Free Book Instantly<<<

The above book is a gift, given to you as a sincere thanks for buying my e-book. I hope it helps you increase of your life. Download this **FREE BOOK** by clicking the link here

So click the link above to get access now and thanks once again for your support.

Enjoy!

Disclaimer

No part of this e-book may be reproduced or transmitted in any forms of whatsoever, electronic, or mechanical photocopying, recording, or by any informational storage or retrieval system without express writer, dated and signed permission from the author.

I'll send you my future projects, in preview, with nothing in return, if you just want a realistic review on them, which I'm sure will be useful to me. Thanks in advance! Leave me your best email, my staff will send you a copy as soon as possible: digitallifemystery@gmail.com

For a Better Experience, Download Audio Book Version of This Book for FREE

If you love listening to audio books on-the-go, I have great news for you. You can download the audio book version of this book for FREE just by signing up for a FREE 30-day audible trail! See below for more details!

AUDIBLE TRAIL BENEFITS

As an audible customer, you will receive the below benefits with your 30-day free trial:

- **FREE** audible book copy of this book
- After the trail, you will get 1 credit each month to use on any audiobook
- Your credits automatically roll over to the next month if you don't use them
- Choose from Audible's 200,000 + titles
- Listen anywhere with the Audible app across multiple devices
- Make easy, no-hassle exchanges of any audiobook you don't love
- Keep your audiobooks forever, even if you cancel your membership
- And much more

Click the links below to get started!

For Audible US

Introduction

"It's all about falling in love with yourself and sharing that love with someone who appreciates you, rather than looking for love to compensate for a self-love deficit."

~ Eartha Kitt

You've done it again. You entered another relationship that seemed destined to fail. This has become your modus operandi, or so it seems. Why do you go for a certain type of person? It almost seems to be your weakness. However, this is not your weakness; instead, it is your own style of attachment.

From your primary relationship, your bond with your childhood caregivers, you have learned to behave in a certain way. This type of behavior has become a habit that is ingrained in your thinking and doing. These behaviors are known as styles of attachment. Psychologists have conducted many tests and research studies over the years to discover why people do things the way they do them, and John Bowlby (a psychoanalyst) finally created the theory of attachments to explain the four styles of attachment that were identified.

In a nutshell, the best form of attachment that is most stable and responsive to change and helps you to be in a successful relationship is known as a secure attachment style. This style of attachment usually develops in children who are raised in homes with dependable parents who quickly address their children's fears and help them deal with stressors in a responsible manner. In essence, these children grow up to be secure self-loving adults, and this enables them to share that love with others in a responsible and compassionate way.

The three other styles of attachment are known as insecure attachment styles and start in children who are raised in homes where there was irregular activity, with parents who were not dependable and emotionally unavailable, where they suffered trauma and neglect. These styles all enable us to deal with the stressors of a relationship in different ways, and because of them, we can engage in harmful behavior. There is also evidence of insecure attachment styles contributing to mental health challenges as people struggle to deal with trauma or to build their self-confidence, and we should all try to move towards more secure attachment styles.

If you find yourself displaying the characteristics of any of these three attachment styles, you tend to engage in self-sabotaging behavior in your relationships. You are drawn to the wrong partners, or even when you have an ideal partner, you tend to mess things up or leave that partner. So, how do you get to a point where you can enter a healthy relationship, or even create your own happiness without being in a relationship or partnership? Certainly, you do not need to be a victim of your past.

By dealing with your attachment issues, you will enrich your long-term relationships and heal the broken connections within yourself and between other people in your life. You need to return to a sense of wholeness, the original trusting and caring person you were before you were robbed of your potential by trauma. And, even if that trauma originated in your childhood, it can impact your life today, creating dissociation and a loss of boundaries.

This book is about reclaiming your birthright, finding healthy connections and redeveloping compassion with yourself and with others. By becoming aware of your behavioral mechanisms and attachment behaviors, you will start to see why you make certain decisions, replace your fear with curiosity, and connect with your peers as you enter into healthy relationships with yourself and with others.

In these pages, you will get a better understanding of attachment theory as it applies in your life and the life of your partner. You will come to understand different approaches to interventions as you learn to form deeper bonds, develop your self-confidence, and learn to trust. Looking at all the relationships in your life, whether platonic, romantic, or familial, you will learn a variety of therapeutic techniques and approaches to help you develop a secure attachment style and heal your core wounds.

Your adult behavior need not be a continued reflection of your childhood traumas, and a deep personal transformation is possible. There are a range of traditional psychological methods and new cutting-edge technologies available to help with your transformation. Change is powerful, and you can build more secure and lasting relationships with the people in your life, especially with the people you care about most. Let me be your guide, your therapist, and your compass.

My name is Kate Homily, and I have been a relationship therapist for 18 years. Throughout my long years of family practice, I have seen and even experienced many forms of relationship anxiety myself. I have successfully helped all my clients overcome their own unique relationship challenges by identifying their attachment styles, exploring how this affects their lives and relationships, and planning a constructive guided path for them to work through to achieve their own relationship goals and find happiness. In this book, I hope to share the wisdom and experience I have amassed in my years of helping people of all ages, genders, and races.

I have applied my theories and experience to my own life with great success. Many years ago, I also experienced relationship anxiety, and the battle I won has shaped my approach to relationship therapy to a large extent. Today, I am a happily married mother, and I have built a harmonious life with my family, my two kids, and also my two rambunctious puppies. I no longer spend my days worrying about the what-ifs or that my life could fall apart. Through my experiences, my training, and my years of helping my clients, I have discovered how to enjoy all of my blessings and practice gratitude every day.

Starting today, you can also develop strategies to strengthen your romantic relationships, understand yourself better, and be a better version of your authentic self with the people you care about. Blessings and daily gratitude is within your reach as you learn to let go of anxieties, create coping strategies, and improve your behavior to become the best version of yourself today. Let go of reacting out of harmful instincts and develop the ability to act with control and compassion right now.

Chapter 1: Attachment Styles: Where Do You Fall

on the Spectrum?

Image 1: Geralt on Pixabay. None of us live in isolation. We connect with and to other people, places, and even things. This great big network affects our psyche, and if we are not consciously aware of it and learn to effectively manage it, we can end up being tangled up in it and losing our ability to determine our life course. We react instead of mindfully acting.

Attachment: A Brief History

Attachments form in your early childhood. Before you can even speak or even before your conscious memories form, you start interacting with the people around you. From your first wail, you are engaging in behavior to find the best way to navigate your life. If you were fortunate enough to have responsive parents or primary caregivers who rapidly soothed your wails, fed you on time, eased you from any discomfort, ensured you had routines to develop trust, and kept you healthy from childhood illnesses, you will most likely have developed a secure attachment style. You have been conditioned to believe in the world around you as being good and predictable, which created a low level of anxiety in you.

This will, in turn, create healthy brain chemistry as your body develops naturally. However, should you have been raised in a home that was unpredictable or traumatic, you will have developed a completely different style of attachment. You have been exposed to loud noises, tensions, irregular feeding, lack of comfort, increased levels of fear, and start to develop trust issues.

This will result in you forming harmful attachment behavior.

With young children, this is known as reactive attachment disorder. You learn to react to a situation in a negative or harmful way, based on the childhood traumas that shaped your instincts. Later, as an adult, this has created a harmful behavior and thinking paradigm. Your distrustful and self-protecting behaviors have become your personality. As a result, you may have become abusive, or seek abusers, you may have become avoidant, or distrust people, or feel ambivalence that keeps you from making any real connection to other people. In relationships, this causes breakups, conflict, and further trauma.

Image 2: Kelly Sikkema on Unsplash. Attachment styles are about more than just romantic attachments; they are about how you share yourself with the world as you understand it. Your

worldview is created by how you see the people, places, and events around you. This, in turn, determines how you respond to that world.

There are four distinctive attachment styles, and you could lean towards any of them, depending on your behavior. It is important to find out what triggers you and then work towards a strategy for coping with your past traumas so you can feel more secure and involved in your relationships. You can create a healthy attachment in your relationships, and this includes your relationship with yourself. Here is a brief overview of the four attachment styles to consider:

The Four Attachment Styles

- **Secure Attachment Style**

A child who sees their parents and experiences positive emotions will likely smile and appear happy. They are content to greet their parents and also to say farewell to their parents, and they are secure in the knowledge their parents will return again at the end of the work day. Therefore, children with a secure attachment style will turn to their caregiver or support person for comfort when they experience anxiety. This gave them the confidence to stand independently, and they have learned effective coping mechanisms to deal with challenges in life as they trust themselves (and others). This is the kind of behavior that is associated with a secure attachment style, and it is the healthiest of attachment styles to develop.

In adult life, someone with this style of attachment will be comfortable with and trust other people, as well as trust themselves. They will be comfortable with being close to others, while being confident enough to stand on their own too. Adults with a secure attachment style will be dependable, and they will often depend on others, delegating tasks, and trusting these will be done. They will also have learned successful methods of dealing with their stressors and coping with pressure in a healthy way. These adults display confidence and are secure in their own abilities, yet they know when and how to get social support. This makes them socially well adjusted.

According to Cherry (2020), mothers have a significant influence on the formation of the secure attachment style in their infants by being responsive and meeting their child's needs. In adult relationships, it is also quite easy to see why a person with a secure attachment style will be a more responsive and responsible partner. Cherry also refers to the Hazan and Shaver study where 56% of participants rated themselves as exhibiting a secure attachment style. Therefore, most people who were raised in stable childhood homes will tend to develop a secure attachment style.

To improve or develop your secure attachment style, you can develop skills like communication, empathy, compassion, understanding, assertiveness, and acceptance. These can be acquired through activities such as counseling, group discussions, reading to expand your knowledge, pursuing activities that build your self-esteem such as art and going to the gym, and also doing family tasks together such as cleaning, cooking, and engaging in hobbies. This is how you will learn to respect others, develop your sense of self, become empowered, learn to listen to other points of view, and build a sense of belonging. By becoming more caring, you can also reinforce your partnership as you engage in selfless activities such as making your partner breakfast, helping them with projects, and comforting them when they are in distress.

- **Anxious Attachment Style**

We all remember growing up with a child in our class who was shifty as they were suspicious and evasive. They didn't rush up to greet their parents, yet they wanted to be with caregivers at the start and end of the day. Children with this attachment style tend to be moody and depressive. They seem to wait for disaster to strike. To try and fit in, people with anxious attachment style tend to be people-pleasers.

A child with this style of attachment will tend towards being anxious about changes such as being dropped off at school. They will struggle to adjust to new situations or display feelings of abandonment quickly. They tend to be clingy and will gravitate towards power figures such as teachers or bullies who they will follow. Children who display self-doubt and an inability to work independently will likely fall in this attachment grouping. By avoiding situations or people who push them towards being independent, they will become easily manipulated by others. Peer opinion of them is what matters most to them. Needless to say, people pleasing can become a serious concern with this attachment style.

As adults, people with anxious attachment style struggle to stand out as leaders, and they will rather assume a follower role. They easily develop a mob mentality, doing as they are told. Secretly, they don't trust others, which is why they will often pick fights or pick on those with a shy nature to meet the approval of their peers. By running others down, they may make themselves feel better. Anxiety is always prevalent in their lives, though they probably deny this. Their insecurities may manifest as temper tantrums and refusing to participate in family activities, and they often withdraw since they don't know how to really process joy as they often live in fear.

Adults with anxious attachment styles have probably grown up in homes where their mother and other caregiver was not available to comfort or assure them. They have developed a reluctance to connect to others and feel like they are not worthy enough to be successful or to be loved by someone else. Fear of rejection and abandonment often manifest in their relationships. This can be displayed as aggression and rejection behavior (Cherry, 2020).

This attachment style is relatively rare, and according to the study mentioned earlier, only 19% of adults find this style as being characteristic of their coping skills. While this style may be less prevalent, we often find adults who display aspects of it in certain situations in their lives based on their own experiences and mental constructs.

You need to display great empathy when communicating with and connecting to someone with anxious attachment style. Building secure connections that are reliable, while gently building boundaries, which all parties involved can respect, will be central to creating a lasting and more secure relationship.

Try to foster open communication, remembering that their thinking will quickly turn your words into confirmations that they are not good enough or threats that you will leave them. Saying something like "Don't you remember, I told you I would be late" can be interpreted as meaning "I am tired of your neediness, and you are a burden." Instead, using careful phrasing such as "I am sorry for being late and causing you to worry. Something outside of my control happened" will be better interpreted as you have removed their cause for anxiety and self-blame. Your communication should soothe their worries and anxieties. It is possible to help your anxiety-driven partner to accept themselves and accept you. This will foster trust, which is something they sorely lack and will diffuse their anxieties.

- **Avoidant Attachment Style**

Starting with parental neglect and emotional unavailability, this style of attachment causes children to treat both their parents and strangers with equal disinterest. While children who form this attachment style become independent adults, they are not connected to their social circles or families. They are not confident, and they merely continue onwards on their own steam with little to no regard for those around them.

Children with this style of attachment tend to be loners, and since they don't trust the world at all, they will easily hide away, struggling to make friends or relate to others. Often, some childhood trauma may trigger this style of attachment (or lack of attachment), and they will struggle to play with others. Praise will always be met with suspicion, and they will not take punishment well either. To them, being corrected is a negative criticism, which confirms their suspicions about the world. These children will struggle to be close to anyone, even their own family, and they will avoid getting involved in anything. Therefore, they tend towards an anxious personality type too. Life is stressful to them since they don't believe the world can be trusted or that they can ever simply relax.

Adults with this attachment style tend towards being loners too. They often become suspicious of their partners if they are in a relationship, and paranoia is often a part of their personality. They will struggle to fit in at work, and they often have very few friends. In their professional careers, they will probably have held several jobs as they may struggle to progress within an organization since they will suspect the structures, their peers, and their bosses. Self-preservation might make them quit their jobs unnecessarily as they anticipate being fired or a company going under without valid reason. We might even find the divorce rate being quite high among people with this attachment style as it is incredibly difficult to remain in a relationship with someone who is constantly busy self-preserving, and they don't trust their partner at all.

To recover from dismissive-avoidant attachment style, you need to cultivate an awareness of others and improve your self-awareness. Charity work can help you develop compassion and empathy. While avoidant behavior may, on the surface, make you feel safe, it is damaging to your personal development and indicates a low self-esteem. In your relationships, being avoidant or dismissive diminishes enjoyment and can even affect your sex life negatively. Everything in your relationship can seem to have a negative connotation when you struggle with forming lasting attachments.

When recovering from dismissive-avoidant attachment style, you should focus on self-acceptance, discovering how you can relate to others, perhaps attend communication classes, and practice healthy expression of your emotions. As a child, your curiosity and interest in the world was suppressed, and you need to excavate this through a process of finding your inner child again. Find out what you want, discover your needs, and find meaningful and safe ways to fulfill these. Whichever interventions you choose, you will need to keep your safety and stress relief in mind. Bungee jumping off a bridge may seem like a drastic solution to finding an emotion; however, the resulting emotion (fear) will not help you connect to others or cultivate compassion.

Sadly, 25% of the Hazan and Shaver study reported themselves as displaying dismissive-avoidant attachment style when it came to their relationships. This does not bode well for the intimate relationships which these individuals engage in.

- **Anxious-Avoidant Attachment Style**

Someone with disorganized or fearful-avoidant attachment behavior will show a mix of avoidant and resistant behavior—they become ambivalent to their lives, events, and people close to them. Children with this style of attachment will be clingy to their caregivers one moment and then avoid them the next. Adults will display traits from the secure attachment style, anxious attachment style, and dismissive-avoidant attachment style, often seeming like a chameleon that can't make up its mind about people or relationships.

With this attachment style, children develop apprehension about their world. They almost expect bad things to happen. This can stop them from living with joy as they tend to become pessimistic. They will struggle to communicate or articulate themselves clearly, and they will seem to be disinterested in everything since they are really just incredibly unsure about the world and the people in it. Children with this attachment style will struggle to form close relationships and friendships, and they often struggle to relate to others. Feeling all alone, they will suffer from anxiety and will not have effective coping mechanisms in place.

As adults, people who have this attachment style will struggle with their relationships. They will not know how to make real connections to their partners, often simply being in a relationship since it is the socially acceptable thing to do, not because they really love or care for the other person. This is not something they intentionally do or feel either. Instead, it is just an inability on their part to connect and this often needs to be redressed. With no solid connections or support, people with this attachment (or avoidance) style tend to be anxious about life. Clearly, they feel all alone, which is a scary way to go through life.

Their past will be littered with instances of parents who were addicts or emotionally unwell. As children, people with this style of attachment probably suffered repeated neglect and illnesses that went untreated. Abuse was a constant presence, but this was hidden by caregivers who, by turns, seemed to act in their child's best interest one minute while neglecting them the next. This created a childhood that confused the child and led them to habitually mimic these conflicting behaviors. Adults with this behavior style struggle to make decisions, and they become inconsistent and can't be depended on to uphold their end in a relationship.

While it is unclear what percentage of the population falls within this style of behavior, it is important to be mindful that people with this style will act with inconsistency, and you may feel confused by them. To help your partner who displays this style, you need to be meticulous in your consistency. Help them build routines, celebrate successes, and be ready to constantly assure them that they are doing okay. Be careful not to create doubts in them.

Attachment Styles and Relationships

Image 3: Mohamed Hassan on pixabay. How you form attachments will also play a significant role in your relationships whether these are platonic, romantic, or familial. Your attachment will determine how you resolve conflict, how you relate to others, and how you use or respect boundaries.

- **Secure Attachment**

John has been happily married for 20 years. He adores his wife, but he also respects that she is a working woman and will be away from home at times. He is concerned about her when she travels, but he knows she is a good driver and will call him to let him know she is safe when she arrives at her destination. While they have been married for 20 years, the couple still enjoy a healthy sex life, and they are not strangers to intimacy. John can quickly see when something is bothering his wife. Though he always asks her what is wrong and can he help, he also knows she wants to be in charge of her life and will deal with things in her own way. While many of John's colleagues have expressed concern with John's wife being away on business often, he chooses not to become jealous as he knows they share a good relationship with open communication. As a whole, John is optimistic about his relationship, and he is happy to see his wife at the end of the day.

The above example illustrates how someone who has a secure attachment style responds in a relationship. People with this style of behavior and decision making are able to respect the boundaries of their partners, and

they feel comfortable creating and maintaining their own relationship boundaries. This creates a healthy structure in the relationship. Securely attached adults will be confident enough in themselves and in their partners, and there is no need for jealousy, clingy, or needy behavior. Despite this, they are not afraid of expressing their intimate needs and affections, and they eagerly support their partners in appropriate ways. These individuals are confident and optimistic in their own abilities and their role within the relationship. They often experience a deep and spiritual connection to their partner, without the pressure of being needy or dependent.

- **Anxious Attachment**

Sara is not content in her relationship. She is convinced her partner is cheating on her, and she suffers from chronic anxiety attacks when she thinks about their relationship as she fears being single. Despite her partner constantly telling her everything is okay between them, she still does not believe him, and she is mentally trying to prepare herself for their eventual break-up. When she finds a lipstick mark on his shirt one day after work, she goes ballistic, packs her bags, and prepares to storm out of their apartment. When her partner tries to explain, she simply cries hysterically.

People like Sara are what could be termed a hot mess. They are clingy, needy, and they constantly want to be told that everything is okay by their partners. Everything in their behavioral repertoire centers around getting outside approval. Everything that happens within the relationship is a drama, and they do not handle changes easily. They seem to be ready to run at the drop of a hat, and though they desire the security of a relationship, they are quick to ruin it by being anxious and emotional. Being demanding, they create relationship stress, and they tend to be jealous and suspicious of their partners. With so many negative emotions stirring in people with anxious attachment styles, it is no surprise that they tend to be pessimistic about their relationships, seeing everything in a negative light.

- **Avoidant Attachment**

James has built a reputation as a cold-hearted man. Though he has had many relationships, he has yet to display anything by way of affection or love to his partners. Secretly, he has had multiple relationships while already with a particular partner, and having a one-night relationship seems to be of little concern to him. When his partner finds out and challenges him, he is quick to end the relationship. This does not seem to bother him at all, and he quickly launches into a new relationship.

He is a social butterfly, and while he engages in many relationships, these rarely become intimate. When he starts to develop feelings for his partner or they ask him questions, he tends to leave the relationship without any warning or he starts to act sullen.

The avoidant-attachment style can be extremely hard on couples and in relationships. Like the above example, someone with avoidant-attachment style tends to be emotionally distant, seeming to be cold and aloof. Becoming emotionally invested is not likely to happen with someone who does not show any affection. People like James seem incapable of really feeling anything, and they often lack the commitment to remain faithful to their relationships. They are not confident enough to build a lasting connection and commitment scares them. This is why they will often bounce from one failed relationship right into the next relationship without seeming to care at all.

Secretly, they are afraid of commitment and getting hurt. This is why they may seem frivolous, and they will sometimes cause their relationships to fail intentionally to avoid commitment. When a relationship ends, they experience fear, and this can cause them to act out in a passive-aggressive way, becoming sulky and vindictive. Despite not being able to be in a meaningful relationship, people with avoidant-attachment disorder also struggle to be on their own.

- **Anxious-Avoidant Attachment**

Lisa has always wanted to be married for as long as she could remember. Sadly, she often ends up in broken relationships where she is abused by her partners. Relationships with her are characterized by trauma and conflict. While Lisa desires commitment, she both chases and pushes away her partners. As a result, she has become bitter and reluctant to communicate and open up. Lisa's biggest fear is losing out on love, and she will launch into a relationship with an almost desperate passion.

When her partners push her towards things she is not comfortable with, she quickly gives in and does as they want. Even when she feels uncomfortable with what someone does to her, she does not say anything, being too anxious they will not like her for it.

The anxious-avoidant attachment style is a combination of being afraid of a relationship, wanting it since being alone seems even more terrifying, yet wanting to avoid contact. It is a most confusing way to enter and sustain a relationship. Therefore, people with this attachment style often find themselves in chaotic or tumultuous relationships marked by conflict, obsession, and neglect.

While people with this attachment style crave the security and comfort of a relationship, they also push their loved ones away, before reeling them in with drama again when faced with the possibility of being alone. Despite wanting love, these people are afraid of being alone, and they keep themselves from committing and becoming deeply involved in a relationship.

Relationships with this attachment style in one or more of the partners is characterized by pessimism, and they lack effective or constructive boundaries. This causes resentment between the partners, and with a lack of communication, drama follows. Obsessive behavior and jealousy, as well as avoidance, are also very common in these relationships.

Each of these attachment styles originate from a specific series of circumstances, and they manifest in different ways during the stages of life. Powerful forces are at play during our life stages, and only in understanding these and how they impact on our continued attachment styles can we begin to lead our best lives.

Chapter 2: An Overview of Attachment Through Different Life Stages

Image 4: maz-Alph from Pixabay. Life is marked by many stages, ranging from infancy and childhood to later life. During these stages, we change, adapt, or stagnate. This is all dependent on our behavior styles and our ability to engage in self-reflection and willingness to improve. By looking at the various development stages, we can also gain insight into how attachment styles form and how these influence us throughout our lives.

Attachment in Infancy and Childhood

During the early formative years, from being born to 18 months old, babies develop their attachment through crying and clinging to their primary caregivers. Most of these behaviors are instinctive and are motivated by a biological need such as hunger or comfort. When the primary caregiver leaves the young infant, they become anxious and cry (Ackerman, 2020a). As children grow older, they start to form their own internal thinking paradigm, and based on the reliability of their caregivers, they form beliefs about the reliability of their world and of themselves.

When the child receives a balanced support and mirroring system from their caregivers, they develop a settled brain chemistry, affecting the hormones and neurotransmitters in the brain. Reese (2007) supports this in finding that the levels of stress-management by cortisol production is set during infancy in relation to experiences. This, in turn, affects the emotional spectrum and control that children develop and carry through into adolescence and adulthood. The emotional range will also influence the attachment styles that develop with anxious-avoidant attachment on one end, secure attachment in the middle, and anxious-resistant attachment at the other end.

Research into childhood attachment styles have delivered much information, but for the layman's application, it is useful to know what to look for in identifying your child's particular attachment style, and sadly, this is something many new parents are completely unprepared for.

- **Secure Attachment**

In children, seeing behavior like being helpful, respectful, trusting, and resilient, as well as class-room participation and the willingness to participate in more novel or complex tasks, all indicate a secure attachment style has developed. Children with this attachment style tend towards developing empathy and the ability to put themselves in someone else's shoes, to see things through someone else's eyes. This leads to the cultivation of trust and reliability.

Parents tend to be responsible and present when their children form this attachment style. If their child cries, they are quick to soothe their anxiety, and this develops the child's ability to trust and interact with people. They engage in healthy play and bonding with their parents and caregivers. When the parent leaves the home, they ensure their child is in the care of a reliable substitute caregiver to ensure that anxiety is minimal, and they return soon, thereby assuring their child that they can be counted on.

- **Anxious-Avoidant Attachment**

With children, this style results in behavior such as struggling in stressful situations, being withdrawn and anxious, not forming friendships or relationships with their caregivers, and the display of negative emotions such as anger, bullying, deceitfulness, and an inability to relate to the emotions of others. These children struggle with expressing themselves, and they quickly pick on others to make themselves feel better. Being with others causes them stress and anxiety, and therefore, they distance themselves more, preferring to be loners.

Children with this behavior style tend to come from homes where the environment is volatile and there is no stability between them and their caregivers. They may be left alone for long periods of time or they may not be soothed when they suffer anxiety. As a result, they do not trust new situations or strangers. Due to these children having such anger in them, they display aggressive behavior towards those they interact with. Mothers are often not available, which is a key factor towards children developing the anxious-avoidant attachment style.

- **Anxious-Resistant Attachment**

Found on the opposite end of the behavior range, children with this style of behavior tend to be excessively needy and clingy. They want to constantly be with their primary caregivers, and they follow after them like puppies. If they are separated from their parents or caregivers, they tend to have an overly emotional reaction such as crying, screaming, or becoming agitated, yet when the caregiver returns, they often avoid them. They struggle to relate to their own age group and prefer to stick to their caregiver or rather be alone. This leads to isolation.

Families of children who display anxious-resistant attachment are often abusive or neglect these children for large parts of the day. This quickly teaches the child they can only count on themselves. Therefore, when they are placed in a situation of needing to depend on or show affection to an adult, they react with uncertainty and even aggression. Early childhood for these children may include physical, emotional, and sexual abuse, which later manifests in deviant behavior and social awkwardness. They may also have been bullied by a caregiver who teased them when they were in distress.

- **Disorganized Attachment**

Children with this attachment style are like confused chameleons. They have no solid strategy for coping in life, and they fall from one type of behavior to the other. Behavior can include becoming aggressive, disruptive, emotional, and isolating themselves. Instead of looking to other people for support, they see people as a threat and respond negatively to them.

The childhood home of children with this attachment style is often a place of confusion. They may be raised by a single parent who has a range of new partners entering and leaving the home. Or, they may suffer with one or both parents being abusive or given to addictions, which cause the parents to act inconsistently. At a very young age, these children both want and avoid attention. They will ask for hugs and then run away. When activities are being performed, they seem confused about participating. A few years later, they will begin taking on the parental role, doing chores that are beyond their years and often parenting their parent if that person is given a reduced mental capacity at times due to addiction.

Attachment Styles: Factors That Influence Your Kids

The attachment style of parents can also have a significant impact on the behavioral style that children develop. It is not a guarantee that a parent who has a secure attachment style will necessarily raise a child who has the same attachment style, though the likelihood of this increases. Likewise, when a parent is themselves given to an anxious-resistant behavior style (or any other unhealthy behavior style), they will have a larger likelihood of raising a child who suffers from an unhealthy attachment style.

Attachment styles also do not happen as a result of one experience, nor do they magically (or genetically) manifest. Rather, it is a gradual process where a multitude of experiences or massively traumatic singular events have a negative impact on a child's development. Abuse is a sure indicator of the possible development of unhealthy behavior styles. These issues children develop and try to process by creating an unhealthy behavior style are not something children will outgrow. It will not improve on its own, and your child will carry it with them into adulthood if you do not take action to intercede and intervene at an early age.

Interventions and counseling need to be directed at an appropriate age group, and it should be remembered that a child is not a mini-adult. Therefore, you can't talk your child out of their unhealthy development style, nor can you beat them out of it (which is what many parents try to do). Rather, you need to focus on the preoperational stage of development that young children experience, which mostly deals with the senses, particularly sight.

Using activities such as playing games, drawing, making art, and singing songs are a great way to communicate with young children. This will help challenge their unhealthy behavior styles and thinking without raising conflict or causing anxiety. In activities such as building puzzles, playing, making and creating art, and performing, young children can be helped to improve their attachment to people and friends. Over time, and through careful and consistent interventions, children can move from the more volatile end of the behavior range towards the healthier secure attachment style of behavior.

Try these activities suggested by West-Olatunji (2019) to heal the wounds caused by harmful or unhealthy attachment styles and facilitate healthy bonding:

- **Popsicle People**

Using popsicle sticks, glitter, wool, and other craft items, create a stick figure for each member in the family with your child. Let your child use this opportunity to wrap up the figures as they feel fit, allowing them to express their feelings and begin to communicate to their caregivers with the dolls acting as intermediaries. By showing your child you can take care of their doll, they will begin to see that you can take care of them, fostering trust and confidence.

- **Feeling Faces**

This is another popular bonding and counseling technique that can be easily used. Printing out several children's faces on A4 pages, you encourage your child to touch and talk to the faces, identifying the emotions, and reacting to the emotions. This is a great way to help your child learn compassion and identify with other people's feelings, which is so vital for making connections to others. For really young children, you can encourage them to trace the emotions on the lips and eyes of the pictures. Then you can help your child to mimic these expressions. As an added bonus, it can help repair your relationship with your child since we instantly feel close to someone we learn positive things from.

- **Storytelling**

While young children lack the vocabulary or ability to tell stories, they need to be given a chance to express themselves. The important thing here is to let them tell the story their way; you should not interrupt them or correct them. Asking questions is fine, but accept what they choose to say, and how they make up the story. The child can use drawings, cartoons, or pictures to tell their story.

Freehand drawings are often used for this. If your child is resistant to communicating or expressing interest in narrating a story, you could try reading a picture book to them and asking them in a gentle and non-threatening way about the pictures. This would draw them into communications and develop a healthy exchange and encourage bonding.

- **Puppets or a Doll's House**

This is an expansion of the above storytelling idea, but here you use puppets, toys, and other tangible objects to tell stories. You can begin to teach moral values and the importance of having people in your life whom you can depend on to your child. Be careful to keep your stories and words age appropriate.

- **Play Dough**

Expression is a healthy way for children to deal with their emotions, and using material such as play dough gives a fun dimension to this exercise. The goal is to draw the child out of their shell and help them externalize their internal conflict. This is how you will help the young child deal with their inner traumas and find healthy expression and connection. The nice thing about play dough is that it encourages tactile interaction, and children naturally love to touch it, which may help you break through some emotional barriers that trauma has created in your child.

Attachment in Adolescence and Young Adulthood

While attachment styles follow the same patterns as established in early childhood, there are a few changes that sneak in during adolescence and young adulthood. For starters, this is when people start to become more aware of and involved in relationships. These relationships are not only physical need based, such as a baby needing to be fed or comforted. It also includes romantic relationships, and since teenagers and young adults are still trying to find out who they are in relation to others, this is a particularly vulnerable stage of development. Attachment styles may change, worsening or improving depending on the relationship experiences and successes that the teen and young adult enjoys.

While attachment styles can be loosely understood as a working model for behavior that we all develop, this becomes infinitely more complicated during adolescence. While a child who has developed a secure attachment base during early childhood is certainly more prepared to face adolescence, they can still become unsettled when they face a situation or experience in their teens they are not prepared for. Once poor self-esteem develops, this may signal the beginning of a web of negative experiences and harmful decisions and behavior.

Since children instinctively model the behavior they see in their parents, they will usually copy their parents' behavior patterns. This could possibly be a worst case of the sins of the father (or mother) being revisited on their children. With parents who are unstable in their behavior styles, the children will inevitably suffer similar behavioral decisions unless intervention is implemented or a stronger role-model affects the child's decision-making formation.

Choosing to intervene and help teenagers form better behavior styles is about breaking the vicious cycle and preventing early adult psychological deviant behavior and ill-health as a result of conditions such as depression, mania, obsessive compulsive behaviors, and even more serious conditions that are linked to early mortality. When considering an intervention, you would have to look at the displayed behavior of the teen and evaluate whether this indicates neediness, avoidance, attention seeking, how the teen calms themselves, and how they handle anxiety or stress. This will provide some indication of whether the adolescent has moved from their stable (or even their unhealthy) childhood behavior style and whether they are coping with the demands and stressors of adolescent life.

Teenagers or adolescents with unhealthy behavior styles will struggle with understanding emotions, relationships, and they will not successfully relate to others. This could give rise to serious conditions such as attention deficit hyperactivity disorder (ADHD), obsessive-compulsive disorder (OCD), and other negative labels being applied to them by their peers and authority figures such as teachers.

When an adolescent or even a young adult is exposed to multiple traumas or challenges that they have a negative reaction to, this is known as cumulative developmental trauma (CDT), and it is responsible for many teens and young adults experiencing a disintegration and dissociation from their previously successful behavior styles. This can often result in post-traumatic stress disorder (PTSD), which will further develop unhealthy behavior styles that are anxiety and avoidance based instead of the individual searching for a positive or secure solution. In practice, we often see this with teenagers who engage in risky sexual behavior or suffer a romantic break-up that results in depression, tension, agitation, anxiety, and in the end, avoidance of relationships in general.

What makes the adolescent and young adult stage of development so traumatic and potentially crucial to the individual's healthy development of an effective attachment style is that this is a stage where there are massive external factors influencing their development.

A teenager will face peer pressure, bullying, sexual pressure, and hormonal pressures as they try to find who and what they are. Likewise, a young adult is at the cusp of being a "child" and becoming a "successful adult." This means they will face new challenges such as tertiary studies, evolving relationships, possible parentage, entering the employment market where bullying can again surface, and the heart-rending question of "what to do you want to be" applying pressures on them.

Attachment traumas at these crucial stages will have a significant impact on the resulting behavior styles. Getting help and support during these life stages is vital to developing or maintaining a secure attachment style. For teenagers, dealing with relationships on a romantic level is often incredibly traumatic. They have moved from the cute puppy-love stage to burgeoning intimacies, and often this is accompanied by raging emotions such as love, closeness, dependence, betrayal, anger, and jealousy. These can lead to serious harm being done to the previous behavior style they had formed. While parents may want to step in and shield their teenagers from the "bad world," this is something the adolescent child or young adult needs to deal with and learn from. So, how does a parent support their adolescent child or their young adult child who is possibly heading out on their own for the first time?

For adolescents, given that they are in new situations and may lack the skills to cope, it is instrumental to combine support with helping them develop coping skills. These techniques can be useful to help foster and protect a more secure attachment style (Reachout.com, n.d.):

- **Encourage Communication**

While you can often see that your child is in pain, you may often feel stuck on the outside talking at the walls they have put up. Fostering and encouraging communication from a young age will help to open avenues for support. In your communications, be careful to realize that this is not about you preaching to them on how to do things (like you did things), but it is rather about giving your adolescent or young adult child a way to vent, release, process, and evaluate their feelings and their possible actions in a healthy way. They talk, and you listen. When you do talk, be careful to talk *with* them and *not at* them. In the infancy interventions, you learned to listen as your child told the story, and this should not change when they become teenagers. Only if they ask, should you offer solutions. You can't live their lives, so don't.

- **Step Away**

When you are young, every issue seems like Mt. Everest, so help your adolescent step away and find a balance between being with people and being on their own. They need to realize that the issue they are dealing with is not their whole life. As the saying goes: it's not a bad life, just a bad day. Developing life perspective is a vital life skill and will help to remove a lot of the anxiety that creates unhealthy behavior styles.

- **Develop Passion Paths**

Finding joy is a great way to build confidence and develop a secure attachment style. Therefore, encourage your adolescent child or young adult to engage in their favorite hobby (which isn't hanging out with friends) or doing a self-building activity such as art or reading. With effective repetition and application of the idea of making a safe place or pattern of doing to which the child can return, it will become a habitual behavior that will build self-esteem and release anxieties.

- **Healthy Habits**

A healthy body houses a healthy mind. Encourage and model healthy behavior such as healthy eating, not binging, exercising, and practicing self-care. These routines also help form healthy attachment behavior styles.

- **Stress Solutions**

We can only use the solutions we are familiar with. So, teaching your child from a young time to practice healthy interventions such as breathing techniques, yoga, tai chi, or meditation can be a great way to help them deal with the tensions of discovering relationships and love. It will also help them stay healthy, reduce anxiety, and build self-esteem as they realize they can control their bodies and engage in self-care, which feels good too.

- **Positive Self-Talk**

Doubt is the result of anxiety, and this often results in anxiety and fear-driven behavior such as negative self-talk. Ensuring that your adolescent or young adult is aware of their inner thoughts and knows they can control what they think is a highly effective way to create healthy behavior management patterns. Using positive affirmations can counter negative external influences such as bullying, peer pressure, and relationship confusion.

- **Creating Healthy Examples**

Children who have secure and balanced parents or caregivers are more prone to be positive, secure, and independent (self-assured). Hence, you should model what you are seeking to create in your child. This does not mean you need to be perfect. Instead, this means you need to show them how you deal with issues and what behavior you use to live a successful and balanced life. Clearly, knocking back several quarts a night after a stressful day is not the example they need. However, seeing you spend some time listening to music and then writing in a journal or dancing while you make supper will help them approach life with confidence and self-empowerment.

Mid-Life Attachment

Mid-life can be an equally trying period of development in life. This is when our values can be challenged by factors such as relationship satisfaction, job satisfaction, introspection, and the involvement and evolution of our growing families, and the supposed mid-life crisis. These all contribute to building tension and anxiety, and in sexual terms, this is often when sexual dysfunction often appears.

In mid-life, relationships also face their most challenging times as parents start to age and also have to deal with their adolescent children's life crisis. The dynamics between relationship partners (including the partnership between children and parents) change, and this can cause serious mental strain and divorce rates often increase in the age group of the 50s and 60s. This can be partially attributed to mid-life strain (Whitbourne, 2013). The reality is that people often drift apart in this life-stage as they struggle to deal with crisis and stressors. Long-term relationships can come undone as partners lose focus on each other, and they often become bored and disillusioned with the life they have created for themselves.

A good example of this is the Oscar winning movie, *American Beauty* (1999). This movie shows several factors that challenge and dissolve the primary relationship, including conflict with the children, partners losing touch, personal inadequacy, and low self-esteem, which all contribute to chaos and interpersonal conflict. Though your life may not be quite as dramatic, there could be similarities in your relationship challenges and how this affects your behavior style. Where you may have been happily married and secure in your attachments, you could find yourself suffering anxiety and dissociation or avoidance, which might lead to the ending of your relationships. So, how can you ensure the success and security of your relationships and attachment style?

- **Positive Partners**

Be mindful to focus on the positive assets of your partner. If you dwell on your partner's flaws, you will not want to spend time with them. However, if you pay more attention to their positive points, you will be more likely to want to be with them and see less of their flaws. This reduces relationship conflicts. People argue about their (or their partner's) flaws, never about their plus points, so focus on those.

- **Think Yourself Together**

The saying "out of mind, out of heart" is a sad reality. When you are thinking of your partner in a positive way, you will not be tempted to stray outside of the relationship. You will also feel more content and be less inclined to question your "success" (which is often more in your mind than a reality). Complement this with phoning your partner to express concern or interest in them. You used to do this when you were younger, only then, it was flirting with your partner, why can't you do so now?

- **Avoid Multitasking**

While we may be pressured by busy lives to multi-task, this takes your focus away from your partner and your relationship. Focus on spending time together that is yours alone. This doesn't have to be a holiday or some novel gesture. Instead, focus on making it a routine (which positively builds your coping skills and behavior style) such as a Saturday bed brunch. No one wants to feel like they have someone's divided time, so focus on your partner and on yourself, not on outside distractions.

- **Use Challenges as Glue**

In mid-life, we often feel like we haven't accomplished all that we wanted. We become more and more aware of time running out and our fast-approaching mortality. However, we will probably live longer than we think, and there is always time to expand our sense of self and do things to make us feel alive again. The important thing is to use challenges and adventures such as going on a road trip or bungee jumping as activities that keep you together with your partner. Just because you have been together for 20 years does not mean your relationship is fixed or should stagnate. Be assertive and communicate about the life challenges you still wanted to embrace.

- **Bond With Time**

Relationships take time. If you are only spending a few hours a week together due to work, activities with the kids, relaxing with your friends, then you are gearing up your relationship for dissociation and are engaging in avoidance. Spend time together as you continue to strengthen ties, reinforce each other's sense of worth, and deepen your love and affection.

- **Turn on Affection and Love**

Flowing from the above intervention, you should continue to share affection and expand on your intimacies within the relationship. While sex is said to stagnate in mid-life and die completely by later life, this does not have to be the case. Be open and communicative about your needs. There is nothing wrong with flirty behavior to please and pleasure your partner as long as this is well communicated and reciprocated. Intimacy is a powerful binding force. It makes both partners feel a boost to their self-esteem to feel needed and wanted by their partner.

Attachment in Later Life

Later life can be a more traumatic experience than many people realize or prepare themselves for. Challenges such as reaching pensionable age, having to adjust to life at home (and not at work), rediscovering your partner, or dealing with the loss of a partner can create massive anxiety and, with a slow decline of mental functioning, this can really challenge your coping skills and behavior style. The people in your life may also have changed significantly from who they were when you started out together, and if you have neglected your relationship, this may bring disparity and discontent. The major stressor is the possibility of losing your partner and becoming single again. In addition to this, we have to deal with the reality that we will face our own death.

Behavior patterns can become problematic at this age as this is often when people stop growing and lack the ability to adjust and cope with their life experiences. Often, people believe the elderly are set in their ways, which can create trauma in the relationship to their significant others, their adult children, and grandchildren.

Some common issues that face late-life adults include:

Depressive Disorders

With failing health and physical decline, the sense of self will begin to decline, and elderly people often begin to suffer from depressive episodes. Combined with the loss of a partner or the financial strain of being a pensioner, this can easily result in serious depression disorders. This, in turn, negatively impacts on health, which worsens the pensioner's emotional state. Late life suicide is becoming much more prevalent than before.

Anxiety Disorders

Due to depression, failing health, and the decline of the chemicals that the brain requires to maintain an emotional balance, anxiety disorders are also prone to increase in late life. Maintaining a healthy life outlook, keeping the brain alert with activities, and engaging with your world will greatly help to boost a sense of purpose and help negate anxiety.

Bipolar Disorders

While this disorder mostly sets in during your early twenties, it can also appear in late life. Perhaps this is due to anxiety, chemical imbalances, and declining health; however, the effects are equally devastating. The dizzying highs and dismal lows associated with bipolar disorders can manifest in late life, with the additional burden of age-related medication such as blood pressure, heart, kidney, and lung medications complicating the chemical processes of the body.

It can place a strain on your relationships, and when combined with other disorders (which it often does), you may begin to lose the ability to function in the stressful situation that comes with daily independent life.

Oppositional Defiant Disorder

This disorder often manifests in the elderly. They may be defiant, engage in rage filled outbursts, lament how no one comes to see them (yet they don't go see anyone themselves), and they might even become spiteful or vengeful (such as disinheriting their "ungrateful" children). This can completely destroy your existing behavior style as you become given over to anxiety and even paranoia. Antisocial behavior will soon follow, and many elderly people become recluse, not wanting to venture out into the world where their tempers are easily triggered.

Age-Related Disorders

Other age-related disorders such as dementia, Alzheimer's disease, and Parkinson's disease can also severely challenge your coping ability, behavior, and decision-making paradigms. This may require careful management and even late life care at a professional facility.

While these disorders can be intimidating, and it may seem to indicate that growing old will be an unpleasant experience, this is not so. By being proactive and informed, you can ensure you remain vital, behaviorally adapted, and maintain close connections to the people you love. Here are some suggestions for maintaining and creating a secure late-life behavior style:

- **Rebuild Your Body**

While many elderly people have simply accepted their physical decline, this need not be the norm. When you look good, you feel good, and this can have amazing effects on both your psyche and mind. Taking care of yourself physically by doing some activity to promote flexibility and mobility can have a significant effect on your self-esteem, independence, and keep your emotions more stable too. Take up a physical hobby such as tai chi, go for massages, spoil yourself with a good skin care routine, and take care of your teeth. Smile daily and allow yourself to have fun, using your mind to interact with other people instead of sinking into your frail body and feeling despair.

- **Adapt**

One of the worst things you can do in late life is to sit still and lose interest in the world around you. This may seem like a great way to minimize anxiety, since the world can become a really scary place to you in late life. Even more so with the recent worldwide shift in isolating behavior due to health concerns for the aged. However, you should engage in novel ideas, new inventions, and exciting changes that affect your world. If you can keep interested, you will be able to adapt to and remain interactive with the world and the people around you.

- **Medicate Appropriately**

Pills, different assistive aids, and other medical necessities are part of later life. However, by having an attitude towards your medical needs of simply clinging to life, you will not be doing yourself (or your behavior) any favors. By working with a skilled doctor, you will be able to plan your medical needs to not only keep you living but also help you stay alive and vital. You should supplement to keep your mind healthy and happy, and you should admit when you are feeling pressured or anxious and discuss treatment options with your doctor. Do not suffer in silence and withdraw. Connect and reach out, take charge of your emotions, and relate to others.

Chapter 3: Getting Started With Some Self-Awareness: Emotionally Focused Family Therapy Techniques

Image 5: sweetlouise on pixaybay. While we often think focusing on our emotions means we should have a cry; this is not always what is behind it. Rather, it is the understanding and appropriate application of our emotions by identifying them in others and in ourselves. Through appropriate techniques, you can learn to respond in meaningful ways to the people you have relationships with and become responsible and aware of your own feelings and the impact of those feelings on your family.

What Is Emotionally Focused Family Therapy (EFFT)?

EFFT is a form of therapy that stems from the humanistic school of psychology, specifically from psychotherapeutic approaches to family relationships. It focuses on the family dynamic, how the individuals within the family interact with each other and themselves, and how this constructs their present experiences. During therapy sessions, attention is paid to the emotions of the family members as this indicates how they see and relate to the family experience. Emotions are the language of our behavior styles, and they inform us about our world, and they prompt action.

By interacting with and exploring the emotions within the family relationship, the therapist can help the family members discover and begin using new and more secure behavior patterns. EFFT is based on the work of psychologist John Bowlby who conducted research into and formulated much of attachment theory (Stavrianopoulos, 2019). The goal of EFFT is to foster increased emotional availability in parents and improved responsiveness in children. With the therapeutic interventions of EFFT, the role players in the family relationship are encouraged to be present and involved. This makes a huge difference in decreasing dissociation and avoidance within the relationship as the family experiences emotional involvement and growth.

When parents are emotionally available for their children, the children will feel assured and comforted. This will lead to more secure attachment behavior manifesting in the children, who will turn to their parents for support. When parents are emotionally unavailable, their children will resort to anxious and avoidant behavior. This creates points of contact between EFFT and attachment theory. According to Johnson (2009), the transactional nature of EFFT and attachment theory can be seen in a cause and effect interaction. The parent becomes more supportive, and the child becomes more open and trusting. When the self is developed, you will have more confidence and a more secure attachment style.

In essence, attachment theory and the development of a secure attachment behavior base thrive under the administration of EFFT. This can be summarized as follows:

- Attachment theory calls for a secure base of reference or safe home base to develop attachments from and EFFT creates this.
- While attachment theory helps us understand our deeper and more negative emotions such as pain, rejection, fear, and avoidance, EFFT helps to address these and build secure behavior.
- Emotions are the central guiding force and also the result of interactions and the resulting behaviors, and EFFT focuses on emotional development and healing.
- While behavior theories center around the person and their interaction with their world, EFFT focuses on the person's ability to change their world and their responses.

The feedback and effectiveness of EFFT is massively successful. The behavior styles of people, combined with emotional development and communication, create healthy narratives within the relationship. Its strong points include being supportive and respectful to clients, a history of 30+ years of empirical evidence, and continuing development in the field to address cultural differences and societal changes. The American Psychological Association (APA) has formally acknowledged EFFT as an effective treatment approach to treating depression, interpersonal conflict, past or suppressed trauma, and avoidant or anxious personality disorders (Church, 2017)

EFFT focuses on the emotions in a relationship (whether romantic or familial) that result from insecurities. Attachment-related insecurities can be addressed through facilitation of emotional development and skills building. Various techniques are used to assess emotional development and check whether the therapy participants are ready to progress to the next technique or level of therapy. It engages these techniques through several stages and steps that the family is guided through by the therapist who acts as a facilitator.

Stages and Steps of EFFT

In brief, there are three stages and nine steps to EFFT. The first four steps (stage one) are about reducing conflict and discovering which attachment styles the family (or relationship) members default to instinctively. Steps five through seven (stage two) is about creating more secure family relationships. In the remaining two steps (stage three), the therapist helps the family members discover more positive strategies and ways to interact. During these last steps, the family members also build their confidence in their ability to handle stressful events in a more proactive and positive way in the future. Therapy concludes when the family members can engage in new and positive ways in their daily life. This therapeutic process can be seen as follow:

- **Stage One: Cycle De-Escalation**

Step one: Identify conflict and issues in the relationship, such as a lack of communication and anxiety avoidance between the husband and wife.

Step two: Identify negative behavior and patterns that are linked to the conflict or issues, such as defensive shouting and neediness that happens when the partners threaten to part.

Step three: Evaluate attachment emotions that underpin the behavior of each partner in the relationship, such as anger masking fear of abandonment.

Step four: Rename the issues according to the emotions and attachment needs, such as seeing the partner's rage as being a declaration of insecurity, a need for belonging, and validation.

During this stage, the couple or family engage with the therapist, talking about the therapeutic setting, the therapist, their expectancies, and their past interactions. The end result of this stage is that the couple is no longer against each other, but rather against their past negative interactions. It is important that the couple is helped to identify the behavior patterns that fuel their attachment insecurities and begin to see this problem in a new way.

- **Stage Two: Changing Interaction Patterns**

Step five: Access and explore avoided emotions or emotions that are uncomfortable for the partners in the relationship such as fear, insecurities, and rage.

Step six: Foster acceptance of each partner's experience within the relationship.

Step seven: Achieve expression of each partner's experience and create new ways to bond within the relationship and nurture acceptance.

During this stage, the focus is on creating new experiences to replace the negative experiences and emotions that had previously existed in the relationship. Through an improved repertoire of communication skills, the partners are helped to better express their needs and feelings and show compassion with each other.

- **Stage Three: Consolidation and Integration**

Step eight: Begin a new relationship narrative to address the old problems. This is a process of actively and positively finding new solutions to the relationship (and behavior) problems.

Step nine: This is the conclusion where the couple take what they have learned and apply this to their problems within the home environment. While they are still unsure, they may cycle back to check in with the therapist and further consider step eight until they are able to effectively apply new solutions to old problems with confidence. This results in a secure attachment style.

Ways to Classify and Identify Attachment Styles

There is a plethora of different ways to classify attachment styles; some even call them love styles, but the reason to identify your style is to help you improve in your attachments and become more secure in your relationships. Taking a quick online test is one way to get an idea of which attachment style you tend to display. However, any test will only be as accurate as the honesty of your answers.

Now that you already know the basic tenets of the different attachment styles, you probably have some inclination of what style you tend towards. However, there are also a range of online quizzes and tests you can consider taking. Though they may not be definitive, they are a good place to start if you are still clueless as to your attachment style. Here are a few good tests to try:

- **Psychology Today**

This online test takes the form of answering a range of questions about your relationships and behavior by rating whether you agree with a statement or not. There are 50 statements, covering a diverse range of aspects of your behavior and relationships. Upon completion, you get a snapshot of your test results, with the option to purchase the full result. Complete the test at https://www.psychologytoday.com/za/tests/relationships/relationship-attachment-style-test

- **Greatist.com**

If you want a bit more variety, you can try five different tests about attachment styles at this site where you follow the links to a range of tests. By trying different tests, you can get a broader view of your behavior and style of attachment. Find the tests at https://greatist.com/health/attachment-style-quizzes#1

- **Simple Questionnaire**

This short test, based on the test originally designed by Dr. Amir Levine and Rachel Heller, is a good place to start. Choose either 1—highly agree, 2—strongly disagree, or 3—neither to the statements below:

1. I do not enjoy it when my partner is close to me and asks questions.

2. Fears about my partner leaving me dominate my mind.
3. When my partner and I argue, I begin to doubt everything about us.
4. I avoid showing people how I feel as I believe they will not reciprocate, and I will be left feeling embarrassed.
5. When my partner is feeling depressed, I find it difficult to relate to them or offer comfort.
6. In my relationships, I feel no need to take action.
7. I worry that people will not like me once they get to know me.
8. Instead of being with my partner, I would rather be on my own.
9. When my partner is upset, I don't know how to help them find peace, so I retreat.
10. Being single is scary to me, and I would rather be in a relationship than on my own.
11. I loathe it when other people are dependent on me.
12. People think I am boring since I don't argue or fight in a relationship.
13. When my partner is away, I miss them, but once they are back, I wish they were gone.
14. My partner knows exactly what I want and need as I tell them clearly.
15. When my partner is standoffish, I believe I have somehow sinned or done something wrong.

16. Breakups are no problem for me. I get over them surprisingly quickly and move on to the next relationship.
17. If I break up from my partner, I fear being alone.
18. I know that when people are distant, it has nothing to do with me.

How did you score?

Scores of 30—36 (score of 2 in most questions) indicate you are predominantly secure attachment styled. You are in touch with your own emotions and those of the people around you. In your relationships, you care enough to participate since you have compassion, but you also realize it is not your responsibility to make others feel better. You invite discussions, and you respect other people's points of view.

If you scored a 1 in statements 1—5, 7, 9, 10, 12, 13, 15 and 17, you display characteristics of the anxious attachment style. You tend to struggle on your own, but when you are with people, you do not connect well and often blame yourself for this. Relationships do not comfort you, yet you hate being alone. Your partners may tend towards being abusive of you or they do not acknowledge how you feel since you don't express your feelings at all.

If you scored a 1 in statements 5, 6, 8, 11, 12, 16, you tend to be ambivalent in your relationships and have developed a fearful-avoidant attachment style that governs your behavior. You don't like being around people, but you also don't do well on your own.

With a score of 1 in statements 1, 5, 6, 8, 11, 16, this is characteristic of a dismissive-avoidant style of attachment. You struggle to form connections to other people, and you prefer your own company. Emotions are a mystery to you, and when people become emotional, you withdraw.

When looking at your past, you may begin to see instances where you have been directed towards the development of a certain attachment style. Abuse, neglect, failed relationships, dominating partners or bosses, and even sibling rivalry can lead to the development of an unhealthy attachment style. Events that made you fearful tend to create a fearful or anxious behavior style, and when you felt you had to crawl in your shell for protection in the past, you will likely still avoid real connection and intimacy.

Core Interventions and EFFT Exercises

There are a range of EFFT exercises that can be used in the therapeutic setting. Always, the goal is to achieve a specific end state based on the intervention technique or exercise.

- **Empathic Reflection**

Goal: The idea is for the therapist to hear their client out and develop an understanding of their client's needs and challenges.

Method: This is done by encouraging the client to talk about how they feel about the therapy process or even the therapist themselves. For example, when clients say things like, "I don't know what I am even doing here; I don't have a problem," this means they are engaging in avoidant and self-denial behavior.

- **Restructuring Interventions**

Goal: Here the therapist will interject new approaches or drive the discovery of new methods to deal with the problems that have been identified.

Method: This takes a discussion format where emotions are discussed in a transactional way. The therapist may lead the discussion or ask the client to do the theorizing, "If you feel like...and you try to...what would happen?"

- **Validation**

Goal: We all need to feel heard and valued. This is the goal of validation. It gives meaning to our pain, which can open the door to intervention.

Method: By acknowledging what a client says, and giving them the chance to really express emotions they may have denied even to themselves, it brings them out of the pit of despair and into a state of feeling supported.

- **Evocative Responding**

Goal: Sometimes, clients are unsure of how they actually feel about a past (or even current) trauma or behavior. The aim is to help them clarify this by probing their reactions and guiding them towards meaning.

Method: Direct questioning and careful summarizing of what the client says will help them to realize the underlying themes and unacknowledged emotions they are hiding.

- **Heightening**

Goal: When clients have hidden away their emotions, they may need to be pushed or directed to excavate these feelings through a heightening of related emotions.

Method: For instance, a therapist may stimulate the client's fear reaction or a feeling of sorrow by helping the client experience this through watching a video or seeing a picture.

- **Empathic Conjecture**

Goal: Helping clients to think critically about their emotions is a great way to help them interact with and consider the aspects of their feelings.

Method: By asking if the client sees themselves as being defensive, angry, avoidant, selfish, or needy, the therapist can help the client think about their own actions, behavior, and feelings.

- **Reframing**

Goal: Often used during the first stage of therapy, the therapist will rephrase what the client says to help reach a new understanding of the problem or to involve the client in the discussion.

Method: When the client says something like, "I feel so alone and no one understands me," the therapist may paraphrase this as, "Am I correct in saying that you feel disconnected and unvalued?"

- **Creating Enactments**

Goal: Creating a safe environment where the client can attempt different solutions to their problems.

Method: Through role-play, dialog, enactment, and even role reversals, the client can gain a better understanding of their problem and find healthy ways to address these, as well as seeing which approaches have the potential to work.

Finding an EFFT Therapist

When your secure attachment base is reasonably developed, you may be able to address minor issues on your own and through family discussions. However, when you have faced significant trauma, have developed an extremely unhealthy form of attachment style, and display attachment behavior that is damaging to yourself and others, you may need to find a professional such as an EFFT therapist to help you. This person is specifically trained to guide you through the process of developing healthier attachment styles and foster positive behavior and thinking mindsets.

Within the U.S. (and abroad), you can find a registered therapist or support center by logging onto the International Center for Excellence in Emotional Family Therapy (ICEEFT) at https://iceeft.com where you can learn more about EFFT, find therapists, become a therapist, and find additional support.

Chapter 4: Cognitive Behavioral Therapy and Self-Improvement

Image 6: Julie Rose from Pixabay. We all carry a suitcase with us through life. It is filled with our experiences and it can determine how we act. When that suitcase is overloaded with things we choose not to think about, we become clumsy and burdened in life. Only when we open the suitcase and unpack our experiences can we begin to lighten our load and step forward with intention and purpose.

What Is Cognitive Behavioral Therapy (CBT)?

CBT consists of many techniques, strategies, and interventions that can be used on a daily basis to help foster self-reflection, build self-esteem, and facilitate communication. It also helps with conflict resolution and finding healthy ways to express emotions. It is an effective therapy to help with the reframing of your current attachment style as the ultimate goal of the strategies and techniques are to foster a healthy and secure sense of self. This, in turn, creates a healthy secure attachment style.

In essence, CBT is talk therapy. It is about finding ways to talk about your feelings, your thoughts, and the way in which you tend to behave in certain situations. CBT is geared towards finding thinking patterns and the resulting emotions that are negative and unhelpful. The ultimate goal of CBT is to help people see how their current way of thinking and doing things results in negative emotions. It then helps them train their thoughts to be logical and positive, creating behavior that is constructive and stable, which enables them to feel contentment, satisfaction, and discover inner peace. In the end, our thinking, actions, and feelings are all related in a transactional exchange. Therefore, when you change one component, you change the outcome.

Changing your thinking will change your behavior and your feelings.

This transaction can be visualized in the following example:

you are not enough	you withdrawing from responsibilities	you feel depressed
Thinking	Behavior	Feeling

How CBT Is Used to Treat Anxiety and Depression Disorders

CBT is highly effective in treating anxiety and depression disorders (Helpguide, n.d.). It focuses on identifying the stressor that influences your thinking, analyzing what you are thinking, and finding ways to change that thought so you will behave differently when in a similar situation in future, thereby feeling better about your ability to deal with a stressor. As example: You feel uncomfortable when you go to a party with a friend (social anxiety disorder), and you panic about the party beforehand. As a result, you become anxious, avoid taking the friend's calls, and eventually feel like you have failed that friend. When you are invited to another party in future, you will recall this incident and feel even worse, therefore, acting in an even more negative way.

So, how do you break this cycle? With CBT, you are encouraged to think about what the problem may be. Perhaps you have an instigating incident or early trauma relating to a party, which is holding you back from enjoying social activities with your friend in the future? Alternatively, you may fear rejection when in a crowd, and this could lead to your negative feelings. CBT would help you to discover the root cause of your thinking, which influences your behavior and your feelings. Therefore, the basic tenet of CBT is that people's thinking about situations is what influences their behavior and feelings. It is not a specific event that influences how we act; it's how we think about that event.

CBT: The Process

The process of CBT is to evaluate thinking patterns, find negative patterns, and replace these with positive ones. With the help of a therapist, you can identify the thinking issues that affect your life in a negative or limiting manner, and you can then create a strategy for dealing with these. Basically, you learn to discover faulty logic and inappropriate or unsatisfactory emotional responses. This process allows you to work on your actions and modify your beliefs.

If we continue with the earlier example of being invited to a party, your thinking might be evaluated as follow:

Negative thought one: I am not popular at parties, so I shouldn't go.

Illogical reasoning: You are jumping to a conclusion, and there's no evidence to support this.

Logical reasoning: If you do go and don't enjoy it, you can always leave earlier.

Negative thought two: I always feel awkward at parties and make a fool of myself.

Illogical reasoning: You are generalizing based on one bad experience in the past.

Logical reasoning: This time could be different, and you might enjoy your time there.

Negative thought three: Parties are filled with drugs, criminals, and they do bad things there.

Illogical reasoning: You are seeing it only in negative terms. This is not how reality works.

Logical reasoning: Parties may have some of those influences, but there are also good people there whom you can relate to.

This reasoning process reveals another basic tenet of CBT—we all have distorted thinking we subscribe to. These thinking patterns are not based on logic but have rather formed from our own negative experiences.

When we surrender our thinking to these distortions, we will begin to engage in attachment styles that support our negative thoughts. What you think, you manifest. How you behave will affect your thoughts, and this can create a negative cycle that spirals ever deeper into unhealthy attachments and behavior. As negative thinking becomes your norm, you will manifest unhealthy behavior styles such as anxious and anxious-avoidant styles of behavior. This, in turn, could lead to associated problems such as depression, anxiety disorders, addictions, phobias, panic disorders, and personality disorders. It is important to discover your thinking flaws or negative thinking styles to improve your behavior attachments and subsequent emotional reactions.

Common Types of Cognitive Distortions Based on Your Attachment Style

Image 7: Rostyslav Savchyn on Unsplash. Cognitive distortions are like looking at the world through the filters of a kaleidoscope, and it can severely affect your logical perspective. While you may firmly believe something to be a certain way, you merely perceive it as such due to your flawed thinking patterns. Once you learn to discard negative and faulty logic, your whole world can change for the better.

There are a range of thinking or cognitive distortions that can influence your behavior style. Each of these distortions, in part, originates from a past experience or by faulty reasoning that has become your way of thinking. While you may not believe your brain has the power to improve your life (and it does), it certainly can ruin your life (when you use it in a flawed way).

Here are some popular ways people engage in distorted thinking pathways and how to counter this:

- **Always Being Right**

While we all want to be right, and being wrong can be an embarrassment, expecting to be right the whole time is illogical. When this form of thinking becomes your norm, you may start engaging in anxiety-driven behavior when you are proven wrong in a situation. You lack the ability to then see things from someone else's point of view, and you have developed an over-dependence on yourself and your "superior" status as being right the whole time. This arrogant thinking will cut you off from the emotions of others, and even your own emotions will become a confused entanglement as you shift between feelings of pride and feelings of despair.

As the joke goes, "I found Mr. Right, but I didn't know his first name is Always." This does not only apply to men though, and being right the whole time is not only a pain to the people around you, but it can also end up being exhausting and isolating to you.

Countering It: To beat something you are secretly scared of, it may be helpful to intentionally do it. Like someone who is scared of heights who climbs tall buildings to become less scared, you can choose to intentionally do something wrong, such as giving an incorrect answer to a question. This experience should allow you to begin adjusting to being incorrect and accept that you are not always right, and with practice, you will be okay when you are wrong.

- **Black-and-White or Polarized Thinking**

People who only see the world in terms of it being black or white tend to have polarized thinking where they can only see one thing as being right and everything else as being wrong. Life, as we mostly find, is composed of shades of gray, and what is right for one person will not be right for you. This is a normal perspective. However, when you believe the other person to be wrong, no matter their circumstances, this becomes flawed or illogical thinking. Often, this form of thinking combines with the notion of yourself always being right.

As a result, this causes great anxiety in your mind as you try to survive in a world that does not seem to agree with your norms. This can again lead to dissociation and isolation. It is instinctive to withdraw from what we see as threatening our way of thinking. In extreme cases, this form of isolating thinking can lead to the formation of cults and extremist thinking.

Countering It: People who tend towards polarized thinking will not step outside their comfort zone, and they struggle with new ideas as this makes them question where they stand on something. Therefore, engaging with new ideas, going to new places, and visiting strange cultures can be a great way to break down these preconceptions. Joining online chat rooms to discuss how people think and feel can also help to widen your perspectives and modulate your narrow view of the world. Should you choose to do this, you would need to become aware of any judgments you have about the conversations or topics being discussed. This will help alert you to your polarized thinking. Once you know you are doing it, you can begin to watch out for these illogical measures in the future.

- **Negative Filtering**

We all have personality types, and being a negative Neil is certainly more common than you might think. There are some people who simply see the world through a negative filter. Regardless of the type of situation or what is actually going on, they see it as being negative and believe it will harm them, so they avoid it, and even then they feel negative about that action too. This is an extreme form of pessimism.

Oftentimes, this form of thinking is "inherited" from a parent who displayed this form of thinking distortion. It can also form as a result of a negative or disappointing event or experience that has so devastated you that you simply can't see the world with a positive eye again. Sadly, this results in instability and unhealthy attachment formation. You will doubt others so will avoid them. You will also doubt yourself, so you will self-isolate and avoid thinking about yourself, which leads to a low self-esteem and reduces your relationship satisfaction. After all, how can you be in a satisfying relationship when you see the world, your partner, and your interactions as being bad?

Countering It: Individuals with this distorted way of thinking need to be consciously reminded of the positivity in life. This does not mean you should wrap them in cotton wool and sing them lullabies the whole time. Instead, they should practice being positive, showing gratitude, and make an effort to eliminate their negative thinking. Starting with awareness of self-talk and thoughts can be really useful. Keeping a gratitude journal, writing down their thoughts, and coloring them according to emotions (red for negative, green for positive), they can begin to visualize their thoughts changing as they consciously think happy or positive thoughts. Even wearing an elastic band on your wrist and snapping it whenever you have a negative thought or a negative reaction to something that you begin to realize is not negative is a great way to retrain your thinking.

- **Catastrophizing**

This form of distorted thinking is the proverbial waiting for the sword of Damocles to drop. You anticipate that something bad will happen as a result of something insignificant. Perhaps this originated from being punished too severely as a child or being told you were not good enough while growing up, but now it persists as an adult, and you think you suck, so you look for things you can fail at—and it will be the end of the world to you!

Even something as insignificant as dropping your boss' files at work will have you convinced that punishment (and hellfire) will follow. Surely, you will lose your job as a result of this heinous crime? And even when someone praises you for doing something right, you still look for ways to minimize their praise or negate your praiseworthiness. You might say things like "Oh, no! It was a team effort" or "I really didn't do much."

As a result of believing and looking for the worst to happen, you don't trust the world or the people in it. You are like a child waiting to be punished for kicking out the neighbor's window. This fills you with anxiety and drains all the pleasure and wonder out of life. You are constantly traumatized, and you quite likely have a depressive personality type as a result.

Countering It: You need to learn to accept praise. Give it to yourself; you need it. Keep a positivity journal in which you write down all the good things you have done every day. Create your own support group of people who build you up and can validate your daily successes with an honest opinion and also help you realize that the thing you think is the end of the world is not all that bad (if it's even anything at all). In all likelihood, you are a worrier, someone who battles their own worry demons each day. You need confirmation that your worries are unfounded.

- **Singular Blame**

With this distorted thinking, you are an either-or person. You either think you are to blame for everything, or you believe the world is to blame for everything. Neither of these thinking paradigms is correct though. When you have a balanced life view, you accept that sometimes you are to blame, such as burning the supper because you were texting on your phone and not paying attention. At other times, the world or outside forces are to blame, such as burning the supper because you had to help your neighbor who was having a heart attack.

Many times, this distorted thinking results from being overly criticized as a child or from some childhood trauma like an overly zealous religious event (or doctrine) you were not mentally prepared for (and you now think you are destined to suffer; hence, you feel you are to blame).

The opposite holds true when you feel you have no control over your life. You have come to believe that you can take no action to influence what happens, so you don't. This can create disinterested behavior and a low self-esteem. Relating to others becomes a problem since you take no responsibility, and you can't be counted on.

Countering It: Therapeutic interventions may be required here, and you would benefit from being professionally guided towards developing an understanding that the world does not hinge on your decisions, so it's okay to fail sometimes. Nor can the world run when you are not participating and take no responsibility for your actions. You need to own up when you are to blame and step back when it's simply circumstances.

Journaling can certainly help as it will make you aware of what your self-talk sounds like and guide your thoughts towards more neutral territory.

- **Fallacy of Fairness**

The world is not fair. How often have we heard that being said? People often hide behind it when they think the world has turned against them. Reality: the world simply is. Fairness has nothing to do with it. True, we get injustices such as crime and inequalities, but again, fairness does not really apply to it. When someone robs you, it is not because they want to be unfair. It is probably because they need money, or they have been living a life of crime and know no different. When a colleague at work gets a promotion, and you don't, this is not an example of unfairness. Rather, it simply means that your colleague was better placed to be promoted. Things go our way one day, and they go against us the next day. Fairness has little to do with it.

When you believe the world should be fair to you, it sets you up for extreme disappointment and disillusionment. When you then decide the world is not fair because you have been disappointed, this negatively influences your thinking, which affects future events beyond the "unfair" event.

Countering It: Learning to let go of the concept of being fair or not is often learned through techniques such as meditation. Instead of focusing on the world outside and potential negative events, you learn to focus on simplistic concepts that are neither fair nor unfair, such as breathing, body awareness, and releasing bad memories.

- **Over-Generalization**

This is fallacious thinking based on one negative event in the past informing all of your decision-making skills. For instance, being robbed by someone who is African American could lead you to conclude that all African Americans are criminals. Clearly, this is not factual or logical thinking (criminals come in all colors and nationalities). Even something as simple as being disappointed by one faulty car, which makes you refuse to drive that kind of car again is an example of this. As shown by the first example, over-generalization can create substantially negative thinking and behavior patterns. It is an unbalanced way to go through life, and it will severely limit your chances and options in life.

Countering It: Play the devil's advocate. When you are given to generalization, you can use the approach of being "against" your view to help you become more balanced in your thinking. It's about putting yourself in the other person's shoes or seeing a situation from the other side. You can do this as a journaling activity. So, when you have come to generalize that all blondes are dumb, as an example, find reasons to counter this belief. You could remind yourself that hair color has nothing to do with intellectual facility. If you believe you suck at job interviews, you could remind yourself of all the times you have had a successful conversation with someone new, and how this is precisely what a job interview is.

- **Assumptive Thinking**

We tend to make assumptions easily. It is really when we are too lazy to think things through. We rely on what we think we know and jump to a conclusion about something or someone. This is the normal end of the spectrum for most of us; however, when you jump to conclusions about everything without any evidence, this is distorted thinking and decision making at play. This can manifest as a "gut feeling" that someone doesn't like us, or they are out to get us, or that we didn't make a good impression on someone (all without having any facts to substantiate this logic).

With this kind of unsubstantiated thinking, it is very easy to become detached from reality and develop a mistrust of people in your life. You might develop a behavior style that is anxiety driven or feel ambivalent about people in general, making real connections virtually impossible.

Counter It: To counter this distorted thinking, you need to become like a scientist. Whatever you believe, you should support it with evidence. If you believe someone doesn't like you, then don't allow this belief without concrete evidence, such as them telling someone they don't like you. Basing your assumption on "a look" is not evidence enough. While gut feelings can help us out, they should not govern our actions in everything in life.

- **Emotional Reasoning**

This distorted thinking revolves around feeling something and believing it to be true. You feel bloated, so you believe you are fat. You feel unhappy, so you believe you are depressed. While your feelings are important, they are not supposed to dominate your thinking. Feelings can't reason, and they can't be logical. Being overly determined by your feelings can lead to unhealthy behavior habits such as anxiety-driven attachments. It also prevents you from seeing the world as it is, and not as you feel about it.

Counter It: Emotions can be tricky to balance, and you may need professional intervention such as EFFT. A trained therapist can help you make healthy associations based on your feelings and also help you discover how to control your emotions, instead of letting them control you. Journaling and using positive affirmations can also help you to find healthy self-expression, while meditation can help you acknowledge and release potentially harmful emotions that have no factual reason to influence your being.

- **Blaming**

As children, we often tend to use this form of behavior to get out of trouble. Mom asks who broke the plate, and we all point at our younger brother, hoping to avoid punishment. Sadly, this kind of thinking still persists into adulthood for many people. When they are faced with possible punishment, they are quick to place the blame on someone who may not even be involved in the issue. We even end up blaming someone for the way we feel or for what we do. When a wife blames her infidelity on her husband's inattentiveness, this is a form of fallacious thinking. Clearly, the husband did not strip her and throw her into another man's bed. Though his inattention is not healthy, it is not what forced the wife to act as she did.

We are responsible for our actions. Therefore, we can't assign blame to others and state they made us do something. To do so is an example of distorted thinking.

Counter It: Start using words of power to help focus your thinking on you and not on the people around you. For instance, when you want to blame someone for making you swear, you should say, "I chose to swear." If you believe someone made or caused you to miss your bus, you can say, "I alone missed the bus." Consciously take ownership of your thinking and actions.

- **Rule-Based Thinking**

Many of us develop rules that seem to govern how we live and what makes us feel comfortable. For instance, we may believe that women should be soft and feminine. When we are then faced by the image of a female bodybuilder, this challenges our rule-based thinking, and we may end up being rude to that woman as we are inevitably angry as she didn't follow our rules. This is also about seeing the world as we want it (and have ordained it) to be. But we are not the kings and queens of the earth. The world does not operate according to our rules.

Any thinking that removes you from interacting with what is real and there in your environment creates behavior based on distortions. It will lead to withdrawal, emotional instability, and difficulty accepting and trusting the world, which creates anxiety-driven behavior styles.

Counter It: When little children learn, they often drive us nuts by asking "why?" This is actually a good thing as you need to explain, and therefore, think about something. Hence, when you feel upset as something seems "wrong" to you, you should start asking yourself "why?" When you see a same-sex couple together and it pushes on one of your personal life rules (or your fallacious thinking), ask yourself why you think it is wrong. When you can't answer it in a satisfactory manner, you start to question your fallacious beliefs and can begin to see the world as it is.

- **Self-Sacrifice as Reward**

Many of us have come to expect that sacrifice brings reward, and this is often not the case. This kind of distorted thinking only brings disappointment and resentment when we do something with an expectation of reward only to receive nothing in return. This is also an example of the world not reacting as we expect, which causes confusion and let-down with us. Accepting that the world will not necessarily reward your sacrifices with bounty or feast will help you to adjust better by forming a secure attachment style.

Counter It: If you enjoy engaging in sacrificial behavior, it may be healthier to satisfy that need by engaging in charity work where there is no promise of return. This way, you will learn you can't influence what other people do or how they return favors.

Self-Improvement Practices and Exercises

Image 8: Hannah Olinger on Unsplash. Self-improvement practices and exercises can include constructive tasks like journaling and meditation or it can include more challenging tasks such as guided discovery journeys. The goal is to experience the emotion or behavior you want to change and then plot how you will go about changing this negative or unhelpful behavior. This plot includes how you will change it, to what you will change it, and how you will feel in the end.

- **Journaling**

This is a little different from a usual journal or diary in that the sole purpose is to capture and gather information about your emotions or feelings, your thinking patterns, and your actions or behavior. This is a great tool to use for self-development as it allows you to tangibly look at your thoughts, behavior, and feelings. When it is made tangible on paper, you will find it easier to start reflecting on possible solutions. It is also useful for evaluating the progress you make as you start trying out different solutions.

In your journal, you can use activities such as word associations, mind maps, and even image-based reflections to help you articulate how you feel, why you feel that way, and what you are going to do about it. Thanks to technology, there are even apps for this now, with several well-rated apps available online. The CBT Tools for Healthy Living, Self-Help Mood Diary by *Excel At Life* is available for download to most mobile devices from Google Play Store and can be downloaded free at https://play.google.com/store/apps/details?id=com.excelatlife.cbtdiary&hl=en_ZA while Apple users can download a similar online product called CBT Thought Diary from Eddie Liu at https://apps.apple.com/us/app/cbt-thought-diary/id1010391170.

- **Meditation**

Meditation as a daily practice, not a once-off fad, is very useful for de-stressing and developing a peaceful mindset. There are various techniques and styles for meditation, and you can certainly find a way that works for you. From simply listening to a guided meditation to participating in specific breathing exercises, there are many different approaches. Guided meditations can be found free on YouTube, and there are several channels dedicated exclusively to this, such as *Meditation Vacation* or *Jason Stephenson's channel* that has an assortment of highly popular guided meditations on.

A similar skill that may help you release tension and bring inner peace is taking up a practice such as tai chi, which is like moving meditation. The goal here is to give your stressed brain a break, allow your body to become grounded, and find a more peaceful way to think. If you are anxious-avoidant in your normal behavior, you will find it holds less power over you when you can reduce your anxiety, opening up your mind to think with greater clarity and perspective.

- **Cognitive Restructuring or Reframing**

Using the journaling you have started doing and the peaceful mindful state of meditation, you can begin to explore your perceptions and beliefs, not only finding and challenging negative ones, but also finding healthy thoughts to replace them with. For instance, if you believe a woman is only as good as the family she creates, but you suddenly undergo a divorce, you may find your negative thoughts are challenged. Instead of only trying to believe a woman is not only her family, you might begin to question yourself what it is that makes a woman.

- **Guided Discovery**

Sometimes we believe things without knowing why we believe them or how we came to believe them. These thoughts are not always negative, but in not knowing where these thoughts came from, you will not be able to embrace your mind's processes. Using your journal and perhaps the help of a counselor, you can begin to find evidence to support your beliefs or assumptions. So, if you believe you have no right to speak in public, you would need to find evidence for that belief. In some countries, this is an actual law, but when considering it in line with your own legal concepts, you might find your evidence does disprove your thinking.

- **Exposure/Desensitizing Therapy**

Anxiety can give rise to a range of behavior that is not beneficial to your health or well-being. Exposure or desensitizing therapy can be really helpful in dealing with negative behavior and mindsets such as phobias, fears, and anxiety triggers. It works on the principle of starting with small exposure to the thing that scares or triggers you. The exposure is short, and afterwards, you discuss how you felt with a therapist. The next day, you may experience the same length of exposure again; this time, you are encouraged to remain calm and not panic. When you feel less frightened or upset over the experience, you will face longer incremental exposure to the trigger.

In reality, if you are terrified of spiders, you may start by looking at a picture of a spider for a few minutes and then discussing how you felt. You might journal about the experience, how it made your skin crawl, and how it made your brain feel numb. The following day, you may have to hold the photo, then next time, you may have to watch a video of a spider moving on someone's hand. Eventually, this would culminate with you going to a petting zoo to have an actual spider walk on your hand too.

With gradually increasing exposure, you begin to feel confident in your ability to handle the emotions of this fearful experience. You are able to analyze how and what you think, which, in turn, influences your actions. Anxiety can be controlled, which opens the road to secure attachment and thinking styles.

- **Activity Scheduling**

Your calendar can be your friend. Sometimes, we have an activity we are not really eager to do as it is in some way linked to having to face a fear or engage with an anxiety trigger. Going to the dentist is for many people a fine example of this. Using your calendar, you can begin to mentally prepare yourself for the activity, while you resolutely refuse to postpone the activity. Once your appointment is set, you can begin to stop focusing on it and rather deal with it on the day when you need to go for the appointment.

- **De-Stressing Techniques**

Anxiety has a biological component too. It affects not only how you feel; it also influences your rate of respiration, blood pressure, heart rate, and even your perspiration. We certainly know when we are anxious we get sweaty palms, and some people even complain of stomach difficulties from prolonged periods of anxiety. To bring some relief on a physical level, you are encouraged to try the following techniques:

Breathing Relaxation: This has already been somewhat introduced to you in meditation; however, there are a range of breathing techniques you may consider. Box breathing has become very popular recently (and not only because it's being used by law enforcement officers and Navy SEALs). In essence, it is symmetrical breathing, and it is very easy to do. When you find yourself in an anxiety-fueled situation, you can benefit by doing it right there. Breathing in through your nose for four seconds, you pause for four seconds, then exhale through your mouth for four seconds, followed by another pause for four seconds to complete one set. Quite simply, it's inhale (four seconds), hold (four seconds), exhale (four seconds), hold (four seconds), and begin again.

Breathing creates mindfulness, lowers your blood pressure, encourages slow deep heart activity, and it even lowers your temperature (no more sweaty palms). When your blood is more oxygenated, you will be able to think more clearly and feel less anxious.

Progressive Body Scan: Like the breathing exercises and meditation, a progressive body scan notes the physical cost of constant anxiety and worry. As you mentally become aware of every part of your body, you note tension, pain, tightness, and discomfort. Using the focus of your intention, you can begin to gently tighten and release muscles, banish pain, and relax your body as you begin to let anxiety go.

- **Role Playing**

As the name states, this is about playing out roles to find new insight and acceptance of what happens in your life. Fear-inducing scenarios become less scary as you develop problem-solving skills, become familiar with new circumstances and gain insight, develop social skills and become more assertive in what you need and want, and you learn to communicate better. This is an effective way to engage in examples of the devil's advocate role play where you reason on behalf of someone else.

Chapter 5: Finding Happiness in Your Single Life

Image 9: Priscilla Du Preez on Unsplash. Being single is a daunting experience for many of us. We desperately want to be in

a relationship, forgetting that relationships are definitely not an easy road to walk, and these come with their own challenges. Being happily single is becoming a buzz concept of late, and more young people are choosing to remain single or embrace being single once their current relationships have ended. So, what does it take to find happiness in your singlehood?

Your Attachment Style and Your Confidence

While you may want to be in a happy relationship, the first relationship you will ever have is with yourself. It is essential to discover happiness in this primary relationship, for it is one you will remain a part of for the rest of your life. Being single and happy with your singlehood is a number one factor for avoiding toxic relationships with partners who are simply available but not suitable for you. Once you know what you are looking for, you will have no issues in maintaining healthy boundaries between you and your partner, and between your relationship and the outside world. This is how you ensure the relationship remains a happy place to live, and stop it from becoming a traumatic war zone.

If you have already developed an insecure or harmful attachment style, this does not mean you are doomed to constantly be unhappy in your relationships. It simply means you have some obstacles to overcome, which might translate into a longer journey to reaching your ideal relationship status.

When you have formed anxious or dependent attachment behavior styles, you will struggle with being on your own. This imposes restrictions on the relationship, and your partner now has to haul your life baggage around with them too. Not everyone is cut out for this, nor need they be. This is your battle to fight. You need to decide what you will leave behind, and what you will take with you.

While you may be looking for a partner who lifts you up, and you may be fortunate enough to find a partner who is willing to do just that, this will be a temporary fix. You can't place your happiness in someone else's hands. That's like expecting to find happiness in a commercially available form to consume when you want it—like eating a lollipop and instantly feeling better. It won't last.

Only *you* can make yourself rise and feel lifted.

After searching for numerous partners and being in one failed relationship after another, you may have become quite skeptical of real love really existing. As a result, you may settle for a relationship that may not be right for you, but it's convenient and right there.

Eventually, you start accepting things you shouldn't. You may stick with a partner who cheats on you because at least he doesn't beat you. Perhaps you accept a wife who doesn't love you and who becomes emotionally abusive because you have children with her whom you adore.

This settling "down" will not end happily in the long run. While this does not mean you need to bail out of the relationship right now, it may mean you need to begin traveling along the therapeutic road to see if you can create a relationship that all the people involved in can enjoy and feel satisfied with.

What You Want From a Relationship, You Want From Yourself

You may have been asked what you want from a relationship, and many of us are quick to list the following conditions:

- Stability
- Love
- Care
- Affection
- Protection
- Support
- Happiness
- Family

These certainly seem like the best qualities in life and having all these conditions met would probably create a holy-grail kind of relationship. While your list may look slightly different, the basic principles will be the same. But, here's the kicker: these relationship goals can apply to your singlehood or relationship with self too. If you can't create these conditions in yourself, how can you offer them to someone else? You are expecting it from your partner, but if they don't already have this in them, they can't share it with you. Likewise, if you don't have this in you, then you can't share it or share in it either.

When you can safely and confidently create these conditions in your relationship with yourself, you will not be dependent on someone else for contentment or happiness. You will also be able to share these qualities with your partner, becoming the ideal partner for your ideal partner. Remember: a relationship takes two people (more when you start having children), and when you are already unhappy, you will not bring anything except unhappiness to your relationship. So, engage in and grow from activities on your own to help you become stable, loving, caring, affectionate, protective, supportive, happy, and family to *yourself*.

Challenges to Overcome

Embracing your singlehood is certainly not going to be easy. There will be many challenges to overcome in addition to the process of becoming all of the above requirements you created. These challenges include:

- **Social Stigma of Being Single**

Choosing to remain single is not condoned, accepted, or understood in most societies on earth. There is the constant social pressure to become a part of a relationship unit, continue the bloodline, family name, and have children. Perhaps you may be fortunate enough that some of your family members will understand and accept your singlehood decision, but many of them will not. This means that family gatherings will usually involve the inevitable, "When are you getting married?"

Society also tends to tie age to this concept, and when you are nearing a certain age, the pressures to commit to a relationship usually build. This can push you towards entering into a relationship without being ready or even if the relationship is not suitable for your needs.

Remind yourself daily that being single is not something to apologize for, nor is it something to be ashamed of. Whether you choose to remain single forever, or you choose to enter a relationship, the goals will remain the same. However, if you can satisfy those goals in your selfhood, you are more likely to be able to have a satisfactory relationship with another unique individual.

- **Your Own Neediness**

We all like to feel validated, to have our existence and our experiences witnessed by another person. This can create pressure to enter a relationship to get this outside validation. However, you do not need to rely on a partner or significant other to get this validation. Even a close friend or someone you trust can act in this capacity, assuring and confirming that you are on the right track and you are doing things right.

In reality, you might get more validation from a close friend than from your relationship partner. Affirmation and positive feedback is more likely to come from a dear friend than from a lover, husband, or wife who is not involved or invested enough to meet and satisfy your neediness.

- **Relationship Urges**

We live in a society that is geared towards couples, and this can make things difficult for singles to feel accepted and happy. Going out can become problematic when you are on your own. Eating out, going to a movie, clubbing, and attending shows becomes awkward when you are without company. Certainly, the "couple's discounts" and "family buckets" clearly indicate which way society is inclined. Again, this can lead to alienation and loneliness when you are still trying to find your own power in a singlehood.

These can all increase the urge to join a relationship simply to not be alone. This is, of course, not the right reason to enter into a relationship. Again, you would be placing your happiness in someone else's hands, and when they can't meet your needs, you open the door to resentment. Compromising by entering a relationship before you are ready will not lead to the happily ever-after you are dreaming of.

- **Self-Confidence Issues**

Over time, especially as your friends get married and have children, you will begin to doubt the wisdom of your decision to self-develop in your singlehood. You may begin to lose self-confidence, and you will wonder if you have waited too long. Perhaps your partner has already come and gone? With aging factoring in, you may begin to feel as if you are not good enough, pretty enough, young enough, or simply enough to attract a partner. This could also prompt you to settle for the first possible relationship that comes along. Again, you have not ensured your happiness; instead, you have placed your happiness in someone else's hands. It belongs in your hands, and the right partner for yourself is you. Once you are happily single, you will be a perfect partner for the right partner.

Singlehood Models

Your attachment style is a valuable motivating factor in being single (Brenner, 2018). Insecure forms of attachment are statistically linked to a lesser chance of being single as you struggle with being alone, while it is also linked to a higher chance of being in a relationship that is unhappy. The secure attachment style is most associated with being happily single, or happy in a stable relationship. People who are prone to anxious attachment styles tend to become single not by choice but because partners leave them or they struggle to secure a partner.

Singlehood can be a choice, and most often, those who choose to be single do so from a secure attachment style. These individuals have the confidence to do so. However, when considering the three models that lead to or create singlehood, we find the following:

- **Anxious and Activated**

People who default to anxious attachment styles tend to make poor partners in a relationship. While they seek intimacy, once they have this in a relationship, they tend to become hyper activated, a condition where their behavior kicks into overdrive. Where they were anxious before, they become neurotic; where they were fearful of being abandoned, they now become jealous and controlling of their partner. Needless to say, the relationship becomes unbalanced, and often the only option open to the relationship is its end, with the anxious styled partner being forced into singlehood.

- **Avoidant**

Individuals who have an avoidant attachment style tend to believe being within the bounds of a relationship will end in unhappiness and pain. They view the intimacy of a relationship with trepidation, and they fear being close to people and revealing their vulnerability. As a result, such individuals tend to naturally choose singlehood not out of any reason other than they fear being in a relationship. Singlehood does not offer them joy or contentment, as they are simply hiding in it from their own hang-ups.

When these people are in a relationship, they maintain a foot-out-the-door philosophy, being ready to leave and flee to the unattached nature of being single. They tend to be aloof, unaffectionate, and disinterested, causing their relationships to fail. Avoidant typed people will also not easily enter another relationship again, preferring to remain single, even though it does not necessarily meet their needs either.

- **Single, Secure, and Happy**

With increasing frequency, as societal norms are being challenged and broken down, we find individuals who have a secure attachment style, who choose to remain or enter singlehood. These are people who can happily meet all their needs from a range of non-romantic relationships, and even their sexual needs, if they have them, are met outside of a romantic relationship.

The reasons for being single may include spiritual, religious, or a heightened need for space to engage in self-discovery and development. While these people would make excellent partners in a romantic relationship, they choose not to necessarily engage in a romantic relationship, instead forming lasting and satisfying bonds with themselves. This choice is also not driven by some buried childhood trauma or anxious avoidance; rather, it is a conscious and carefully considered choice.

How to Become Single, Secure, and Happy

More and more people are choosing singlehood as a permanent lifestyle choice; however, some choose to combine it with a therapeutic treatment to find, care for, and develop their own selves and create healthier attachment styles. In these cases, it can be considered an intermediary stage between an unhappy relationship and finding a satisfactory relationship when they are ready. Whichever your choice for being or becoming single, your happiness and satisfaction is in your hands, which requires you to develop or maintain a secure attachment style:

- **Mindfulness Techniques**

When you are ready to engage in developing yourself, you will need to start a process of finding yourself, consciously identifying the root causes of your insecurities, and actively repair your insecurities. Using methods such as meditation, journaling, and therapy you will be able to start finding out who you are, what happened to you, what you need, and how to give that to yourself instead of looking for it elsewhere.

This is not an instant fix, and humming while you sit in the lotus position will not quickly make everything better. Instead, it is a life-long commitment to yourself. It is like admitting you have a preexisting condition that you need to nurture and take care of for the rest of your life. You can choose to ignore it and hope for the best, or you can be proactive and learn to cope with and adapt to your behavior style, making it become as close to confident and secure as you can.

Creating healthy self-care and self-soothing routines such as daily journaling, reflection, mindfulness through meditation, breathing exercises, and intentionally facing your fears, you will be able to be the best possible version of yourself, the most secure you that you can be, and you will find a state of contentment with yourself (and eventually in a suitable relationship if you so choose).

Even if you already come from a stable background, have suffered no past traumas, and you are very secure in who you are, creating mindful routines of self-care to practice daily will help you remain secure in the face of daily pressures and challenges.

- **Therapy and Relationship Counseling**

Okay, so you have some issues that you need to deal with before you can securely enter a new relationship. This is not the end of the world, but if you are not proactive, it can be the end of yet another relationship. If you don't become responsible enough to admit you need help, you may even further damage your relationship with yourself.

Going for therapy or signing up for relationship counseling need not be an admission of defeat. There is no shame in needing help. In fact, you should be applauded for being brave enough to do it. The benefits of having therapy to help you face your troubled past, and finding out what you want, or making sense of your own tumbled thoughts is immeasurable. You will become stronger, wiser, and much more confident in who you are on your own and who you are in a relationship. How is that not a win-win situation for you?

Relationship counseling will not only assist you in finding out how to make your existing relationship work, and discover what you actually want from a relationship, but it will also help improve your relationship with yourself. Remember, your relationship partner is not there to fix you. And you are not there to fix them, either. A healthy, satisfying, and dependable relationship is about being together, facing outside (and inside) challenges together while being dependable enough to be counted on. When you build that relationship with yourself first, you will be ready to engage in the challenges of two independent and secure people becoming a unity in the relationship. Entering a relationship with a partner who is not secure in their attachments brings with it a whole range of complications. You are not their savior.

You should not engage in a relationship bearing a messiah complex, for then you are not able to help someone out at all. Instead, you can point them in a direction to engage in self-development, support them through the healing process, and then see if the relationship will work. A trained therapist can help you in this regard, assisting you to steer clear of pity pitfalls and traps of dependent anxiety your partner may already be creating for you (usually quite unintentionally on their part).

- **Analyze Your Needs and Wants**

What you need and what you want is not always clear, especially in the technological age, where the media is constantly telling us what to think, how to be, and what we need or want. However, looking back at your past relationships, what strikes you as being an obvious need (that was probably not met) or a want (that you had satisfied or not). A previous partner may have been domineering, and now you know you do not want this.

Perhaps they were caring, which you enjoyed, and you want this. Maybe the lines of communication were not available to you during the relationship, and you missed being able to simply talk to them. Even non-romantic relationships can help you find out what you enjoy and don't. Camaraderie, sharing, talking, caring, respect and trust, intimacy, sex, and friendship may be on your list of things you need and want. Surprisingly, you can satisfy these needs in non-romantic relationships, or even with yourself. When you know how to tend to your own needs, you will know what you expect from and need from your partner.

Take some time to journal about this. Write about past relationships, even relationships that didn't involve you, such as that of your parents, siblings, friends, or colleagues and find the things that stuck out to you as being something you would want and need. Having a partner who walks into your office and tongues you down to your toes is not a healthy or viable need. If this is something you believe you need, you may need to dig a little deeper as there is an insecurity you are not dealing with. However, wanting a partner who sends you a daily message with kind wishes and shows their affection by talking to you and discussing how they can help you build your relationship is a secure and positive need.

- **Engage in Meaningful Activities**

Happiness is determined more by your feeling about an activity than who you necessarily do it with (if anyone). Enjoyment comes from doing something that matters to you. Find what gets you excited, passionate, and interested and go do it. Whether it's going on a weekly hike, taking up sky-diving, or simply browsing the local flower shops every weekend to make yourself a beautiful bouquet for the week, you can enjoy and find personal meaning on your own. When you are happy, you will also have a greater chance at attracting someone who is like-minded and secure in their attachment style.

- **Supporting People**

While you are busy journaling, take some time to really think about the people in your life. Are they helping or hurting you? Often, we attract people into our lives with the best intentions only to find they are not helpful to our personal journey. They may be emotional leeches, they may be dominators, or even secretly frenemies who are only waiting for you to fail so they can rejoice. You may also be blessed with dear friends who support you when you need it; people who care enough to either voice an opinion or keep quiet and be exactly what you need in the right moment.

Having a strong support circle is important when you engage in a selfhood relationship. You are not planning on being a hermit (hopefully), and you will need people to meet your needs to communicate, share ideas with, spend time with, develop friendship with, laugh with, and turn to when you are having a bad day, or needing assurance and validation. Choose people who help (not hurt), people who care and don't scare, and people who support you with no ulterior motives. You are worth it.

- **Live Now**

Don't be a one-day person. Someone who has all these great plans of what they will do when they are in a relationship, but then wait for that relationship to happen. These one-day people are living in a dream of one-day. What about today?

If you are planning to take a trip, then do so, whether you are single or not. Don't wait until you find a partner. Live now. Find ways to satisfy your life goals now and don't wait for someone else to make it happen for you. You are all you need.

- **Stop Speed Dating**

If you are busy working on creating a better selfhood, or making yourself into the best version of yourself, you may be tempted to start dating before you are ready. This can be overwhelming, and it can really knock you back from all the good progress you have made. Instead, wait a bit longer until you are ready to date again. Don't allow society or anyone else to push you into meeting someone because they are "nice" or because you are simply "available." You are already dating someone—yourself. And that is the best relationship you should be focused on until you are ready to step back into dating and then only *if* you want to.

- **Declutter Your Mind**

Become mindful of your thoughts. What you think will influence your behavior, and your feelings. If you sit all day pining away with thoughts of how sad you are at being single, you will not be engaging in building a healthy selfhood. Note these negative thoughts and take action against them. Journaling is a great way to deal with these. You could write them down and turn them into affirmations, or counter them with affirmations. So, if you are thinking "I am going to be single and sad for the rest of my life," you could counter it with an affirmation like "I choose to be single and happy until I am ready to meet my perfect partner."

Calming your thoughts can also help you to create mental space to actually start paying attention to yourself, thinking about what you want and what you need, and enjoying your own company. When you are in a relationship, a lot of your mind is occupied with thoughts of your significant other, who may deserve your time and thoughts, but you also need time and the ability to think about yourself.

Make space upstairs for your life too. By spending more time (and mental space) thinking about yourself, you will also cut down on all the senseless worry you may be engaging in relating to your partner (are they safe, do they love you, are they cheating on you, did they pack lunch, will they still love you when you're old?). Lastly, remember, a cluttered mind can't think logically or clearly, and reasoning distortions may begin to creep in, ruining your progress and happiness.

Chapter 6: Strategies to Build Stronger, More Meaningful Relationships

Building meaningful relationships will for many of us be a lifelong process, and the question arises, "What do healthily attached couples do that is so different from what everyone else is doing?" There are a few significant differences in the approaches favored by healthy couples. However, there are also similar approaches to what everyone else is doing, just differently applied that these couples use.

Key Concepts in Promoting a Secure Attachment

You will be developing your attachment style for the rest of your life as you experience new things, recall old things, meet new people, and deal with the people who started out life with you. This ongoing process can be challenging, and it can often seem like you are falling so short of the mark; however, it's important to remind yourself of these basic tenets:

- **You Are Lovable for You**

One infallible truth you need to recognize and embrace is that you are enough for you. You are lovable enough for you. There is no one's approval and love you need more than your own—yours is what matters. You should not waste time or energy trying to win the approval or love of anyone who doesn't love you for you already.

- **You Are Deserving of Understanding and Compassion**

For some strange reason, we tend to apologize when someone offers us their understanding or compassion when we are feeling down or insufficient. It's almost preprogrammed into us to say, "Oh, I'm sorry for being such a mess." You are allowed to be a mess, and you deserve to have the important people in your life show you understanding and compassion. Even if you have chosen singlehood, you are not alone. Whether you are single or in a relationship, you deserve support.

- **Your Boundaries Should Be Respected**

While a traditional relationship makes an "us" out of you and one other person, you are still entitled to have boundaries. Your personal life, body, and mind does not become open range to your partner. They should respect your boundaries enough not to challenge these. You should have the wisdom to clearly mark what you are confident and happy with sharing and what is private and not up for casual debate. A partner who respects you will respect your boundaries as well.

- **Healthy and Rewarding Communication Is Possible With Someone Who Gets You**

It is the most incredible feeling to speak to someone who gets you. Someone who really understands and gets what you are saying without the words being any different or special than normal. In some cases, that process of being "gotten" happens so seamlessly, you hardly need to speak at all. Some people refer to this as being in sync or on the same wavelength. This is what communication is all about. It is the golden medal at the end of a time of hard work. Building a relationship where you "get" each other is not something that happens over night, but it is so absolutely worth it.

Healing From Trauma Through Emotionally Corrective Relationships

Healing is important, and if we don't address the pain and injuries of the past, we will not be able to engage in meaningful relationships. Engaging with and healing your past trauma is vital to leading a life of empowerment and relationship bliss. Corrective relationships are aimed at helping to support your emotional recovery and healing.

- **Therapy to Face the Past**

A relationship should be a space where growth and recovery can happen. This is what it means when you hear a relationship is a soft place to fall. In a corrective relationship, you find the courage to face past traumas such as abuse, neglect, previous failed relationships, and even current relationships that are on the rocks. If your primary relationship, such as your marriage or life partner, is unable to meet this requirement of being your recovery point, you may have to turn to your therapist or counselor to create a healing or corrective relationship. Having a space to engage with and heal from the past is important to finding your feet in a meaningful relationship.

- **Choosing the Right People for Support**

While your partner is an obvious choice as a support person, you will be well-served to create a support network of people whom you can turn to in a time of crisis. This does not mean people you can go borrow sugar from when you're baking a cake kind of crisis. This is about knowing who to turn to when you need to cry and cry until your emotional rivers run dry. It may be about having someone who can support you to release and laugh with about stressors of your day. It can also be someone whose wisdom and judgment you trust when you don't know which way to go next. Believing your life partner must fulfill all those roles is not only unfair to them but also improbable to be true.

Therefore, you should have a support network that expands beyond your relationship. This does not mean your partner is not enough; instead, it means you know to accept and value all they are *and* turn to others to take unreasonable pressure off your partner. Remember, they are also dealing with their own crisis, past and present, and while they will turn to you, your partner also needs to have their own support network.

- **Healthy Boundaries**

A healthy relationship is built by knowing where you stand. This is achieved by having clear communications and knowing where you are permitted and not permitted in a relationship. Building healthy boundaries is not about saying no; it is about earning respect and understanding from the people in your life who matter most to you. When the lines are drawn within your relationship from the start, you will not have to suffer through the confusion of being pressured when you don't feel comfortable about something.

- **Creating a Conflict Resolution Toolkit**

As with boundaries, when you learn to communicate, you can quickly diminish the impact of conflicting situations and resolve these more peacefully. It is a great feeling to know you and your partner had a difference of opinion or a misunderstanding, but you were able to resolve this in a mature way. Creating a relationship toolkit for conflict resolution may be a great idea. Create some ground rules to stop you from needlessly arguing. This could include rules like:

- Never go to bed still angry.
- If you are not sure, or feel hurt, ask for confirmation first.
- Speak, don't shout.
- Confirm what you heard before you jump to a conclusion.
- If you are unhappy about something, speak about it.
- Listen to your partner too; don't just speak.

Attachment Style Interactions and Their Relationship Challenges

People of different attachment styles interact with each other in dynamic ways and this can become part of the relationship challenges they will face together. Being together despite and in spite of each other.

- **Secure and Secure Attachment**

This is the most secure and successful relationship combination. When both partners in a relationship have a secure attachment style, they will be confident and supportive, caring and considerate, and they will be able to commit and show affection without secretly having concerns the relationship will fail or secretly trying to make it fail.

- **Secure and Dismissive-Avoidant Attachment**

When one partner is secure and the other dismissive-avoidant in their attachment styles, this may become a complicated relationship. The secure partner will want to engage in genuine intimacy and trust, but when they try to draw close to their partner, the dismissive-avoidant partner will draw away, avoid them, and even dismiss their efforts. The dismissive-avoidant partner may also be abusive in making light of the other partner's feelings and needs. Emotional intimacy will be complicated. Since the dismissive-avoidant partner is not fully capable of committing to the relationship, this may cause the relationship to break up.

- **Secure and Fearful-Avoidant Attachment**

With one partner being secure in their attachment style and the other fearful-avoidant, many complications can be expected. The secure partner will try to assure their partner of their love and affection, while the fearful-avoidant partner will shelter a secret fear of being single or being alone, yet they want to get out to avoid anticipated pain. This could mean that the partner with the harmful attachment style will intentionally cause conflict, but then cling to the secure attachment partner. They will quickly misread whatever their secure attachment partner says to them, looking for conflict so to speak.

- **Secure and Anxious Attachment**

Should one partner be secure in their attachment styles while the other is anxious avoidant, you have a complicated situation where the insecure partner is constantly trying to get more intimacy and becomes overly demanding for reassurance. They are constantly afraid of being left by the secure partner, who assures them this will not happen, yet over time, they become worn down by the lack of communication and development. Should the relationship end, the partner with an anxious attachment style will quickly jump into the first available relationship, becoming progressively more and more anxious and fearful of being dumped.

- **Dismissive-Avoidant and Dismissive-Avoidant**

When both partners in the relationship have a dismissive-attachment style, the relationship will be cold and hostile. Both partners will lack the initiative to create intimacy and closeness. Communication is also likely to be problematic and somewhat argumentative. Given their withdrawn and dismissive natures, both partners are unlikely to approach a therapist for help either. Problems will not be discussed, and both partners will refrain from spending time together or engaging in joint activities. For children born of such a relationship, their childhood will be filled with cold arguments between their parents, a lack of affection, and a slow response to their needs.

- **Dismissive-Avoidant and Fearful-Avoidant Attachment**

This type of relationship will be a clear case of abuser and victim. The dismissive-avoidant partner will be aggressive to and manipulative of their fearful-avoidant partner who will cower and be unable to stand up for themselves. The relationship will not be likely to survive for long, and the fearful-avoidant partner will either self-isolate themselves within the relationship or they will bail on the relationship.

- **Dismissive-Avoidant and Anxious Attachment**

When one partner is a dismissive-avoidant and the other is anxious behavior styled, you will have a situation where the dismissive-avoidant partner will be dominating towards the anxious behavior-styled partner. Abuse may be present, often spilling over onto the children of such a relationship. The home of the relationship will be a place of nervous tension, and the dismissive-avoidant partner will be unable to tolerate any form of criticism, responding to it with aggression. As a result, the anxious partner will become even more anxious, and though they want to leave, they will not do so as that would mean being on their own, which they can't handle.

- **Anxious and Fearful-Avoidant Attachment**

With a relationship made up of an anxious and a fearful-avoidant styled partnership, there will be less violence, but both partners will display negative characteristics such as jealousy, fear, anxiety, and lack intimacy. While the anxious partner will need assurances, their fearful-avoidant partner will be unable to provide these as they already believe the worst will happen. This will, in turn, make the anxious partner more anxious, causing the fearful-avoidant partner to become even more terrified and withdraw even more. This is a worst case-scenario of two partners bringing out the worst in each other.

- **Anxious and Anxious Attachment**

While a relationship with two partners who are both anxious in their attachment styles may seem like a place where mutual anxiety could lead to understanding, this is not the case. While both partners need assurance, they don't have the confidence to meet this need for each other, which will again see an escalation of even more anxiety and feelings of inadequacy in the relationship. This form of relationship is also quite rare as anxious styled people tend to be attracted to either secure or dismissive-avoidant styled partners who project confidence or dominate them into submission.

- **Fearful-Avoidant and Fearful-Avoidant Attachment**

In a relationship where both partners have fearful-avoidant style approaches to behavior, there may be a substantial lack of communication. Both partners will be afraid of the relationship failing, and both will avoid doing anything about that. They will lack commitment and confidence, and as a result, they may engage in extramarital relationships when pressured to do so. This is often not based on any sexual needs being met but more on avoiding committing to the relationship. Yet, when their partner discovers the infidelity, they may become fearful of the relationship ending.

While being in a relationship with someone who is not secure in their attachment style can be difficult, it can work out when both partners are there to support each other and look on the upside and not on the downside.

Exercises to Strengthen Your Relationship

It is possible to strengthen your relationship with someone whom you may have become disillusioned with. After all, there was something that attracted you to them in the beginning, and it was not what is now pushing you away.

- **List Exercise**

Try this exercise to strengthen your relationship (Vilhauer, 2017). It could possibly give you the inspiration to fight to save your relationship:

Use Your Journal

Sit comfortably somewhere quiet, close your eyes, and begin to think back to when you first met. Can you recall what your partner was like? What was it that attracted you to them in the beginning? There was something you felt when you knew they were coming over, or you were going somewhere with them—write it down now.

List

In your journal, create a list with all of the best qualities your partner had when you were dating that attracted you most to them. It could be how they were considerate of your comfort, how they smiled when you complimented them, or how they were funny. Try to make your list as detailed as possible.

Add to It

Every day, when you are getting ready for bed, use your journal and the list you created to add three new points you appreciate about your partner today. It does not have to be big things like them buying you a car. It can also be something small like smiling at you, or how they made you coffee to go because you were running late for work.

Read It

The following morning, take some time as you get up to read your list and reflect on it, recalling more precious and meaningful moments as you ponder on this little list.

Grow for 30 Days

Faithfully keep adding three things to your list about your partner *every* day. After 30 days, there will be a much less negative impression about your partner in your heart and mind. You may find the list growing much bigger than you had anticipated. Where it may take you three hours to write down the three things on the second day, you may find you are burning to write down three things by day 20. It will also make you much more observant of the good things about your partner and about your relationship with that person.

- **Learn Something New**

Communication and learning is what keeps a relationship interesting and novel. Try spending some time every night learning something new about your partner. Even though you may have been together for five years or fifty years, you don't know everything about each other yet. So, open the avenues of communication by finding out:

Something funny

Something embarrassing or awkward

Something they love

Something they hate

A random childhood story

If you are not sure about where to start, paging through some childhood photo albums may be helpful. If your partner has had a traumatic childhood, you may need to proceed carefully, gently guiding them to recall the best memories and not dwell on painful past events.

- **Ask Questions**

Learning about your partner can also be driven by questions that may be difficult to answer. Be open about this, encourage them to ask freely, and be prepared to answer truthfully. Use some time over coffee or while getting ready for bed. On pieces of paper, write down some difficult questions you have never asked each other. It may be a good idea to place the questions into a jar and select one every night to both answer to each other. This could become part of your pillow-talk routine. Questions could include:

Name your biggest fear and explain.

Tell me about your biggest dream that still hasn't come true.

What is your biggest regret in life?

Share your fondest childhood memory.

Who is your hero and why?

If you could change one thing in your life, what is it and why?

- **Soul Gazing**

Even if you have been in your relationship for years, you may not be familiar with your partner's soul, and this can be a daunting yet important aspect of them to meet. While the eyes are said to be the windows of the soul, we so rarely gaze into our partner's eyes with any lasting intensity. So, try this exercise in soul gazing:

Sit comfortably with your knees touching and look into each other's eyes. Keep your eyes focused but soft, not trying to intimidate or judge with your look. Instead, simply look with a steady visual presence into your partner's eyes. Don't break eye contact, but you may blink. However, look into their eyes as if they are the only person on earth. This is not a contest; it isn't about who looks away first and losing. Instead, you may find yourself realizing aspects about your partner you had not previously known. You may see their and your vulnerabilities, which creates trust and companionship.

- **Attentive Listening**

How often have you longed to speak to your partner, to unburden your mind without them interrupting or offering advice or telling you off or doing anything other than listening to you with complete attention? This exercise is precisely about this, and you can and should use a timer set to five minutes to ensure both partners get their fair share of listening and talking time.

When it is your turn to speak, simply let yourself ramble on about what has been on your mind. It does not have to be anything serious or hugely deep, although you may find your deepest thoughts flowing out before you know it. Whatever you or your partner says, the listener should simply remain quietly listening. Do not ask questions, don't offer suggestions, and don't offer encouraging sounds like "oh," "ah," or "hmm." Instead, just listen, making gentle eye contact or being physically close. When the timer sounds, change positions with the listener becoming talking and vice versa.

- **Spend Some Time on Worksheets for Couples**

The internet abounds with free downloadable worksheets to help couples connect and improve their communication skills. Two excellent examples of this is the *About Your Partner Worksheet*, which is designed to help you discover things about your partner and also show how much you know about your partner (or don't). This worksheet focuses on six subcategories ranging from questions about fun and games to your feelings and careers.

Another useful worksheet is the *Good Qualities Worksheet*, which is designed to help you remember positive points about your partner with guided questions. These worksheets and many others are available from Positive Psychology at https://positivepsychology.com/couples-therapy-worksheets-activities/ and though they may not be a quick fix for your relationship problems, they can breathe new life into your relationship and help you find common ground as well as improving your communication skills.

Chapter 7: Long-Term Relationship Happiness: What's the Secret?

Image 10: Karan Mandre on Unsplash. The expression "you can't make an omelet without breaking a few eggs" may seem to apply to the whole messy business of dating and finding your perfect partner. You may even have broken several dozen and still not found what you need to make you happy and create a meaningful and successful relationship. Perhaps you have found your partner, but you fear losing them, and you wish there were a way to keep your heart fires burning strong. So, what is the secret to long-term relationship bliss?

A relationship requires skills you may not have been magically born with. But don't fret; you can develop them with dedication and an openness to learning. There are several skills that will serve you well in creating and maintaining a long-term relationship. Here are some of the most important ones:

Your Emotional Intelligence

Being in command of your emotions, you can make decisions based not only on an involuntary reaction but also on your reaction to others and with your own internal environment. Having an evolved emotional intelligence (EQ) will lead to you being able to know what you feel and why you feel it. You will also be able to interpret how other people are feeling. You are a master of empathy. However, sadly, EQ is not necessarily something you are born with, though we all have it in differing degrees. Practicing it will certainly improve it, but how do you polish up this skill that can have a huge impact on your relationship and maintain your connected bliss? Golhar (2018) has suggestions to try:

- **Be Assertive in Your Communications**

Being assertive is not being aggressive. When you have a well-developed EQ, you know the difference. Practice communicating clearly but respectfully.

- **Respond, Don't React**

When tempers run high, we are all inclined to respond in haste and in anger. Our emotions can be a hot pot of trauma, and if we don't take control of this, we spill words we can't ever take back. When you are emotionally mature, you learn to think before you speak and before you act. Reacting is based on emotions, such as running when you hear a gunshot because you are afraid. Thinking will help you develop and maintain integrity within your relationship.

- **Listen**

Often, the death of a relationship is due to a misunderstanding, which could have been prevented if you had simply listened and gotten clarity before reacting. Listening before you react or before you allow your emotions to race off will help you communicate better and avoid confusion and misunderstandings.

- **Self-Motivate and Be Positive**

Be your own cheerleader. The world is not always likely to cheer you on, so it's up to you to motivate yourself and find positive energy to push on through with. In a relationship, we often demand our partner to be our supporter or fan, neglecting that they have their own draining issues to deal with. By self-motivating and building a positive mindset, you will be able to value your partner so much more and not just because they make you feel good. When you are positive, you will also have a different life outlook that will open up your energy for the day ahead. You will be less grumpy and more accessible to your partner too.

- **Embrace Criticism**

None of us are perfect. Being mature enough to embrace this, you will seek to engage in self-improvement, and you will not be upset by constructive criticism. Since you are then looking to improve your skills, you will be much more observant about yourself and the world around you. People will become signboards to you, advertising what they are thinking and feeling, which will help you make better decisions. When you get it wrong, you need to choose not to react in a negative or defensive way. Instead, you can use this as feedback to help you improve and develop more, constantly becoming a better version of yourself.

- **Empathize but Lead**

Feeling bad for someone who is in crisis is not a weakness. It is strength to be able to see what someone is going through and feel an emotional connection to them. This does not mean you (should) feel sorry for them. Instead, it is about understanding what they are going through. This understanding will help you to be a better partner.

When someone is in despair, you can help ease their burdens by leading. While you understand what they are going through, you need to be strong and lead until they are able to get on their feet. Sitting there crying with them will not avail either of you of anything.

- **Remain Accessible and Social**

While we all want to be with someone whom we can drop all of our guards with, letting our hair down and not being as guarded with our emotions, we still need to consider the impact of this emotional rawness on our partners. They may not be as comfortable with seeing the unrestrained us. Having some social skills and knowing that having a bad day is not an excuse for shouting at our partner will help us remain accessible. In addition, emotionally intelligent people know they should communicate with their partners especially. Saying to your partner that you had a bad work day and need 15 minutes of quiet time before you join them to prepare dinner is being mature. It shows a heightened EQ. Your partner will thank you for being up front and honest, avoiding later misunderstandings.

Strengthen Your Communication Skills

Communication is one of the most vital relationship skills, and when you are able to do it effectively, you will be assured of being understood and understanding your partner correctly. Much of the conflict and trauma in relationships are from misunderstandings and an inability to communicate effectively. When you want something, you should be able to ask for it clearly and negotiate to get it without hurting or harming your partner. Likewise, as a responsible partner, you need to be able to listen to and understand your partner's needs, being careful to ask when you are not sure. To communicate better, consider the following carefully:

- **Honesty As Much As Possible**

Complete honesty is not always possible or advisable. When your partner asks if their body is getting old, you may need to avoid that cut-like-a-knife honesty of telling them they are getting old to their face. However, when your partner asks your opinion about something meaningful in the relationship, or if you need to tell them how you feel about something, you need to be honest and explain. Vague statements like, "I'm not going to the park because I don't like it" will not help communication much. However, if you explain honestly that you don't like the park because you feel uncomfortable with so many people you don't know around you, it will help your partner understand without mistakenly thinking it is about them.

Deliberately lying to your partner is unacceptable. Saying one thing and not sticking to it will only make you seem unreliable, and this is what honesty means. It boils down to the old adage of "Your word is your bond." Honesty can be a beautiful thing as it assures your partner, and they always know where they stand with you. They will also be more inclined to ask your opinion on matters then. However, don't respond in ways that seem like honesty but are actually malicious comments. Telling your overweight partner, they no longer turn you on is not honesty. You could rather express this as being concerned for their health.

- **Apologize When You've Been Wrong**

We are often so set on winning that we don't realize when we argue with our partner we are actually both losing. Many times, we argue to hide that we have actually been wrong. Own up to your flaws and mistakes. There is nothing more sexy than someone who apologizes with complete honesty when they were mistaken or acted incorrectly. You will find your partner trusts you all the more when you are mature enough to tell them you were wrong and you are sorry. This is not about begging. It is about admitting your flaws and asking for forgiveness when your words or deeds have wronged your partner as a result.

When you apologize, mean it. So often people say "I'm sorry," but they hardly know what those words mean. It's become a preprogrammed response that we use like a "get out of jail free" card. Apologizing means admitting honestly you have been wrong, asking for the other person's forgiveness, and fully intending not to repeat this harmful behavior you did again. Asking for forgiveness when you had an extramarital affair, but still have your fling on the side, is not a real apology. Know the difference. One type of apology will allow your relationship to grow through difficult times, while the other will most certainly lead to its death.

- **Resolve Conflict Calmly**

Shouting and arguing in a relationship will not create a happy relationship. While you have probably heard that arguing is great for the make-up sex after, this will not help to strengthen your relationship. Instead, you should work towards facing conflict as two mature adults who are able to calmly talk about their conflict and find a way to resolve this without resorting to screaming, name calling, or haranguing.

- **Walk in Your Partner's Shoes**

We each have our own truth, our own version of reality. While you might see something a certain way, your partner may see it differently. Their life view is determined by their experiences and unique personality. When you know them really well, you will be able to consider a situation from their point of view. This is the proverbial version of walking in their shoes. It is great for your relationship as it ensures you can really consider your partner's needs and anticipate how they would react to a certain situation. This becomes a really important skill when you are arguing with or angry at your partner. It's easy to remain angry when you simply believe the other person is the bad guy. However, when you can begin to see why they did something or said something, you can more readily forgive them or let go of your anger. Without this understanding, you will likely turn to resentment instead.

- **Question, Don't Assume**

"Assumptions are the mother of all..." Well, we all know how that ends. Sadly, it is true. When we assume something, we are acting on what we believe we know. We put our thinking over the truth, and that does not end well. Here are a few cases of assumptions ending badly:

Your husband does not listen to what you are saying, so you assume he is not interested and feel hurt by him.

Your wife is not interested in being intimate tonight, so you assume she has found something on the side.

In both these cases, your thinking may be faulty. There are other reasons why people may be distracted or unwilling. Your husband may be busy watching a business report on the news that will affect your family's investments. Your wife may be tired after a long day, or she may be worrying about a lump in her breast and be unsure of how to tell you about it.

To avoid making assumptions and engaging in flawed reasoning, you should ask. Tap your husband on the shoulder and ask why he is not listening and if something is wrong. Hold your wife and ask her if something is wrong that she is not interested in having sex tonight. Be patient and encouraging with your partner. Remember, they may need some coaxing to admit to what is really bothering them. But ask, don't assume.

- **Take a Break When You're Angry**

Anger is one of our most powerful emotions, and often, it shows us when something is wrong. However, it can also be incredibly destructive within a relationship. As a golden rule: don't speak to your partner when you are angry. Instead, call a time-out. Spend some time alone until you can let go of your anger and speak to your partner calmly. In addition, respect your partner's need to decompress their anger before they speak to you. Don't pressure them into an argument either.

Healing Your Trauma and Moving Towards Secure Attachment

While most of us are not secure in our attachment style, we can improve on our behavior styles. This is not an overnight process; however, you can seriously improve your relationship by dealing with your past traumas and making your partner part of the healing process. Remember, when you enter a relationship with unresolved past traumas, you make your pain their pain. Your partner becomes a part of the process; don't shut them out.

- **Share Your Fear and Pain**

Sharing is caring. This is a simple truth. When you share with your partner, you enable them to care about you, and this is nowhere more true in your relationship than when you share your fear and pain with them. Your partner does not expect you to be Mr. or Mrs. Perfect, so don't try to be. Trust them enough to be vulnerable and open up. This will help them understand you and help you heal.

- **Include Them**

While the past traumas are yours to heal from, your partner can help. They want to help. It will bring an additional closeness in your relationship. So, include them. Let them go with you to therapy sessions and attend couple's therapy sessions together. Build stronger bonds by including and sharing.

- **Let Go**

Your partner married or chose to be in a relationship with you. They didn't necessarily sign up for marrying your pain or the past trauma. When you do not deal with this trauma, you are effectively making it a third party to your relationship. Your partner didn't sign up for a threesome. At some point, you need to let go of the past and release your pain or trauma. Your partner can help you, but only up to a point. You need to let go.

- **Create Proactive Co-Habits**

When dealing with past traumas, you need to build supporting habits with your partner. Making healthy routines to replace the pain or trauma of your past will help you move on and move more towards your partner. Go for walks together when you are feeling stressed, or turn off the TV and snuggle on the sofa when you are feeling lonely or inadequate. Habits of support with your partner will increase your positive energies and help you release the burden of your past.

- **Kick Back Together**

Working on your past is hard. It can be emotionally and physically draining, and you need a time-out from this. Having a partner whom you can kick back with and just be fun and silly with will help you be more relaxed and balance the negative you are dealing with internally. Watch a movie, dance like teenagers to the latest dance tracks in your living room, bake cookies together and decorate them like angry birds. Find something to do that releases your frustrations in a fun and healthy way.

- **Be Kind When You Experience Darkness**

No matter how much effort you put in to resolve your past trauma, there will be days when you slip backwards in the process. You may wake up and feel totally overwhelmed, or you may see something that reminds you of the pain and trauma anew. This is when you need to be kind to yourself and your partner. Don't lash out because you are suddenly hurting. Communicate about how you are feeling and what is happening.

Compromise

A relationship is about give and take. It is very much a business interaction. Both partners need to share equal benefit or it does not work. This means you need to compromise to maintain a balance. BOTH partners compromise, not one partner giving and the other constantly taking. This is how you do it:

- **Meet in the Middle**

Compromise means meeting each other in the middle. You need to give equally, take equally, and agree on who gives when and how much. Without being thoughtful towards your partner, you can quickly become a bully who always takes from their partner. This will lead to resentment.

- **Introduce Healthy Compromise**

When you change to meet the needs of both parties in the relationship, this is compromise. It is healthy when it benefits both of you. By entering a give-and-take discussion as part of daily life, you will easily and elegantly begin doing it in the relationship.

- **Know Your Boundaries**

There are some things we will not be happy to let go of or compromise on. These are your boundaries, and you should communicate them clearly to your partner. If you are an avid cyclist, and your partner wants you to stop doing this to spend more time with them, you need to be clear in communicating how this is crossing a boundary you are not willing to break. Rather compromise with your partner, cycling when they are at work or when they have an afternoon nap. Being asked to give it up completely will be a breach of boundaries your partner knew existed and it is not a mutually beneficial compromise.

Privacy and Personal Time

While we are often working on the creation of an "us" within the relationship, we should not lose sight that we are also two individual and unique people within that "us." When you are securely attached, you do not need to spend every waking moment together. You are then confident enough to give each other some alone time. We all need time to be on our own or engage in our own hobbies and do things that may be more for our pleasure and not necessarily interesting to our partner.

You do not have to share all your friends, and it is impractical and illogical to think you will both have the same friends. You have needs your partner may not be able to meet. These could include some bro-time with your buddies or some girl-time with your sisters. Your securely attached partner will respect this.

Be Open and Honest About Difficult Questions

Communication is easy when it comes to the easy stuff, but it really matters when you discuss the less common or difficult topics. Speaking to your partner about things like sex, money, time, chores, to parent or not, and even where to live can be difficult. However, you can't shut your eyes and refuse to discuss these topics, or they will become issues in your relationship. Here are some useful suggestions for sensitive topics and how to discuss them:

- **Fair Division of Chores**

In a modern relationship, the division of chores may not necessarily work when you are not functioning in a purely traditional role. Expecting the woman to take care of housework is not practical when she is also earning money. Insisting the man deals with all "manly issues" such as plumbing and fixing is also not feasible. This will require discussion and compromise.

Today, it is quite natural to find men participating in and doing their share of the household chores. While they may not have acquired the skills to deal with all "manly chores" and the woman may not be a skilled "homemaker" who sews, cooks, and cleans, there needs to be a middle ground. Agree on what will be outsourced, what will be shared equally, and what is within one partner's particular skills set. Do not assume someone *must* do something.

- **Sex and Intimacy**

There is a lot of conflict in relationships that originate from sex and intimacy. We all have our own preferences, and wanting someone else to perform what and when we want is not healthy. Openly communicating what you like and don't like will help to find a way to satisfy and meet the needs of both partners. Again, this is a give and take too. While you may not be particularly turned on by something, your partner may find it very satisfying, and you should discuss this, finding a solution that suits both of you.

It is easy to say that both partners should initiate sex and intimacy; however, this is not always the reality of your relationship. Each of us have our own inhibitions and past experiences that influence how we behave and what we feel comfortable doing. Don't hide from this. Talk about it and be supportive of each other.

- **Finances**

Traditionally, the man has been the partner who dealt with financial decisions. However, with changing times, and with the woman also earning money (sometimes even earning more than the man), this needs some discussion. You should openly discuss your investment goals, what to do with your monthly expenses, who pays for what, and importantly, you should ensure each partner has their own money they do not need to account for.

Remember, you are individuals within the "us." If you want to buy new make-up or a Harley Davidson (and if there is money available after your monthly expenses), then you should be allowed to do so without your partner scolding you about it like a child. Again, consider your partner, and remember, an equal division of expenses only works when you earn an equal income.

- **Your Joint Future**

Making plans for your future needs to include both parties. When you plan where you see yourselves in the near, middle, and far future, you should include your partner. Discuss your relationship goals, how you plan on dealing with complications such as ill-health, loss of income, the introduction of external pressures, and conflict resolution strategies. While you can't plan for every eventuality, you should at least talk about it.

- **Becoming Parents or Not**

Deciding whether you will have children is not a simple choice today. Women have the right to decide what happens to their bodies, as do men. Discuss if, when, and how you will decide to have children. Your discussion might include whether you perhaps want to rather adopt or foster children. Your partner should support your decision, and you should be open and communicative about your reasons for your decision. Importantly, don't fall into the trap of believing children are the cement of a relationship. If your relationship is already not working well, adding children to the mix will not end well.

Spontaneity and Doing Fun Things Together

Relationships are a lot of work, and some of it is really serious. This can quickly suck the life out of your companionship. Remember, you probably started off enjoying each other's company. This should not stop. So, make time to do fun activities together where you can just be two people having a good time. Do fun stuff together and build common interests.

If you are so bound up in your chores and work and planning how to save or maintain your relationship, then you might want to plan for fun. Writing down some crazy (but doable ideas) on scraps of paper, stick them in a jar. Every week you take turns to draw one scrap of paper. Set aside some time over a weekend to go do this activity. Some ideas could include:
- Going go-karting
- Ice-skating
- Watching a movie
- Dancing at the local club
- Going on an adventure at the paintball club
- Having a fancy dress party at home
- Taking a mini road trip

- Planning a scavenger hunt around your home or neighborhood

The Importance of Touch and Physical Intimacy

Relationships have a physical component, and we can easily forget this as we age and when we become busy with life. Even when you are entering the later part of your life, you can still benefit from touch and physical intimacy. Holding and being held is a gift to your bodies. Physical touch activates feel-good endorphins that help you connect and deal with stress. Explore where you and your partner enjoy being touched and how.

When you are younger, this may also improve your sex-life, but it is essential to touch and support each other physically. This will meet your need for intimacy and companionship for your body. Couples who regularly touch each other and practice physical intimacy (not sex) have less likelihood of infidelity within the couple. So, touch is important when building a long-term relationship.

Don't Try to Change Each Other, Respect Your Differences

There was a joke going around a few years ago, where it is said that during the wedding ceremony, women who walked down the aisle next to their husband would think, "Aisle, alter him." You marry someone for who they are. You enter a relationship with someone based on who they are. It is not up to you to alter them or make them into who you want.

Relationships are most successful when you can accept your partner, be respectful of your differences, and be there in a supportive capacity to the life changes your partner chooses to engage in. You may be part of their healing journey, but you are not there to fix them. Your partner is not a broken-down car you can fix up and impress everyone with. They are real humans too, and they deserve your love and respect.

Cultivate Patience and Respect

Your partner is not perfect; nor are you. Having a little patience with each other will help you to develop together into a successful unit of respect and support. There may be small things that niggle at your patience. Evaluate these calmly and don't become angry over petty things. We all have boiling points when we have just had enough, but we should deal with this as a loving partnership. Venting on social media or to a friend will not only do irreparable damage to your partnership, but it will lessen you as a person. Respect each other enough to deal with all things inside your relationship, and if you can't, then approach a relationship professional.

Know When It's Time to Get Out

You can and should try your best for your relationship. However, sometimes your attachment styles are simply not compatible, and when your partner is not willing to put in the work you are, it ends up being a case of leading a horse to water and not being able to make them drink. This is the point where you need to consider whether you should end the relationship or not.

- **Recognize Signs**

If you already have a secure attachment style, you may discover your relationship is not working, nor is it meeting your needs. Being responsible and caring, you will have tried to build on the relationship deficit with your partner, but sometimes, this is not enough, or they are not willing to show the same commitment as you. This is not a sign of failure on your part. It is simply an indication of signs that the relationship can't be made to work. Incompatibility is more common than many people realize, and sticking together can be harmful to all parties involved, especially if there are children involved.

- **The Best Decision**

It sounds really tragic to say you can end a relationship. However, this need not be a death or complete severing of ties. After all, you have a history together, and unless you have been in an abusive relationship, you can redefine the relationship to become platonic and not romantic. There are many instances of couples who divorced and became good friends after, even including their new partners or spouses in their friendships. In the end, being miserable together is not healthy for either party involved in a relationship. Separating or ending the relationship is the only viable and responsible option then.

- **Irreparable Damage**

When you evaluate your relationship, you will quickly be able to identify if the damage has been irreparable, or if there is still hope to repair misunderstandings and miscommunications. Irreparable damage to your relationship could include trust that is broken, there is no attraction of connection between you and your partner, communication is impossible or one-sided, you constantly feel unhappy and bad in the relationship, and if you have developed a loathing or contempt for your partner. When your partner is continually abusive, you also owe it to yourself to walk away. If you find yourself in any of these irreparable situations, you know it is time to leave; the damage is done and there is no way to save an un-savable situation.

- **Walking Out**

When you have made your decision to leave, you should do so in a responsible and mature manner. Now is not the time to be vindictive or immature about your relationship. Discuss it clearly with your partner, drawing a line where intimacy will end (if it hasn't already), and resolve the division of material and financial assets in an amicable manner. Though you are no longer together, there is no reason to be enemies.

When there are children involved, you have a responsibility to keep channels of communication open to their other parent.

Conclusion

"Our minds influence the key activity of the brain, which then influences everything; perception, cognition, thoughts and feelings, personal relationships; they're all a projection of you."

~ Deepak Chopra

We are each of us unique projections of the summation of experiences in our minds. What has happened to us has shaped us and formed us into who we are and how we behave. This not only influences how we act, but also how we react to the people around us. In relationships, this can create chaos or harmony.

By knowing your attachment style, you can be aware of your flaws and strong points, and with a little guidance, you can also improve the chances of finding and keeping love. Your behavior is a result of your mind and your emotions warring over control. When you begin to take responsibility for both these, you can become rational instead of reactional. However, this is a battle with yourself, and though we often want to blame others for our flaws, we are solely responsible for who we are.

Sharing ourselves within the confines of a relationship begins with the relationship with yourself. You have the power to make yourself happy, to meet your needs, and to find satisfaction in your own company. When you are ready, confident, and secure in who you are and how to interact with the world, you are most suited to entering a relationship, if you choose to.

Thinking, Feeling, and Doing

When you have formed a secure attachment style, you are able to manage conflict in your relationships, give freely, and love completely. You do not jump to conclusions or impose your will. The Ancient Delphic maxim of "know thyself" has never been more valid than here. When you have self-awareness, you are more geared to being a responsible and valuable partner for your right partner regardless of the life stage you are at.

Finding, Fixing, and Healing

When you are already in a complicated relationship, you can engage in several therapeutic approaches to help you find yourself within the relationship. Great value can be gleaned from consulting with an EFFT therapist to help you deal with emotion-based thinking in your relationship with your partner and in your relationship with yourself. Cognitive behavior therapy is a great asset to anyone wanting to build up their own skills in thinking clearly and acting mindfully. Self-betterment and the improvement of your relationships is always a worthy cause and one you should make time for and commit to.

Whether you are single or in a relationship, you can learn the skills to find you and your relationship challenges and traumas, fix them, and heal them. A relationship with another person is a constant investment of time, effort, and care. When you do it right, and when your partner is there for the journey with you, your relationship will gift you with love, contentment, belonging, and happiness.

MY FREE GIFT TO YOU:

As my way of saying thanks for buying 'This Perfect Relationship Workbook' **I'd like to give you a FREE COPY of my book** 'Keeping Love and Healthy Relationships Alive'

>>> Click Here to Get the Free Book Instantly<<<

The above book is a gift, given to you as a sincere thanks for buying my e-book. I hope it helps you increase of your life. Download this **FREE BOOK** by clicking the link here

So click the link above to get access now and thanks once again for your support.

Enjoy!

Disclaimer

No part of this e-book may be reproduced or transmitted in any forms of whatsoever, electronic, or mechanical photocopying, recording, or by any informational storage or retrieval system without express writer, dated and signed permission from the author.

I'll send you my future projects, in preview, with nothing in return, if you just want a realistic review on them, which I'm sure will be useful to me. Thanks in advance! Leave me your best email, my staff will send you a copy as soon as possible: digitallifemystery@gmail.com

Do not go yet; One last thing to do…

If you enjoyed this book or found it useful I'd be very grateful if you'd post a short review on Amazon.com. Your support really does make a difference and I read all the reviews personally so I can get your feedback and make this book even better.

Thanks again for your support!

References

Ackerman, C. E. (2020a). *What is Attachment Theory? Bowlby's 4 Stages Explained.* Positive Psychology. https://positivepsychology.com/attachment-theory/

Ackerman, C. E. (2020b). *Emotion Focused Therapy: Understanding Emotions to Improve Relationships.* Positive Psychology. https://positivepsychology.com/emotion-focused-therapy/

Ackerman, C. E. (2020c). *25 CBT Techniques and Worksheets for Cognitive Behavioral Therapy.* Positive psychology. https://positivepsychology.com/cbt-cognitive-behavioral-therapy-techniques-worksheets/

Brenner, G. H. (2018). *The Art and Psychology of Being Single.* Psychology Today. https://www.psychologytoday.com/za/blog/experimentations/201808/the-art-and-psychology-being-single

Cherry, K. (2020). *The Different Types of Attachment Styles.* Very Well Mind. https://www.verywellmind.com/attachment-styles-2795344

Chopra, D. (n.d.). *Personal Relationships Quotes.* Brainy Quote. https://www.brainyquote.com/quotes/deepak_chopra_599977?src=t_personal_relationships

Church, D. (2017). *American Psychological Association Standards and EFT.* EFT Universe. https://www.eftuniverse.com/building-a-thriving-practice/american-psychological-association-standards-and-eft

Golhar, A. (2018). *10 Ways to Increase Your Emotional Intelligence.* Inc. https://www.inc.com/young-entrepreneur-council/10-ways-to-increase-your-emotional-intelligence.html

Helpguide. (n.d.). *Therapy for Anxiety Disorders.* https://www.helpguide.org/articles/anxiety/therapy-for-anxiety-disorders.htm#:~:text=Cognitive%20behavioral%20therapy%20(CBT)%20for%20anxiety&text=Research%20has%20shown%20it%20to,at%20the%20world%20and%20ourselves.

Johnson, S. M. (2009). Attachment Theory and Emotionally Focused Therapy for Individuals and Couples. *Attachment Theory and Research in Clinical Work with Adults.* http://www.creatingconnections.nl/assets/files/Sue%20Johnson%20ObegiCh16.pdf

Levine, L. & Heller, R. S. F. (2010). *Deciphering Your Own Attachment Style.* Attached. https://www.attachedthebook.com/wordpress/compatibility-quiz/?step=1

Reach Out. (n.d.). *Teach Your Teenager Coping Skills for Fellbeing*. Reach Out. https://parents.au.reachout.com/skills-to-build/wellbeing/things-to-try-coping-skills-and-resilience/teach-your-teenager-coping-skills-for-wellbeing

Reese, C. (2007). Childhood Attachment. *British Journal of General Practice,* 57(544): 920–922. https://doi.org/10.3399/096016407782317955

Stavrianopoulos, K. (2019). *Emotionally Focused Family Therapy: Rebuilding Family Bonds*. Intechopen. https://www.intechopen.com/books/family-therapy-new-intervention-programs-and-researches/emotionally-focused-family-therapy-rebuilding-family-bonds

Vilhauer, J. (2017). *This One Exercise Can Improve Your Relationship Today*. Psychology Today. https://www.psychologytoday.com/us/blog/living-forward/201710/one-exercise-can-improve-your-relationship-today

West-Olatunji, C. A., Wolfgang, J. D. & Frazier, K. N. (2019). *Interventions for attachment and traumatic stress issues in young children*. Counseling Today. https://ct.counseling.org/2019/04/interventions-for-attachment-and-traumatic-stress-issues-in-young-children/

Whitbourne, S. K. (2012). *The 12 Ties that Bind Long-Term Relationships*. Psychology Today. https://www.psychologytoday.com/za/blog/fu

lfillment-any-age/201206/the-12-ties-bind-long-term-relationships

Whitbourne, S. K. (2013). *What Rising Divorce Rates in Midlife Mean for You*. Psychology Today. https://www.psychologytoday.com/za/blog/fulfillment-any-age/201311/what-rising-divorce-rates-in-midlife-mean-you

Yerkovich, M. & Yerkovich K. (n.d.). *What is a Love Style?* How We Love. https://howwelove.com/love-styles/

Image References

Image 1: Geralt on Pixabay. https://pixabay.com/illustrations/woman-face-photomontage-faces-1594710/

Image 2: Kelly Sikkema on Unsplash. https://unsplash.com/photos/XX2WTbLr3r8

Image 3: mohamed_hassan on pixabay. https://pixabay.com/vectors/silhouette-relationship-conflict-3141264/

Image 4: maz-Alph from Pixabay. https://pixabay.com/vectors/stage-of-life-childhood-life-1287959/

Image 5: sweetlouise on pixaybay. https://pixabay.com/photos/friendship-brotherhood-love-freedom-2156171/

Image 6: Julie Rose from Pixabay. https://pixabay.com/photos/couple-romantic-together-vintage-5302344/

Image 7: Rostyslav Savchyn on Unsplash. https://unsplash.com/photos/E2zvqyY5zUY

Image 8: Hannah Olinger on Unsplash. https://unsplash.com/photos/8eSrC43qdro

Image 9: Priscilla Du Preez on Unsplash. https://unsplash.com/photos/5eO8WdwszAQ

Image 10: Karan Mandre on Unsplash. https://unsplash.com/photos/FUYSmgif7c8

© Copyright 2020 by

KATE HOMILY

All rights reserved

www.ingramcontent.com/pod-product-compliance
Lightning Source LLC
Chambersburg PA
CBHW071802080526
44589CB00012B/646